Harald Bluetooth, Sweyn Forkl[...] Valdemar the Victorious – in older tim[...] kings of Denmark had irresistible name[...] an added attraction to English readers of Danish history is that many of them have a familiar ring.

Later on the Danish royal line became a tidily alternating row of Christians and Fredericks – so tidy indeed, that even the Danes tend to get them muddled, despite the fact that many of them were just as colourful characters as their gaily named ancestors.

Here however, in this authoritative account, they are all sorted out according to their deeds and misdeeds, and they all come alive – which makes them rather fascinating.

Many great names in English annals – King Canute, James I, Lord Nelson, the Duke of Wellington, Queen Victoria, to mention but a few – had some share, large or small, in shaping the history of Denmark. In this smoothly flowing, highly readable narrative, *Palle Lauring*, a Danish author of established repute, combines the enviable knack of marshalling the facts that matter (and presenting them attractively) with the ability to maintain a refreshing twinkle in his shrewdly observant, historical eye.

of local Danish interest.

Of recent years Palle Lauring has furthermore written a couple of historical children's books, thereby earning himself an award from the Danish Ministry of Education. Palle Lauring has also been given a distinguished Danish literary prize, "The Holberg Medal".

Apart from writing books, Palle Lauring also finds time to contribute articles and essays to the Danish press and write educational textbooks, radio features and radio plays.

Palle Lauring is chairman of the Danish Authors' Association, and is an important and versatile personality in the sphere of Danish letters.

A HISTORY OF
THE KINGDOM OF
DENMARK

A HISTORY OF
The Kingdom of
DENMARK

by

Palle Lauring

TRANSLATED FROM THE DANISH BY
DAVID HOHNEN

HØST & SØN
COPENHAGEN

FOTOGRAFISK OPTRYK
S. L. MØLLERS BOGTRYKKERI. KØBENHAVN

CONTENTS

I ANCIENT HISTORY 11

The Land is Formed 11
The Great Forest 11
The Forest Submerges.. 15
Coastal Folk and Fishermen 16
The Big Stone Graves 18
The Battle Axe 25
Bronze 26
The Golden Land 28
Early Navigation 31
The Celts 34
Mass Migrations 37
The Romans 38

II THE VIKING AGE 45

Unification of the Realm 49
The Conquest of England 51
Canute the Great 54
The Collapse of the Danish Empire 57

III THE EARLY MIDDLE AGES 61

Christianity 62
Canute the Holy 64
The Crusaders — Church-Building 66
The Age of Chivalry – The Pretendant Feuds 67
The Great Period of the Valdemars 71
The Churches of Denmark.. 77

3

Valdemar the Victorious 79
The Conquest of Estonia 83
Ingeborg of Denmark 85
Collapse 87
The Jutlandic Law 89
Valdemar's Sons 92
Crown versus Church 93
The Royal Charter – Murder of the King 95
Dissolution of the Realm 97
Murder of Count Gert 98
Valdemar Atterdag 98
The Conquest of Gotland 100
The Coalition against Valdemar Atterdag 103
Queen Margaret 105
The Scandinavian Union 107
The Union after the Death of Queen Margaret 109
The Sound Dues 110

IV THE LATE MIDDLE AGES 114
The Oldenburgers 114
Defeat in the Ditmarshes 117
Rebellion in the North 120
The Church of the Late Gothic Era 121
Peasants and Townsfolk 124
Christian II 125
Subjugation of Sweden 128
The Nobility in Rebellion 130

V FROM THE REFORMATION UNTIL THE DEATH OF CHRISTIAN IV 134
Unrest in the Church 136
The Count's War 139
The Fall of the Catholic Church 141
Norway and Slesvig 144
The Renaissance 145
Seven Years' War about the Scandinavian Coats of Arms 146
Intellectual Life 148
"His Royal Majesty's Seas" 150

4

Christian IV 151
The Great Builder 154
The Fatal Turning Point 157

VI THE WAR AGAINST SWEDEN AND — ABSOLUTE MONARCHY . 161
Absolute Monarchy 166
The Scanian War – Griffenfeld 167
Molesworth 169
The Great Nordic War 170
Intellectual Life 173
Greenland 175

VII DANISH ROCOCO 175
Shipping and Porcelain 176
The King, the Queen and the Doctor 180
Coup d'Etat 186

VIII THE WAR AGAINST ENGLAND 189
The Battle of Copenhagen 190
Peace between the Wars 193
The Bombardment of Copenhagen – Loss of the Fleet 193
The Seven Year's War of the North 198
The Separation of the Twin Kingdoms 200

IX THE FINAL YEARS OF THE ABSOLUTE MONARCHY 206
X THE CONSTITUTION – THE SLESVIG WARS 211
Between the Wars 216

XI DEFEAT AND REVIVAL 222
Political Fights 231
Revival 232

XII THE WORLD WARS AND DENMARK TODAY 236
The Return of North Slesvig to Denmark 237
National Crisis and the Interwar Period 238
World War II and the Occupation 241
A Clearer Policy 245

General Strike   248
The German Collapse   251
The Aftermath of War   254
Present Status   257

APPENDIX   261
The Kings and Queens of England and Denmark   261

PLATES

The photographs reproduced on pages 32, 46, 48, 96, 97 and 153 II were taken by INGA AISTRUP. The remainder have been obtained from the following institutions:

FREDERIKSBORG MUSEUM: pages 105, 152 I, 216 I, 217 I, 233 II

THE LIBERATION MUSEUM (FRIHEDSMUSEET): pages 242, 246

THE COMMERCIAL AND SHIPPING MUSEUM (HANDELS- OG SØFARTSMU-SEET), KRONBORG: pages 200 I, 201 II, 232 II, 248 I

THE ROYAL LIBRARY: pages 152 II, 169, 201 I, 233 I

THE NATIONAL MUSEUM: pages 16, 17, 33, 34, 35, 47, 49 II, 64, 65, 120 I, 121, 136, 137 I, 168, 200 II, 232 I

THE STATE ARCHIVES: page 104

ROSENBORG PALACE: pages 137 II, 153 I

THE SHIPPING MUSEUM, GOTHENBURG: page 216 II

BRITISH MUSEUM, LONDON: page 49 I

The numbers of the pages refer to the pages opposite the plates in question, the Roman numerals to the order of the pictures on the page itself.

MAPS

Denmark and former provinces   10
Main routes of Viking expeditions from the three Scandinavian countries   44
Plan of the Viking camp "Trelleborg"   53
The last Ice Age in Scandinavia   264
South Jutland   265

FOREWORD

A couple of years ago I told an English friend I was thinking of writing a history of Denmark for English readers, and his comment was: "That's very nice of you – but why bother?"

Here there is no point in making romantic reference to Viking expeditions or to the countless Danish peasants and townsfolk who emigrated to England a thousand years ago. It was, incidentally, an English author who pointed out that in about 900 A.D., more than a quarter of England's inhabitants were Danish or descended from Danes, but that this enormous influx consisted of peasants and townsfolk, not upper classes (as in the case of the French immigrants, who were not really numerous) with the result that the Danish contribution has been more or less forgotten. More important is the fact that, whilst there had been a regular flow of ships back and forth across the North Sea for several centuries, this intercourse came to an abrupt end shortly after 1000 A.D. Cultural and commercial bonds were severed; England and Scandinavia turned their backs on one another, went their own ways and wrote their own histories. Up through the Middle Ages and recent times there were occasional marital contacts between the royal houses of England and Denmark, but these failed to create new political or cultural bonds between the two countries – who found that, despite their being neighbours, they had precious little in common and hardly knew one another. It was not until the chaos of the Napoleonic Wars that these erstwhile kinsfolk met again, at sea – somewhat violently – and the meeting was a bitter one for Denmark and Norway. Afterwards there was silence again until the second half of the 19th century, when Danish trade started to ply the old routes across the North Sea again, and at the same time, Scandinavian interest in English cultural life intensified. But during the thousand years these two northern

7

European worlds – England and Scandinavia – were out of contact with one another, much happened. England became a great power, and the English became far-sighted, accustoming themselves to gazing out beyond Europe towards distant horizons, to Asia, Australia, Africa and America. More than half England's history has been written beyond England's shores, and to many an English mind Europe merely implies France, Spain and Italy – Germany at a pinch. The Scandinavian countries are "somewhere in the north".

For those who live "somewhere in the north" this is a little hard to understand – not that it really should be, for England and the Scandinavian countries respectively are so utterly different as regards their origins as well as their histories. Scandinavia was always left outside the main stream of European activity, and the big waves of history that washed over Europe were no more than ripples by the time they reached Scandinavia. On the other hand the Scandinavian peoples succeeded in making their own domestic history so dramatic that they never had time to be bored. For the people of Scandinavia it is a most natural thought that generation after generation should have continued living in the lands of the north ever since the Stone Age – only mild waves of immigrants forced their way up and became absorbed. England suffered a completely different fate. An ancient country, peopled by ancient Britons, invaded by Celts, then conquered and occupied by the Romans for 400 years, then invaded and conquered by Angles and Saxons, then by Danes, and finally by Norman knights – so tangled are an Englishman's origins that he can no longer be expected to display an interest in the original native habitats of each and every one of these conquering peoples and hordes – it would involve more or less half Europe. The part played by the Danes and the other Scandinavians in England's fate is but a small one, and furthermore the one to have left the faintest visible traces. Denmark's western adventure of a thousand years ago must, to English eyes, appear as a brief, confused episode, broadly speaking an unimportant one, probably most evident in the language (and in very nearly a quarter part of every Englishman, no matter how indignantly he may protest) and an Englishman is right to claim that he can eat Danish butter and bacon without being obliged to take the trouble to delve into a Danish farmer's or dairyman's ancestors.

But the people of Scandinavia look towards the English as their nearest kinsmen outside Scandinavia – certainly not because of the Vikings and all that, but because English language, culture, thought, philosophy of life and humour all appear so surprisingly familiar to Scandinavians. Small wonder that, across the span of a thousand years, it makes a homely impression upon Danes to find, to this very day, that more than 2,000 place-names in England are Scandinavian – mostly Danish. As a Danish farmer said to a Danish journalist after a trip to England: "They've pinched all our old village names – they just don't know how to pronounce them!"

This means nothing to the Englishman. No matter how one tries to present things, the relationship remains lop-sided, unbalanced. The warm interest in English history and literature that Scandinavians have displayed during the past hundred years is simply not echoed by a corresponding English interest in Scandinavia. This is easily explained: Scandinavia is not three mighty kingdoms. England does not need to know anything about the Scandinavian countries. What remains is a desire (which I do not care to define more closely) to explain who one really is. The following is an attempt to do so.

I would like to thank Mr. David Hohnen, who translated the book into English, for his warm interest and for a number of serious as well as ironical bits of advice. English readers will be able to judge for themselves where I have been too stubborn to follow them. Mrs. Jemma Starcke of the British Council in Copenhagen was kind enough to read the proofs, and finally I am indebted to Mr. Peder Hansen, M.A., who likewise read the proofs and drew my attention, partly to a number of debatable points, and partly to a number of errors, thereby enabling me to correct them.

PALLE LAURING

Virum, April 1960.

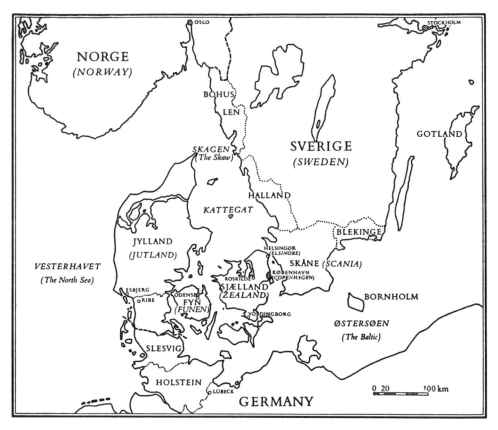

South Scandinavia

(100 km = 62.14 miles)

Halland and Scania originally Danish provinces, today Swedish, surrendered in 1658. Blekinge's original nationality uncertain – at any rate Danish from about 1050, now Swedish, surrendered 1658. Bohuslen originally Norwegian, now Swedish, surrendered 1658. Gotland originally independent, later Swedish, conquered by Denmark 1361, Swedish after 1658. Slesvig and Holstein, see special map page 265. Norway united to Denmark 1380-1814, united to Sweden 1814-1905. Sweden united to Denmark 1397-1521, though with several interruptions.

I. ANCIENT HISTORY

The Land is Formed

Denmark is one of Europe's youngest countries. Only the granite rocks of the island of Bornholm are as old as the earth itself. The rest of the country is not particularly old. During the Cretaceous Period there was no land here, only sea (not particularly deep) and at the bottom, during the course of thousands upon thousands of years, the shells of countless microscopic creatures piled up. When these creatures died, their small white skeletons sank quietly to the bottom, a continuously moving veil that kept sinking and sinking, thereby causing the layer of chalk slime on the sea bed to grow and become hundreds and hundreds of feet thick. This layer of chalk extends today beneath Denmark, northern Germany, northern France and England. It can be seen in the white cliffs of Dover, the chalk downs in Normandy, on the island of Rügen, and in several places in Denmark, particularly in the dazzlingly white cliffs at Møn.

The Great Forest

Later the land here probably became a steppe, whereafter the Ice Ages finally passed over Europe. The great glacier pushed its way down from the north, from the mountains of Norway, and then melted away again during the interglacial periods. When the last Ice Age began, probably a little more than 30,000 years B.C., the ice did not cover the whole of what is now Denmark. The edge of the glacier passed down through the middle of Jutland and formed the heavy banks of clay known as "the Jutlandic ridge". To the east and north, where the ice once lay, the country is hilly, built up of clay, gravel, and stone. To the west lies what is left of an older land from before the time of the last Ice Age, and in between these remains are the moorlands of Jutland, formed by melt-water sand.

There are no traces in Denmark of that ancient Ice Age culture to which cave-paintings in France and Spain, and small, strong figures carved in bone and stone, bear witness. In Denmark we have found a collection of bones belonging to a deer that has obviously been killed and eaten, the bones having been crushed and split for the sake of the marrow. Presumably they are the remains of a Neanderthal man's dinner – nobody can say. But they form the only slender trace of human beings discovered to date in Denmark or thereabouts dating from before the last Ice Age.

When the ice started melting for the last time, in 12–14,000 B.C., the land began to emerge. It consisted mainly of enormous masses of clay and gravel which the ice had carried down from the north and which remained wherever they were deposited. The ice melted slowly: thousands of years passed from the time the Jutlandic ridge was liberated and left stretched out, glistening in the sunshine, until the ice had melted sufficiently to leave what is now southern Sweden ice-free. But it was not until about 8000 B.C. that the ice had retreated thus far north, and by that time human beings had come to Denmark.

Of course it is wrong to use the word *Denmark*. The name did not exist, nor did the country itself as we know it today. From what is now the Baltic Sea there was a channel across Sweden through the big lakes out to the Kattegat; but Denmark was one continous stretch of land. The western Baltic did not exist, nor did the Sound, nor the Belts (Great Belt and Little Belt), and most of the Kattegat was dry land. Where the Belts have since appeared there were a couple of large rivers flowing northwards through the endless tundra and birchwood scrub; and from Jutland, forest and tundra stretched right across to what is now England. Only in the northern part of the North Sea was there any water; the coastline went roughly from what is now the Skaw over to the English coast approximately by Flamborough Head. South of this line there was land.

Living on this big, continuous stretch of land were human beings.

They came from the south, for they were reindeer hunters from central Europe; but the reindeer disliked the warm weather and therefore followed the retreating ice northwards, probably in order to escape, amongst other things, the Arctic mosquito, which in all likelihood was just as unbearable then as it is today. During the winter the reindeer lived in the forests. Every summer they made their way as far up into the mountains, or as near to the ice, as possible; and the hunters followed them. Year by year the reindeer migrated further and further north and drew human beings after them. We find their earliest traces in Holstein, just south of the present Danish border; the first ones to reach further north were probably summer visitors.

The reindeer-hunter's weapon was made from reindeer antlers. The hunter of the coniferous forests made his spear-tip out of bone.

In the meantime the atmosphere over Europe became milder. The Ice Age was at an end, or rather: it retreated so far northwards that Germany and Denmark and the southern part of Sweden became covered with coniferous forests, mostly pine, forming a tangly jungle that extended for mile upon mile, interspersed by wide, heavy rivers, by lakes and swamps; but there were also clear patches where there grew scrub and berries.

In about 8000 B.C. there lived, not only in Denmark, but throughout the great "Nordland", from the landlocked Baltic right across into England, hunters who sought their food in the forests. The reindeer had long since disappeared. There were elk and red deer, roe, bears, lynxes, wolves and beavers, and all the other animals we know from the forests of northern Europe up until our times; also the mighty aurochs, long extinct.

These hunters lived in small communities, generally in huts made of branches, the floors of which were strewn with bark, probably to keep out the damp. Their tools and weapons were primitive, not much better than those of the oldest reindeer hunters, but the bone tips of their spears were smooth and delicately carved, beautiful in shape; loving care had gone into the fashioning of an instrument that meant life to the settlement.

It is unlikely that they created art in the sense we understand it from the older civilizations of central Europe. At all events we have come across no traces of their having tried their hand. We have some bones with figures scratched on them, but the oldest pictures of human beings in Denmark or thereabouts are extremely childish, mere helpless signs meaning *man*. What the intention was, we have no idea; perhaps magic, for hunting magic must have played an important part in the existence

The oldest Danish pictures of men, as primitive as a child's drawing. Three men seen from the side, two from the front; only one has been given arms.

of hunters whose life and death depended upon the success of their hunting and fishing.

For century after century they continued to live in their villages, for generation upon generation smoke rose from their fires, their children grew up, reached maturity, aged and died, whereupon new generations would succeed the old in the scattered, barren settlements. Often there was a day's journey from one village to the next, for these hunters required a big district to themselves if they were to secure enough food. It is unlikely that they remained permanently in any one place, but at times (perhaps according to season) they probably migrated elsewhere, thus causing a slow displacement of the human mass in the tremendous European jungle.

It is a strange thought that where ships now ply across the North Sea between Denmark and England, there once lived, six to eight thousand years ago, human beings. The bottom of the sea, today covered by some 300 feet of water, was then pine-forest. Nowadays, when we sail through the night from Harwich to Esbjerg, we are floating 300 feet above old settlements long since drowned, where human beings once lived their lives in sun-warmed, scented forests. Once (but only once) a fishing-trawler happened to catch a bone spear-head in its trawl together with some peat from a forest floor thousands of years old; but this is the only sign of life the old hunters have ever sent up to us from the deep.

The Forest Submerges

The pine-forest land subsided.

While the mighty glacier of the Ice Age lay stretched across northern Europe, a tremendous pressure was exerted upon the globe, millions of tons of ice, thereby forcing in the very crust of the earth, denting it. When the ice started melting, thereby relieving the pressure, the dent began to rise, and while a solid lump of ice continued to extend from the middle of Sweden northwards, the surrounding lands were pressed up into a gentle ridge surrounding the ice-covered region. When at last the ice disappeared completely, the last large basin began to rise. This was the Gulf of Bothnia and the sloping land of Sweden, which today, thousands of years later, is still rising. In the meantime the land a little to the south began to subside, and this rocking motion has not yet stopped. The mighty forest land subsided and the sea broke in, for as the land began to sink, the seas all over the earth started rising by reason of the fact that the tremendous ice masses of the Ice Age were in the process of melting.

Of course it did not take place that suddenly. Nevertheless, century by century, it could be observed that the sea was managing to eat its way in. The coasts were washed away. The settlements had to move further inland, into the forests. Where the country was very flat, every now and again catastrophic storm floods would swallow tremendous areas. The sea surged in amongst the trees and washed whole villages away, drowning human beings and animals; or else all living creatures, panic-stricken, fled even deeper into the forests, the roaring seas at their heels. These were natural catastrophes, the extent of which can only be guessed at, for nothing has been recorded concerning Denmark's oldest history. There are no names, no details; all that is known is that the land was lost beneath the sea and was slowly, totally changed. Most of what is now the North Sea was covered with water before the end of the Stone Age, whereafter the Denmark we know today began to take form, a completely new land. The sea pushed its way into the hilly terrain; the Jutlandic ridge and surrounding countryside remained, and beyond Jutland there were hundreds of clay banks high enough to save their lives. They did not drown. But the sea flung itself in, filling the old river courses until they overflowed their banks. The Baltic came into contact with the ocean via the Sound, Great Belt, and Little Belt; and Denmark became a sea-washed country of five hundred low-lying green islands.

Northern Europe must have been greatly affected by the subsidence of such large expanses of land into the sea. It meant that there was less room. Hunters had to trek southwards, or eastwards, had to escape to such forest-land as was still left; and there were too many of them. Hunting was no longer enough.

It has been observed that during the thousands of years following upon the subsidence of the land the larger animals became scarcer. The aurochs became a rare beast, the elk almost disappeared, and in general, as a result of excessive hunting, stocks of big game meat became exhausted. But new horizons opened up. Perhaps new peoples arrived, for along the old shore-line, now lost in the North Sea, there must have lived a coastal race of people about whom nothing whatsoever is known, for their settlements have vanished beneath the waves. Whatever the case may be, when Denmark changed shape, or rather, when Denmark was finally created in more or less the shape we know today and became a sea-bordered country, because land and sea had romped playfully together, thereby producing hundreds of fjords and inlets, large islands and small islands, there must have lived, at the time, human beings along her shores, people who had learnt to seek their food in the sea.

But perhaps some of them were merely descendants of ancient coastal peoples from further north.

Coastal Folk and Fishermen

We find their settlements along the Danish coasts. Or, to be quite accurate, in northern Denmark their settlements lie a short way inland. To the south they lie a little way out to sea, for Denmark has still not settled completely; as the land to the north rises, the land to the south subsides. The settlements are fairly easy to find, and there must have been thousands of them. Along the shores of Roskilde Fjord alone the existence of over a

Wickerwork fish trap dating from Stone Age, found in a bog.
Traps of exactly the same type are made by Danish fishermen today.

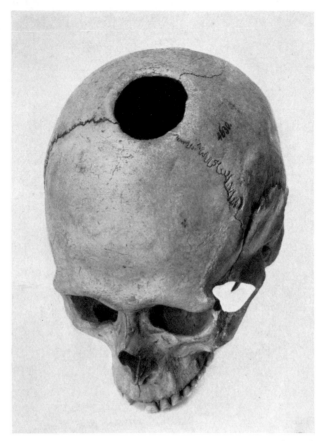

Trephined Stone Age cranium. The operation was successful and the man survived for the bone to heal.

Danish forest hunters used boomerangs for hunting.

hundred of them has been proved. Nearly all can be identified by a single feature: oyster-shells. For in those days, oysters were found much further inland. Today they are only found in the Limfjord, in Jutland. Denmark's first coastal inhabitants, who inhabited the country more than 5,000 years before Christ, lived on oysters, fish, and seal-meat; and (for they were hunters at the same time) on the animals of the forest. But during this period there also existed forest hunters further inland.

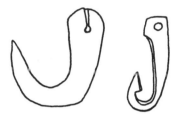

Fish-hooks of bone were probably used until quite late – until metal became cheap enough for all. But even in the Stone Age, hooks were almost the same shape as today.

Even the oldest forest dwellers knew how to sail. They had canoes which they used on rivers and lakes. But those who lived by the sea were obliged to develop even greater skill, for sailing on the sea is much more difficult and much more dangerous. The small Danish islands dotted about the blue sea may have tempted people to migrate from one island to the next; on the other hand they may have been inhabited since ancient times, isolated by the sea. Traffic between the islands must have been by boat, though very likely it was possible to walk across the ice in winter.

The people in the coastal settlements admittedly learnt the use of a few new tools and weapons. They became more proficient at flint-cutting (and there was plenty of flint). But even so, the settlements would appear to have been poor and primitive. The thick layers of oyster-shells on the vast refuse-dumps have made the soil so chalky that bones simply have not had a chance of disintegrating; so it has been possible to learn a great deal merely by digging. The bones of all manner of creatures have been unearthed, bones of marine animals, deer, and birds. It is even possible to calculate the comparative numerical strengths of the various animals, although here caution must naturally be exercised. For example, there are very few *hare* skeletons, so the opinion has been formed that the hare was no doubt rare in these forest lands. This is not certain. We know that in ancient times the hare was not eaten, and that it was in fact taboo. In Germany it has been sacred until comparatively recent times. There may well have been hunting taboos of this nature just as there are all over the world.

More than 5,000 years before Christ, while the coastal folk were getting acquainted with the sea and Danish shipping traditions were being founded, the land changed. With the sea and water getting in everywhere, the climate became much damper. This was too much for the pine tree. Oak became the stalwart of the forest, together with ash, lime, and other deciduous trees. The creatures of the forest remained much the same, but by now the land was only attached to the rest of Europe by a thin stalk down by Holstein, thereby isolating the Danish tribes. Migration could no longer play the important rôle it had done in the past; of course generally speaking you could always just stay put on your island, for the art of navigation had not as yet been sufficiently developed to enable a whole people to emigrate.

The Big Stone Graves

Even so, something of decisive importance took place round about the year 3000 B.C. Until this time the oyster-eaters had stayed happily in the coastal regions without changes of note taking place. But in approximately 3000 B.C. something new came to the country. In all probability it came together with a wave of immigration from the south, one of the few immigration waves about which we know a good deal. It did not mean that the population of the country was completely changed, nor even that it was appreciably reinforced; new people merely infiltrated, but they brought something new with them: agriculture.

This caused an upheaval in the lives of the old inhabitants, a revolution that was little short of overwhelming. Apparently there was not to be so much wandering around the countryside looking for edible berries and roots, for you could now have plants growing just outside your house. Furthermore, in the wake of agriculture followed the keeping of domestic animals. No longer was it necessary to stay out hunting for days on end, for instead, you kept animals near you, and let them reproduce themselves. Presumably you then milked the cows, slaughtered whatever you needed, and used the skins for clothing. Many of the old hunters must have had some difficulty in understanding these strange new ways, but even so, one gets the impression that their popularity spread quickly. It is possible that hunting had gradually become so poor, and that hunters got so much in each other's way in a country already overpopulated (from a hunter's viewpoint), that the innovation really proved a salvation.

The beautifully polished flint head of the big forest axe was wedged through the top of the handle.

Nevertheless, the coastal tribes stayed where they were along the coasts. They continued to live their same old lives, fishing in the sea. And deep in the forests there were apparently still tribes that continued to live by hunting as of old and who wished for no part in the new system.

All over Denmark, the first farmers got down to work.

Farming makes demands. Firstly, land is required, which means that the forest must be cleared. To begin with the lighter scrub regions were prepared and later on a start was made on the big forests. Nobody ever dared try where the soil was heavy and clayey, for the slender tools available would never have made any impression. However, in order to clear the forest, it was necessary to have proper tools. The problem was solved by the axe. Fire was also used, i.e. the forest was simply scorched away; but deciduous forests are not as easy to burn as coniferous forests, so the axe became essential. It was not possible to use the hunter's flimsy, primitive-bladed little hand-axe, so a new tool was created: the big, polished flint-stone axe.

To this day, flint-stone axe-blades are found buried in the soil all over Denmark. There are not many farms in the country without a few specimens lying around. They have been found in their tens of thousands, sometimes in peat-bogs, complete with their wooden handles – and the handles are not mere sticks. They are the handles of proper tools, and it is astonishing to find that they are exactly the same shape and have the same curve to them as a good axe-handle must have to this day. The big flint-stone axe was an excellent tool. Correctly used, it bit through fresh wood almost as well as a modern steel axe. Stone-axes were able to deal with big trees.

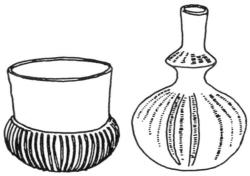

Peasant culture produced earthenware vessels of many shapes.

Simultaneously, the axe apparently became sacred. One has been found "planted" in a little hollowing in the floor of a Stone Age hut. It had been placed with the edge pointing upwards, and before it there was a little sacrificial bowl, for the axe meant life to the settlement and death to the mighty trees; without it, the peasant could not convert the forest and the scrub into usable farmland.

Daily life took on new form. The cows had to be tended (even though they probably grazed in the forest most of the year), and meat and milk had to be treated to make them keep fresh. The art of salting and drying meat was probably already known to the ancient hunters, but milk demanded a new kind of knowledge. Above all it required the use of vessels. Earthenware vessels had been known earlier, in the coastal settlements. Coarse, thick-walled earthen vessels had been used, their bases pointed so that they could be stood in the sand. But the household stock of vessels was now greatly increased, and greater proficiency in their making was acquired. It was woman's work. The decorative, meticulously finicky patterns on these vessels reveal the hand of woman, and presumably those of the housewife; for together with the introduction of this new pattern of life, the status of the woman became radically altered. The hunter's wife may well at times have accompanied her husband on his excursions, but when it came to roasting a leg of venison he was capable of managing by himself. She was probably sent to gather herbs and roots. *The peasant's wife* acquired importance. It was she who knew the profounder secrets of the kitchen, she who knew how to make milk into butter, how to make cheese out of it, how to store butter and cheese so that they would keep – at least for a while. Furthermore, the many vessels became her pride, the home's wealth. They were handled with loving care in order that they should retain their beauty.

The work of the husband was to clear the forest, sow the corn in the warm ashes, and fence the field in order to prevent forest animals from coming and gobbling up the lot. Everybody probably lent a hand with the harvesting of the corn, using a flint-stone sickle; for such an implement existed, a noble little tool with a distinguished handle, once again an instrument highly developed in its design. The sound of the axes rang in the forests, trees crashed to the ground, and new clearings appeared; the fields were small and produced primitive, meagre harvests, but the era of the hunter was over.

Together with peasant ways of living, a new attitude developed towards the powers-that-be. No longer was it the souls of the salmon and the hart you had to get to know, be aware of, and coax. The mystery of corn, the sprouting seedling, the risk involved in casting the seed upon the earth and then waiting for months, perhaps only to see the whole field become choked with weeds, or have deer break through the fences and eat everything in a single night – all these were matters demanding the protection of greater powers. To plough the earth was to cause it pain, to clear the forest was to offend it, therefore sacrifices had to be made to the trees and to the stones – and you had to be friends with the sun. The sun was obviously the power that gave its blessing to the sprouting corn. Together with the new way of life came a new way of thinking, what we would call a new religion, for nothing was known about the chemistry of the soil, nothing about draining, nothing about the biology of sprouting seeds, nothing about cereal diseases. Whether everything went right, or everything went wrong, was a question of *fate*. The powers-that-be decided your luck, and therefore you had to pacify them, protect yourself against them, and, if possible, be on good terms with them. There was hardly a question as yet of real gods. Spirits lived in the streams and marshes, and offerings were made everywhere. The woodland lake was black and dangerous, so earthenware vessels containing food and amber pearls were lowered into the bogs and marsh-ponds, magnificent great stone-axes were consigned to the streams, meat was deposited on sacred

There are dolmens scattered all over Denmark.

stones, and in spring and autumn, the all-important periods when all matters were decided, it is likely that sacrificial feasts were arranged.

At the same time some new thinking was being done about the dead.

Hunters had buried their dead in the ground, often quite simply. The dead might be given a knife and a spear as burial gifts, but behind this there was also some simple reasoning: allow a dead man or woman to take what was his or hers along, for in the next life you need your things, and nobody wants the dead to come back in order to claim former property. The dead are dangerous.

Peasants became more settled folk than hunters had been. After all, a field needs looking after, and even though you may change fields now and again, you need a bigger house to provide a roof for your cattle and crops, and there has to be quite a number of you for the actual forest-clearing work. Settlements expanded, and a new custom made its appearance: dolmens were built over the dead.

This is not a typically Danish custom. Dolmens are known in many regions of the world: along the shores of the Mediterranean, in France, Germany and England. But strangely enough, in no place in the world are they as numerous as in Denmark. The simple dolmen – three of four stones with one big stone laid on top as a cover – is so common in Denmark that there are still no fewer than about 5,000 of them spread out round the countryside. They are found standing in the fields, some drooping slightly, but as a rule more or less upright. Around the dolmen there is often a circle of raised stones half covered with earth so that only the heavy stone on top is left sticking out, thereby forming a sepulchral chamber in the little enclosed space beneath the dolmen. It was here that the dead person was laid.

Naturally a dolmen cannot have been erected every time somebody died, partly because in such case the country would have become badly

The burial chambers of megalithic tombs are concealed within the mounds.

littered with dolmens, and partly because it would have involved far too much work. To be quite frank, we do not know exactly what the purpose of these dolmens was. They may have been the graves of chieftains or "priests"; but each may also have been a holy altar, and the dead person beneath a sacrifice intended to imbue the altar with strength.

Dolmens were the first to appear, but they were soon replaced by something even more impressive: megalithic tombs. These were built of upright stones arranged in an oblong square over which enormous slabs of stone were placed so as to form a ceiling. It was rather a bombastic form of architecture, partly because of the need to find ceiling stones large enough to extend right across the entire space. More complicated constructional techniques had not as yet been mastered.

The building of a megalithic tomb meant many years of toil for the whole village. The stones had to be dragged from wherever they could be found, and it is almost unbelievable that such operations should have been possible merely by means of ropes and crow-bars. Once the tomb had been constructed it was completely covered over with earth. There is always a passageway constructed of stone leading into these pitchblack houses of death, the ceilings of whose chambers at times are high enough for a man to stand upright. Many dead persons were laid to rest in one of these tombs, presumably everybody in the district, for the skeletons of men, women and children have been found, all duly provided with their respective burial gifts and earthen vessels containing food. While these ponderous stone houses are impressive enough in their way, it should be borne in mind that during this same period the Egyptians were building their biggest and most fantastic pyramids.

The average peasant settlement was rich, solidly founded, and therefore soon became a regular feature of the country. But agriculture and cattle-rearing were not the only pursuits. Ever since Denmark became a maritime country the Danes have been able to pick up from their beaches the stuff we call amber, a golden resin which originated from the coniferous forests of the Tertiary Age. It gets washed out of the soil of Germany and flushed into the sea, whereafter it drifts ashore on Danish beaches. Sometimes it gets washed up from the bottom of the North Sea and comes to rest on the west coast of Jutland.

In these tombs we sometimes find enormous ornaments consisting of hundreds of amber beads. Girls wore this Danish "sea-gold" in the form of colossal multiple chains with large centre pieces, in all probability also as belts. But practically all amber then suddenly disappears from Danish graves. The reason was not that amber had become old-fashioned, but something far more important: it was being sold to countries further south. Southern people awoke to the beauty of this strange substance born of the sea, for round the shores of the Mediterranean it was impossible to find as much as a single piece of amber. This was in approximately 2000 B.C. Egypt had been a state for almost 1,000 years, civilization was well under way in many parts of the Mediterranean world, and gradually a demand arose for this wonderful substance that was available only from the lands around the Baltic and the North Sea. Early sea captains probably found their way up rivers and round Spain and Brittany into the North Sea to the amber land the Greeks later gave the name of *Basileia*.

Thus Denmark started trading, that is to say the Mediterranean countries obtained merchandise from round the Baltic in much the same way as Europe fetched goods from Africa until a century ago. However, the initiative did not *only* come from abroad. Denmark had another export article, namely flint. Danish flint was easily obtained, and as a rule of excellent quality. Danish flint was (and still is) found round the shores of the Baltic, and far up into Norway and Sweden. It was exported both in the form of finished products, i.e. axes and knives, and as a raw material, hacked into small square chunks which people abroad could fashion into whatever they liked. At this time, Danish flint technique had attained a state of proficiency only surpassed in the Old World by the Egyptians, although in the New World certain implements and other objects cut out of stone are undeniably superior to the work attempted by the more down-to-earth flintsmiths of Denmark.

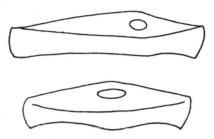

The battle-axe of the followers of single grave culture is like the American Indian tomahawk, a beautiful, frightful weapon.

Stone-cutting had by now become an industry. Not every Danish peasant made his own axe, for specialized craftsmen existed. Both the cutting and polishing of the axe-head and the fashioning of flint-knives were such difficult tasks that only those who devoted themselves completely to the craft were able to master the technique. We have found traces of ancient flint-cutting grounds, and it is not unthinkable that big-scale farmers who were engaged in trade kept many flintsmiths busy.

The Battle Axe

And then, round about the year 2000 B.C., the good old Stone Age peasant settlements received a shock in the form of a new wave of immigration. Once again, it was no stormwind that swept through the country, obliterating the old inhabitants. The influx of newcomers was more in the nature of a trickle. Nevertheless, various things seem to indicate that all did not proceed quite peacefully. The newcomers brought along something that was able to speak for itself: the battle-axe.

The older peasants probably knew the use of a small fighting-axe, but it was merely a pleasant, heavy little thing that nestled comfortably in the hand. The newcomers had a weapon the peasants had never seen before, and it was quite fantastic: a battle-axe, a masterly piece of stone sculpture, ingenious, splendid, beautiful in line, deliciously worked, a masterpiece and a work of art, an instrument of murder on which loving care had been expended – and only people who intend to make good use of such a weapon do that. In the wake of agriculture came war. Hunters had probably had their intertribal feuds, but a hunters' settlement was hardly worth conquering; at the most you might manage to seize a few women if you happened to be short. The peasant had his cattle and his corn, the fruit of bitter toil; there it was, waiting to be grabbed by those who could not be bothered to toil themselves, but were impertinent enough to take what others had created, thereby demonstrating the mentality of the thief, the ruthless brute.

The newcomers forced their way up through Jutland, and it appears that centuries passed before the whole country came to feel their presence. They lived side by side with the old inhabitants, but the solid peasant settlements altered their ways. No longer were grandiose megalithic tombs erected. You made do instead with a smaller affair that would take a dozen persons or so. This was not necessarily the influence of the new-comers. Building megalithic tombs was hard work, and it was perhaps only to be expected that such peculiar contrivances should eventually de-generate. The newcomers settled in Denmark alongside the old inhabitants – who, in spite of everything, were apparently still very much in the majority.

Bronze

But almost at the same time another novelty started finding its way into Denmark: bronze.

Metal had already made its appearance during the period of the mega-lithic tombs. A couple of half-moon-shaped jewels of pure gold and of Irish origin have ended up in Denmark – just how, nobody knows. They cannot have been brought over much later, just by chance, for they were discovered in Danish Stone Age graves. Had people then really managed to sail across the North Sea? Was part of the southern half of the North Sea still land at the time? Did these golden collars come all the way from the island way out beside the Atlantic Ocean as traded goods, or did they hang round the necks of itinerants?

Axes made of pure copper turned up. A discovery has been made in a megalithic tomb of the hip-bone of a man who has seemingly been struck by a bronze spear. The broken tip was apparently not extracted from the hip-bone and thereby caused such damage to the leg that the man suffered from a large, suppurating wound for a very long time.

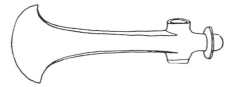

The big axes of the Bronze Age were hollow, only for ceremonial use.

The Bronze Age came to Denmark during or just after the period otherwise known as the "Dagger Age" on account of the splendid big flint-stone daggers that have been found lying beside the corpses in the graves. The dagger had apparently become a weapon worth owning.

Some uncertainty exists. On the one hand, there is no doubt that these splendid stone daggers were copies of bronze daggers and this, one might suppose, would hardly be feasible if bronze daggers had still been unknown in the country. It must be assumed that the Dagger Age and Denmark's early Bronze Age coincided, i.e. that bronze began to make its importance felt whilst the stonecutters were still desperately trying to refine their craft in order to keep up with the new fashions and compete with weapons made of metal.

What the stone-smiths managed to produce during this period of transition is simply astonishing. We have found copies of whole swords made of flint fashioned so delicately that the actual technique of cutting must have been confidently mastered by then. Knife blades became thin, flint arrow-heads almost papery; they were regular, delicately formed and painfully symmetric.

The question is whether most of the 'Dagger' part of the last Stone Age may not have coincided with the dawning of the Bronze Age. After all, it is unlikely that the novelty should have been introduced throughout the whole country at one and the same time.

27

It was probably only the better-class peasants (who perhaps likewise controlled the commerce of the country) who experienced a "Bronze Age". The new metal must have been so costly that few can have been able to afford it. In addition (as also applies to the whole of the Bronze Age) certain implements were lacking. No large forest-axes made of bronze have been found. It seems that they went on using the excellent big flint-stone axe-heads with which they were already familiar.

Furthermore, all the early bronze objects were imported goods that for the most part originated, as far as can be ascertained, from Italy. We have

During the Bronze Age, a woman was armed with a solid dagger.

come upon solid swords, small battle-axes, and jewellery. But shortly afterwards, Denmark secured bronze craftsmen of her own. It is hardly likely that her stone-smiths switched trades. Presumably those who founded the Danish metal industry were immigrant craftsmen who had settled in the country. From the very start, the work bore a professional stamp. Soon the Bronze Age community settled in the lands around the western Baltic, a community of which the Danish islands and Scania together formed the splendid hub. In this respect Denmark has something exceptional to boast of, for no museum in Northern Europe contains Bronze Age collections worthy of comparison with those that can be found in the National Museum in Copenhagen – which in turn is supplemented from whatever happens to be available in other museums all over the country.

There was still hardly any question of a unified nation. But nevertheless there was a certain amount of cohesion, and as regards Scandinavian culture as a whole, Denmark at this time was in the lead. Norway and Sweden tried to keep up, but they were still a long way behind.

The Golden Land

This Bronze Age land of Denmark was rich. Not only did bronze make its appearance, but gold too. It has been loosely calculated that all the gold dating from the Bronze Age that has ended up in Danish museums does not represent even as much as one percent of what existed at the time; riches in gold were truly astonishing. The Bronze Age settlements must have wielded authority over foreign traders. Goods from Italy and other southern European countries still found their way up to Denmark, and Scandinavian amber still found its way down to the Mediterranean. Denmark did not possess one single ounce of tin or copper; this meant

The burial mounds of the Bronze Age are found in rows, presumably along the ancient road lines.

that raw metals for the making of bronze had to be obtained from abroad. It is also astonishing how much finished bronze got into the country.

A number of simply unique archaeological finds have been made in Denmark dating from the first half of the Bronze Age. They give us a strangely vivid picture of life as it was 3,000 years ago, well over 1,000 years before Christ, at the period when Egypt had got as far as Amenhotep IV (Ankh-n-Aton) and Tut-Ankh-Amon. When Danish Bronze Age noblemen died, they were buried in an oak coffin formed by the simple expedient of taking the trunk of a mighty, newly-felled oak, splitting it and hollowing it out. The dead person, clad in everyday apparel, was laid in the coffin together with his burial gifts, whereupon the two halves were closed together again, and a dome-shaped grave-mound was heaped over the coffin. In the majority of cases the coffin and everything else has naturally long since disappeared; at most some verdigrised bits of bronze may remain. But in certain cases in Jutland, *hard pan* has formed in the grave-mound. This takes place when the mound becomes overgrown with heather. If the mound itself has been erected on heather-covered ground in the first place, it means there will be a layer of hard pan both under and over the mound, whereby the mound gradually fills up with rain-water that cannot escape. The coffin is thus left standing in water, whereupon the tannic acid in the oak starts acting, with the result that the coffin, the corpse, and everything else buried alongside quite simply become tanned. It is from coffins such as these that the oldest European costumes we know of have been recovered. Few Egyptian costumes are as old or older.

We notice that the men wore a garment round their hips held in place by a leather belt. This garment sometimes extended right up under the arm-pits and the cut occasionally bears a resemblance to certain Egyptian costumes. Round his shoulders the man wore a flared cape covered with frayed tassels to make it look like the hairy skin of an animal, and on his head he wore a round, brimless cap, covered similarly with a mass of

A number of small statuettes date from the Bronze Age. Several of them are presumably gods, but we know nothing definite about the pantheon of the Bronze Age.

minute knots just like the finest terry cloth. The arms and legs were bare. Leather sandals were known.

A woman wore a blouse with half-length sleeves, cut exactly like blouses of the present day. It was sometimes embroidered round the neck-band. She also wore a very wide skirt with voluminous folds reaching down to the ground, and in addition a cord skirt made of woollen threads held together at the top and bottom by a piece of braid, rather like a woollen latticework. Women and girls wore this well-ventilated skirt wrapped round their loins. Sometimes it was used together with the blouse (if one chooses to believe that the living were clad just like the dead) but from some very small bronze figures we know that Bronze Age girls also sometimes wore the cord skirt and nothing else, just bare legs and a bare top. The bronze figures likewise reveal that the men sometimes wore a brimmed hat and that they used something in the nature of underpants or legless trousers, although the garment may have been a swathed, very tight-fitting loin-cloth, roughly like those seen in the East today. Etruscan bronzes reveal the same short pants.

It may sound peculiar, for the Danish climate hardly seems appropriate for such flimsy wear. But then the weather during the Bronze Age was much warmer than it is today; it was drier, summer practically the whole year round, more or less like the climate nowadays in the southern part of Central Europe. Roofed quarters for animals were unknown, and the light cord skirt was no doubt a pleasant summertime costume.

Early Navigation

Ships were known during the Bronze Age, from now on navigation was a factor to be reckoned with. We have not as yet unearthed any ships dating from the Bronze Age, but we have many pictures of ships, partly

Rock engravings reveal to us (amongst other things) the ships of the times. Here probably a cult ship with a sun disc on a pole.

carved on stone, partly engraved on weapons and on elegant little razors – for the men were clean-shaven and always took their razors with them to the grave.

Shipping was doubtless bound up with trade, but the ship was possibly also a religious symbol. When the forests cleared, the axe became sacred, so it was not surprising that the ship should quietly slip into place beside the axe as an object of religious worship. How the ship of the Bronze Age was built cannot be stated with any certainty, but it must have been capable of carrying many men. It was long and had a high, sweeping prow shaped like a swan's neck with the heads of animals carved on it. And it possibly had a sail. *Possibly*, for the pictures we have that look like ships with sails may merely represent ships with a tree raised in the middle. The practice still exists on Russian lakes of using a young leafy tree as a

31

combined mast and sail if one's boat happens to be going the same way as the wind. But the tree in the ship was also a religious symbol. Pictures of boats with trees in them were discovered at Mycenae.

Many things point to the fact that Denmark enjoyed commercial relationships far to the south. A little folding stool has been discovered in a grave; the design is Egyptian, but the workmanship Scandinavian. Trade with Italy was still lively.

The sun chariot from Trundholm in Zealand, probably a small model of a big, horse-drawn cult image of the sun.

What with trade, shipping, and relationships with a larger world beyond, faith changed once more; the *Sun* apparently now became a power of no mean consideration. A complete sacred figure has been unearthed, a golden disc drawn by a horse, the whole mounted on six wheels. It presumably represents an image of the sun's path across the heavens. In all likelihood cult-inspired chariots bearing images of the sun were driven round the fields.

In the Bronze Age, a curious form of picture-writing existed that was not really writing at all, merely pictures of animals and people, ships and sledges, of ploughing and holy ceremonies. Such pictures are commonest and best in Norway, both in the present kingdom of Norway and in the ancient Norwegian *Bohuslen*. They exist in Sweden and they exist in Denmark. Exactly what the idea was is impossible to say, but the pictures were probably drawn in connection with sacred events, perhaps painted at feasts; pictures on wood probably existed too, pictures that are now no more.

Faith developed and changed, and with it a burial custom was adopted which we now have deep cause to regret: the practise of cremation. The dead were depatched to the Kingdom of Death by means of fire –

Copy of Bronze Age costume found in grave-mound:
string-skirt, blouse and belt-plate.

Bronze Age razor with stylized picture of ship.

Detail of the big Celtic sacrificial silver kettel found in Jutland, showing the horned Celtic god Cernunnus.

Various gold vessels have been found in sacred banks and in the earth. Danish bronze lurs are usually found in bogs, often in pairs, sacrificed to the gods.

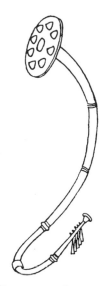

and that put a stop to our oaken coffins with well-preserved corpses, weapons, costumes and burial gifts. In the urns used to hold the ashes of the dead lie burnt stumps of jewellery and the odd burial gift, tiny model swords for instance, for a cremated man did not need his own big, expensive weapons in view of the fact that he himself had been reduced to a symbol, in other words, to ash; and of course his real sword was much too good to let him take along with him seeing that, after all, it was not strictly necessary.

Big bronze lurs have been found in bogs, usually in pairs, magnificently curved blow-horns that bear witness to the fact that music was not unknown.

The occasional lur has been found in southern Norway and Sweden, and one primitive lur has been found in northern Germany. But the classical land of the lurs is Denmark, including Scania. About thirty have been found in present-day Denmark alone, several of them admittedly more or less destroyed, but others so well preserved that they can still be played to this very day and thus enable us to hear the same sounds that once echoed three thousand years ago. The lur produces a very powerful sound, clear and resonant, much like a French horn, but more masculine. The lurs mark the culminating point reached in the technical proficiency of Scandinavian bronze-casting, for they were not built up of forged

3

plates. The entire length of the conical tube was cast in several pieces that were fitted together afterwards. The castings are extremely thin, several bronze alloys being used – always at least three. They are masterpieces that even today are extremely difficult to copy.

But apart from the fact that we see a rich land apparently engaged in steady trading, its peasant settlements efficiently organized, we know practically nothing about this golden, Bronze Age land of the North.

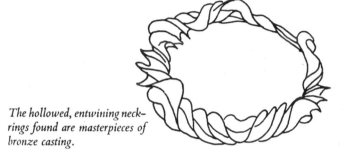

The hollowed, entwining neck-rings found are masterpieces of bronze casting.

Gold and bronze were acquired by trading, so presumably flint was still exported to those regions that had a use for it, and amber was sold in the south. Perhaps other things were traded, such as slaves, furs, fish, and maybe cattle. The climate was fair, and, as already indicated, livestock stayed outdoors the whole year round, so at any rate it can presumably have entailed neither extra trouble nor capital to breed far more livestock than a peasant settlement required for itself – but we know nothing definite.

All we know is that this paradise was suddenly shattered.

The Celts

It was at this time that the Celts started marching through Europe. A new people, possessing their own distinctive culture, shook the European world. They forced their way into Greece, conquered Rome, established themselves firmly in the south of Central Europe, conquered the whole of Gaul (as the land later came to be known after them), and landed on the British Isles in order to extinguish the golden light of the Bronze Age there too.

*Head of bog corpse found at Tollund in Jutland,
dating from about the time of the birth of Christ.*

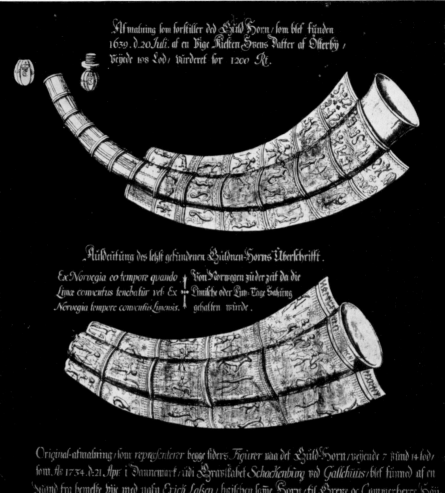

Gold horns found at Gallehus. Old picture from the Royal Treasure
Chamber, where the horns were kept until they were stolen.

While the Celts became the masters of vast regions in a broad belt reaching clear across Europe right out to the Atlantic, they never forced their way up to the North. A chain of old defenceworks across northern Germany, peasant castles, probably marks the border across which the Celts never managed to penetrate northwards. But at the same time the Celts formed a barrier between the north and south of Europe, which meant that the Scandinavian Bronze Age trade with Austria, Italy and other southern countries was stopped.

More or less simultaneously, "Nordland" was struck by another catastrophe. The mild, summery climate came to an end. The cold weather set in with rain and fog and harder winters. The Bronze Age land was, even without any enemies to the south, seriously shaken.

It might appear as though something or other had already taken place beforehand, an overwhelming exodus for instance, perhaps of the leading families; we do not know for certain. Nevertheless, the countries of the north, and at all events Denmark (the land that formed the hardy core of the Bronze Age) apparently became far more thinly populated. There are several places – in Scandinavia and in England – where the population disappeared or thinned out, so it is possible that the newcomers, the Celts, brought disease with them, plague of a sort, but we know nothing.

The Celts brought one novelty with them to Europe, something which was the secret (or one of them) behind their victories and superiority: iron. A few items of ironware had probably already reached Scandinavia a little earlier, but the Celts used iron weapons: swords and knives and axes.

Scandinavia passed into the period we call the "Celtic Iron Age". As already indicated, it does not mean that Celts settled in the country, but it seems that trade with the newcomers soon started up, and in Denmark, as in the rest of Scandinavia, many things began to show Celtic influence. Denmark was unable to produce bronze herself. On the other hand, strange as it may sound, she was able to provide herself with iron. There is no iron ore anywhere in the country, but the marshes and bogs provide the so-called "bog-ore", a layer of iron that has become deposited over long periods as the water oozes down. When bog-ore is dug up and melted, it makes good quality iron provided the process is carried out properly. But it is rather complicated and therefore out of the question that the Danes should have discovered it by themselves. They learnt it in

35

the south, from the Celts, and soon furnaces started smoking in the marshes throughout Denmark. On the other hand it looks as though, to begin with, we fumbled in our efforts to grasp the essentials of the smith's trade, for the oldest weapons we find are poor and very clumsy. It is unlikely that the bronze-casters learnt a new trade, for, strange as it may sound, the country was still able to obtain all the bronze it wanted. It was not a shortage of metal that encouraged the production of iron, merely the wish to own weapons made of the new metal. Bronze was used for jewellery, buckles and the like; no attempt was made to save on bronze – quite the contrary.

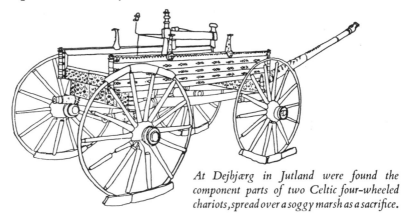

At Dejbjærg in Jutland were found the component parts of two Celtic four-wheeled chariots, spread over a soggy marsh as a sacrifice.

Strangest of all was the fact that the country managed to find its feet again incredibly quickly after the shock. Moreover, the whole country did not adopt the change-over all at once. The Bronze Age continued to thrive on the main Danish islands for a good while after the new influences had made themselves felt up through the mainland of Jutland. But soon, trading with the Celts became extremely lively, with the result that we have had the good fortune to discover objects of Celtic origin on Danish soil that quite simply are among the most sensational Celtic finds in all Europe. At the close of the 19th century, two big four-wheeled chariots were found in a marsh near *Dejbjærg*, in Jutland. They had been dismantled and their various parts laid out on the soggy turf of the marsh as an offering to the gods. There must have been a sacred place near the marsh, for Dejbjærg, or *Dødebjærg*, means Death Hill, and nearby is a *Vognbjærg*, meaning Chariot Hill. The chariots must have been magnificent vehicles in their time, richly mounted with bronze, gleaming lushly gold as they rolled past. One is reminded of what Tacitus had to say later on about the charioteering goddesses of the Teutons, for the chariots were in all probability sacred vehicles. A big silver kettle was found a little further to the north in Jutland, in a marsh near *Gundestrup*. It is 32 inches in diameter, has been forged in pure silver and decorated both inside and out with chased pictures of heads of gods and goddesses, scenes of sacred rites, warriors or holy men in procession, and the interesting point is that the whole world with which these pictures are concerned is Celtic. It is impossible to say whether the kettle was forged abroad and imported, or whether it was made in Denmark. It is possible that Celtic craftsmen came to Denmark, either as prisoners-of-war, (i. e. bought slaves) or else because there was a good market up here. Denmark was apparently on the way to becoming a rich trading country again, and we presumably still had wares to offer that were in demand further south – first and foremost amber, and possibly slaves.

Mass Migrations

There was trouble in the country at this time. It seems the Bronze Age must have been relatively peaceful. The many weapons found never bear signs of use, and towards the close of the Bronze Age swords became smaller, mere ornamental objects, badges of rank. During the Celtic Iron Age there were apparently feuds in the provinces. Perhaps it became necessary to defend the country against foreigners, and some 100 years before the birth of Christ the world received a message from the North to the effect that the Cimbrians and the Teutons were marching southwards.

Roman authors claim (and likewise the traditions of itinerant tribes) that astonishingly many of these tribes came from the North. This applies to the Haruds and the Vandals.

It would not be unreasonable to assume that the Vandals were in some way connected with North Jutland, in particular with that part of the country called Vendsyssel. It has been proved that it must have been the same people who were living both at Vendsyssel in Denmark, and at a place near the River Oder, in northern Germany. Probably it was a Vendsysselian tribe that went south. At all events it was the Vandals who later suddenly broke up, travelled through France to Spain and settled there in the province that still bears their name, Andalusia (formerly Vandalusia). From thence they made their way over to Africa, created the Vandalian Empire and conquered Rome.

But there was a long period between the time the inhabitants of Vendsyssel broke up from North Jutland (if it was them) and the time the Vandalian Empire shocked the Mediterranean world with its ravages.

On the other hand the Cimbrians and the Teutons came fresh from their northern villages. Whether the Teutons really came from Ty in northern Jutland, as is claimed, is hard to say. On the other hand the Cimbrians in all likelihood really did come from Himmerland in northern Jutland. They moved south demanding land, new settlements. They defeated one Roman army after another and spread panic throughout the Empire until the two peoples separated and met their fate in the person of a rugged little army commander named *Marius*. The Teutons were beaten at Aqua Sextia in 102 B.C., and the Cimbrians at Vercellae.

The great empire of the Celts never became a unified state. They managed to consolidate in France and England, but otherwise the whole Celtic world was so loosely knit that foreign tribes were able to march straight through their territories; and by more or less the time of the birth of Christ, the glory of the Celts was past.

The Romans

Rome assumed world dominion, Caesar occupied Gaul and invaded the British Isles, and shortly afterwards they became a Roman province for 400 years. The Roman legions marched east, south, west, and through Gaul. Their roads spun a web over England, but they never penetrated properly into Germany, nor up to Scandinavia either. This is one of the reasons why the prehistory and ancient history of Scandinavia is completely different to that of Western Europe.

But this does not mean that Rome never managed to reach Scandinavia at all. Admittedly it was only the occasional Roman ship's captain that was able to relate on his return that he had been "in the land of the Cimbrians", (i.e. Jutland), but Roman merchants made their way up here,

Roman traders sent goods north in exchange for amber, fur, slaves and possibly other wares, and Denmark passed into the period which we know as the "Roman Iron Age".

For, with the fall of the Celts, and the Romans in command of the world, the balance of power was clearly endangered once more. But two factors enabled Scandinavia to hold a special position: firstly, Roman culture had made its way up here via peaceful trading over long distances; and secondly, large-scale migrations, which later were to embroil the whole of Europe, only caused slight repercussions in Scandinavia.

One of the good Roman silver drinking-vessels from Hoby,
on the island of Lolland.

Once more it is astonishing to note the excellence of the Roman wares that Denmark managed to secure for herself. The Roman bronzes that came to rest in dark, low Scandinavian farmhouses are first-class, and one of Europe's noteworthy Roman finds was made on the Danish island of Lolland, namely the chieftain's grave at *Hoby*. Here, beside the body of a Scandinavian nobleman, lay a drinking-set of finest Roman make consisting of a bronze tray, a lovely little pitcher, a pail, a wine-ladle and two silver beakers; even at Pompeii nothing finer has been found in the way of drinking-vessels. The Danish peasant communities managed very nicely for themselves by trading; they were not poor.

Even so, things looked a little poverty-stricken, for Roman metropolitan culture never reached this far north. Houses were not built in Denmark the way they were in the south. There is not one single stone house, not one Roman bridge, no theatres and no Roman baths as in England. The Danes lived in low, dark, windowless huts with a hole in the purlin to let the smoke out. The floor was of earth or clay, and the house was divided into two parts, one for cattle and horses, and one for human beings. Another thing: only the upper classes wore fine clothes, brooches and jewellery. Ordinary Danes went about in simple woollen garments or animal hides – sheepskins, for instance.

There have been a number of finds in Denmark dating from about the time of the birth of Christ that have caused something of a sensation: corpses in bogs. In many cases both the corpses and their clothes have been preserved by bog acids, thus enabling us once again to find out a little about the costume habits of the time. Many of the corpses have been so well preserved that literally speaking the whole body is there. A photograph of the head of the Tollund Man was sent speeding all round the world, for here we are confronted with a man who was lowered into a bog 2,000 years ago. His countenance is better preserved than those of Egyptian mummies. He wears a serious, calm expression and a faint smile as though he were asleep – the sort of man you might meet in Jutland to this very day.

But the period of Roman trade came to an end. Rome fell, and greater troubles descended upon Europe, a period of large-scale migrations, with the main pressure coming from the east. There were migrations taking place in Denmark at the time, for the most part probably local in nature. It appears that the Scandinavian tribes drove each other out. It was a period of trouble and fighting, and the period from which the great bog discoveries date.

Roman authors tell us that the Teutons were in the habit of sacrificing spoils of war to their gods after a battle. In Denmark, such spoils have been discovered in several places, having been consigned to the bogs and marshes. The black, wallowy soil must have fairly teemed with swords and shields, coats-of-mail, spears, horse skeletons and other items of a more domestic nature; for those that showed fight were often migrating peoples.

Many sacred bogs were "in use" for a long time, in fact they continued to have things consigned to them over periods of several hundred years. The most famous finds are those made at *Viemose*, at *Kragehul*, at *Illerup* near Aarhus, and at *Thorsbjærg* and *Nydam*, in South Jutland.

The bog at Thorsbjærg contained a complete Teutonic costume consisting of trousers and tunic, a magnificent cape and several helmets. At Nydam a couple of big boats were found – as long as the Viking ships found later – and many weapons. The find was made in 1863, and when the Germans conquered South Jutland they demanded that the find be handed over, which it was. When the northern part of South Jutland was returned to Denmark in 1920, Denmark duly recovered Nydam bog, but not the find. It is still in a museum at Schleswig.

Much of the find, including one of the big boats, was destroyed during the war of 1864, for excavation work had still not been completed. But one of the boats still exists and reveals that Danish shipbuilding had made great strides at the time. An older boat, dating from about the time of

A model of the boat found at Hjortspring on the island of Als, a type of craft similar to that seen on Bronze Age rock-engravings.

the birth of Christ, was found in Hjortspring Marsh in South Jutland, a boat much as we know them from Bronze Age pictures: a 42-foot, slender canoe, as delicately and expertly built as a racing skiff, but naturally more primitive. Its narrow planks have never been nailed together, but sewn and then lashed to the framework. But the *Nydam boat*, which was some 500 years younger, was a proper ship, not unlike the boat discovered at Sutton Hoo in England. The Nydam boat is over 60 feet long, a good craft bearing an outward resemblance to the big boats of today. It was propelled by oars, and was perhaps able to carry a sail; on the other hand it has practically no keel and is somewhat rounded, so it probably capsized rather easily. It was in boats of this type that the Angles of South Jutland sailed westwards and, together with the Saxons, occupied England.

This took place round about 400 or 500 A.D., forming part of the Scandinavian tribal migrations. While the Saxons were Teutons, the Angles came from further north. Something they brought with them to England was a knowledge of Nordic mythology – the Song of Beowulf, for instance.

The period after the "Roman Iron Age" in Denmark is called the "Teutonic Age". During this period an independent Germanic culture grew up upon the remains of what the Teutons had learnt from the Celts and the Romans, based upon their own, even older, cultural inheritance.

The famed golden horns found at *Gallehus*, in South Jutland, date from the period between 400 and 450 A.D., when the Angles emigrated.

Two heavy horns of pure gold, bearing chased pictures as fantastic as those on the Gundestrup kettle, were found at the same place in 1634 and again in 1736 and handed over to the King's collection, where they were highly treasured until they were stolen at the beginning of the 19th century by an artisan who melted them down. The horns were worth a fortune in their day and were presumably sacred too. Perhaps they were buried on some occasion when a tribe decided to forsake its land and its gods.

One of the two horns bore an inscription. The Scandinavians had evolved their own form of writing, *runic characters*. They had learnt the art in the south and instead of merely adapting letters they evolved a whole set of new ones to represent the sounds of the Scandinavian language. The runes were edged and particularly suitable for carving in wood. The writing was used in sacred formulae intended to make weapons powerful, for inscribing owner's names on weapons and jewellery, and on tombstones over the dead.

By this time the Danes had already made their presence felt along the coasts of northern Germany and Flanders, right down as far as the shores of France. They were the forerunners of the later Vikings and had already discovered that booty could be won by the simple expedient of sailing to foreign countries and raiding. Gregory of Tours mentions that a Danish king met his death during a campaign in northern France.

But meanwhile, something important had happened.

It all started when Emperor Constantine transferred the capital of the Roman Empire from Rome to Constantinople. This dislocated Europe's entire trading system, and Denmark, having sought her trade in the south for thousands of years, found that this too had now been transferred eastwards to the Baltic and thereafter via Russian rivers south to the new hub of the Mediterranean. In this way the trade lines started to move from east to west through the Baltic, so that all of a sudden Denmark was no longer in such a favourable position for trade. It led to trouble in the Baltic. Islands such as Gotland and Bornholm became trading stations *en route*, which in turn meant that they were worth plundering. And it appears that they were indeed plundered, time and again, by pirates. At this time Denmark was quite well-off for gold. Silver appeared, and it seems that real money (Roman) was used as a form of "part payment" in Scandinavia. It gradually became the custom to seek one's living on the sea. No doubt it had always been so to a certain extent, ever since Denmark became a sea-bordered country, but it now became a definite profession.

This is apparently the main cause of the evolution of the Viking Age. This, and one other thing: Denmark, as far as we can deduce, had for a very long time had a population surplus, a surplus she had been obliged to get rid of. An attempt had been made in former times by means of large-scale migrations southwards (like those of the Cimbrians), but with time, as the German tribes gained control of their territory, tribes were no longer free to wander at liberty down through Europe. They sought other paths, across the sea, eastwards, northwards, and westwards.

Within the confines of the Baltic a competitive battle gradually developed against the Swedes, who were particularly interested in trading along the Russian rivers. Thus the Danes and the Swedes were continually running foul of each other in their struggle for commercial power. However, the big Dano-Norwegian drive was made to the west, where its impetus produced one of the strangest chapters in Scandinavia's history: the Viking Age.

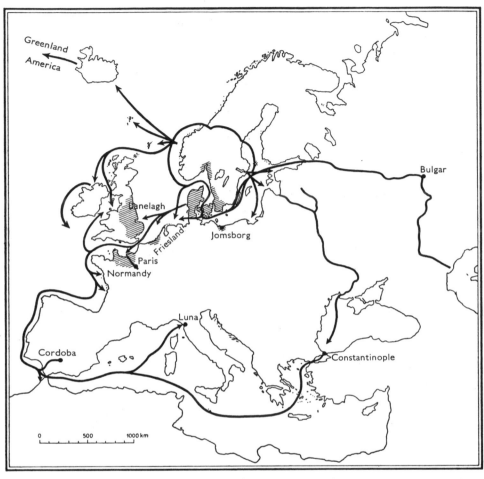

The main routes taken by Viking expeditions from the three Scandinavian countries, Denmark and Danish areas of expansion have been shaded.

II. THE VIKING AGE

The Viking Age is generally said to have begun on June 8, 793, with the attack on Lindisfarne on the northeast coast of England. This attack provoked consternation, for although by no means the first Viking raid on an English or French coast, the fact that on this occasion the plunderers' objective should have been a famous convent, an episcopal residence and well-known seat of learning, and that its holy inmates were killed or dragged off as slaves, produced a shock. The report sped down through western Europe and everybody was horrified.

But it was only a start. The Danes and the Norwegians had learnt that there were spoils to be won by crossing the sea and that coastal raids involved relatively little danger. The armies of the English and French kings could not be everywhere at once. Viking fleets would suddenly appear off the coast, their warriors would leap ashore, plunder a village or a convent, or a couple of big estates, and then make off again before news of what had taken place reached further inland.

Later on they became even more impudent. They joined forces to form big fleets and attacked Flemish and English and French coastal trading stations. And thus, year after year, always in the springtime, these pirate fleets descended from the North.

What the word "Viking" really means, nobody knows. Probably "the men from the fjords", for *vik* or *vig*, both in Danish and in Norwegian, means a *little fjord* or *creek*. To the west they were often known as "Normans" for it was difficult to tell the difference between Danish and Norwegian Vikings, despite the fact that in Scotland, for instance, distinction was made between "black" and "white" *Lochlans*. The colours probably referred to the ships, their sails or the way they were tarred.

But it was not only by means of these warlike raids that the Scandinavian Vikings made their presence felt in western Europe. Very soon they started settling. Danish chieftains became rulers of sizable areas of Flanders and obtained control of several trading ports. They literally streamed into England and soon there were so many Danish immigrant peasants that the whole area comprising Northern England, the Midlands, and Eastern England broke away from the English community and constituted itself as an independent Viking kingdom called "Danelagh". It became a

It was with "the Viking ship" that the Scandinavians aroused terror along the European coasts.

"chieftaindom" or kingdom organized the same way as the peasant settlements at home in Denmark with their free peasant farmers who met at their *thingsteads* and settled all legal disputes there. Danish peasants continued to stream west, and at the same time the Viking raids were kept up. The threat to England became deadly earnest.

And then, in the person of Alfred the Great (871–901), the English found a man capable of putting a stop to the onrushing might of Scandinavia. He organized a defence system that was based upon the principle of tackling the Vikings in their own sphere.

One of the secrets behind the Viking Age was *the ship*. In the course of thousands of years of sailing, the Scandinavian peoples had succeeded in creating a craft that, for its day, was undoubtedly the finest in Europe. It was light, very fast, seaworthy, strong, excellently built, solid and yet at the same time slight; there was not one single superfluous inch of wood. Every little detail was the result of endless generations of life spent on the sea. The people of Scandinavian were furthermore seafarers by nature, completely fearless. They voyaged across the seas in their boats,

The big runic stone at Jelling has an image of Christ and a lion fighting a serpent on the reverse sides. The runic letters read: "Harald King (Harald Bluetooth) had this stone made after Gorm his father and after Thyra his mother. That Harald which conquered all Denmark and Norway and made the Danes Christians." – Behind the large one can be seen the smaller Jelling stone, raised by Gorm over his wife Thyra.

Mane-chair of wood and gilded bronze dating from the Viking Age, and one of the bronze heads of the mane-chair.

Casting mould for Thor hammers and Christian crosses – the silversmith supplied both Christians and heathens.

Silver Thor hammer, worn by worshippers of Thor round their necks.

which though sound, were after all still open boats. They were accustomed to life on the sea and knew how to sleep in their cold craft, soaking wet, night after night, until they reached their destination.

But Alfred the Great built an English fleet and started intercepting the Vikings at sea before they reached England's shores.

At the same time the Danes and Norwegians living in Danelagh, Scotland, and Ireland began to think that it was no longer so pleasant having these wild visitors from their old home country. Anglo-Danes and Anglo-Norwegians had by this time become thoroughly settled, owned their own farms and land, and had no wish to take part in feuds and wars. In the beginning they welcomed the new immigrants from home, and it must likewise be admitted that they frequently joined forces with the raiders in the springtime when they landed in England. But in time, the whole affair became a threat to Danelagh too.

It became a real trial of strength between Alfred and the Danes, and it looked as though Alfred was going to lose. He lost a great many men and nearly all his land, and when forces from Danelagh started joining up with their countrymen from home, he hardly knew which way to turn. The whole affair seemed hopeless, but then the Danes' luck began to change. A Danish fleet in the Channel was supposed to follow the Danish land forces and join up with them, but it was driven off by a storm, whereupon Alfred won a number of decisive victories. Danelagh was obliged to surrender and once more place itself beneath the English crown, but managed to insist on retaining its own Danish laws and customs. The English king was allowed very little say in the northern part of his own country. By way of compensation, Danes now began to stream south. Many of them became members of the English King's highest advisory council. Several sons of Danes became bishops; in fact at one time, the archbishoprics of both York and Canterbury were held by the sons of Danish Vikings.

Up to now the enterprise had met with amazing success, despite the fact that the entire Scandinavian action in the West had been backed by no concerted plan and had no strategic, political aims. Everything happened in some overwhelming fashion – and the final result was the same anyway. The King of France lost the whole of *Normandy*. He had the Viking fleets on his coasts every single year; in fact they finally had the impudence to make camp and spend the winter so that his only resort was to buy them out. In desperation, he negotiated, in 911, with one of the Danish chieftains, (probably of the Danish royal house), Rolf by name (Rollo in French) and granted him Normandy as a duchy and a fief on condition that he, in exchange, would protect the land from further Viking invasions. Rolf accepted, but took his oath of fealty extraordinarily lightly. In reality he was an independent chieftain in his own slice of northern French territory, which soon filled up with Scandinavian immigrants, mostly Danes, who proceeded to build up a well-organized Scandinavian peasant settlement along the lines of Danelagh in England. Little quarter was given. *Regnar Lodbrog*, whom *T. D. Kendrick* in his book "*A History of the Vikings*" calls "one of the most renowned Vikings of all time ... a scion of the Danish royal family" (Regnar's father was probably King of Zealand) sailed up the Seine in the spring of 845 with 120 ships, plundered Paris, ravaged the country on both sides of the Seine, and when King Charles challenged him with an army that he had divided into two halves, one on each bank of the river, Regnar went ashore and defeated first one half, whereafter he sacrificed 111 prisoners to his Nordic gods by hanging them, and then crossed the river in order to defeat the other half of the army. The result was that the French king had to seek refuge in a convent. Regnar sailed down the Seine once more with his fleet. King Charles wanted to stop him, but somehow did not dare. Instead, he paid Regnar 7,000 pounds of silver to keep away, whereupon Regnar sailed home to Zealand in triumph, his ships heavily laden with both booty and prisoners.

A Danish Viking named *Hastings* sailed along the coast of France, down the coast of Spain, into the Mediterranean and then launched a surprise attack and plundered the Italian town of *Luna*. Fleet after fleet went ravaging up and down the French and English coasts. At this same time the Swedes were in action in the east. They sailed up the Russian rivers, gained control of large districts and got as far as the Black Sea. Norwegian Vikings sailed to Iceland, onward to Greenland and thence to America, which they called "*Vinland*" (meaning "Wineland"). But they were unable to retain their position at such a great distance from home. Nevertheless, for five hundred years or so there were Scandinavian settlements in far-distant Greenland, solid trading peasant communities that sent merchandise back to the markets of Europe: excellent woollen cloth,

Viking Age graveyard at Aalborg, Jutland. The graves are "ship tumuli",
i.e. the stones were arranged in the form of a ship.

Nordic king and queen, chessmen of Scandinavian workmanship found on the Isle of Lewis, Scotland.

Danish hand-axe inlaid with silver found in a Viking Age grave in Jutland.

walrus-tusk ivory, incredibly tough ship's hawsers of walrus skin, and other items.

The Norwegians also established themselves permanently in Ireland and founded kingdoms. The Danes retained their footholds in England and northern France. Everything in fact was proceeding splendidly, and the sons of Danish peasants, rather than stay at home, were keener on going to sea or helping themselves to the fine lands that were available in the West. For Denmark was still over-populated, despite the fact that much new land had been brought under the plough.

Unification of the Realm

But then the situation at home in Denmark changed; it was the incessant raids themselves that were largely to blame. Admittedly Denmark was rich, towns were growing up, and in the southern part of Slesvig especially, trade was lively, for trade between western and eastern Europe was by sea, and sailing northwards round Jutland was dangerous. Most trading vessels therefore preferred to sail to the root of the Jutlandic peninsula, load and unload their wares there and let them be transported over the short distance from one sea to the other by road. This provided excellent opportunities for the trading centre of *Hedeby*, just on the southern Danish border, and this wealthy town changed hands several times. For a while a private Viking king (a Swede, from all accounts) ruled the roost, and enjoyed handsome commercial profits.

It was a Danish King named *Harald Bluetooth* (approx. 935–985), a son of Gorm the Old, who first became aware of the danger that threatened. As a young man he had taken part in Viking raids himself, but western Europe, which was more or less defenceless against the eternally venturesome Viking fleets, began to wake up to the fact that every summer, Denmark herself was practically unmanned. The German Emperor Otto made for the Vikings at their home base, and marched north into Jutland. Admittedly he marched south again, and conquered no land, but King Harald realized the dangers involved in the situation. He became, from all accounts, deeply interested in assuring Denmark's safety and slowing down emigration.

Until now Denmark had been all one country. Nevertheless it was divided (just as England once was) into several kingdoms. This was only natural for a country that consisted of two large, separated areas of land, Jutland and Scania, plus five hundred islands. Harald wrote on the runic stone which he caused to be erected at his father's old heathen shrine at Jelling, that he "had united all Denmark and Norway under himself and made the Danes Christians". He gained control of the whole

Wooden remains from King Gorm's barrow at Jelling.

of Denmark and for a time was actually king of Norway too. And he personally became converted to the Christian faith.

The Danes had known the religion of western Europe for several hundred years. They had become acquainted with it in the course of their raids, and monks had come to Denmark in former times as missionaries. However, at a time when England had had solid Christian churches for several hundred years, the Danes, the Norwegians and the Swedes were still heathens. They regularly permitted themselves to be "marked with the sign of the cross" prior to baptism when they were in foreign climes, but it is said that when they came home they "washed off the baptism" and once more became heathens that paid their respects to *Odin, Thor* and *Frøj*. It was not because their souls were false but simply because they regarded Christ as God in western Europe, and therefore it was as well to be on good terms with him while in his countries. But at home in Scandinavia, Thor and Odin were still gods, and naturally one could not fail them.

Christianity now came to Scandinavia, but understandably enough it was impossible trying to convert an entire community of tradition-bound peasant farmers and sailors all at once.

King Harald's interests at home led to a difference of opinion amongst the people. The country was divided into two parties: on the one hand those who shared the King's ideas about staying at home and enjoying peace, and on the other the war-minded who regarded the Viking trade as being more fun. The latter made King Harald's young son Sweyn Forkbeard their leader, with the result that a conflict arose between father and son. The final battle took place at sea, for when Vikings fought amongst themselves they did not care to do so on dry land, but instead went aboard their ships and fought on the water – even though they might only lie to just off the coast for as long as the fight lasted. War for them was mainly naval warfare; it was what they knew best, for they were not so well acquainted with the more modern western European forms of fighting.

Neither won. But that evening, King Harald, who had gone ashore, was hit by an arrow that came whirring out of the darkness. A few days later he died at Jomsborg, a Viking fortress he himself had built down in "Vendland", the present North German coastland.

Jomsborg was a brotherhood or guild of chieftains' sons. It had very strict laws and was a firmly established clan. The Vikings of Jomsborg resolved to avenge the death of their king and therefore took young Sweyn prisoner. He had to purchase his liberty by paying them a large fine in silver.

The Conquest of England

So then, *Sweyn Forkbeard* was King in the land of Denmark (approx. 985–1014) and in him the warlike Vikings obtained a leader after their own hearts. He first dealt with domestic problems. He won back Hedeby and then turned his attention to his rival for power in Scandinavia, the Norwegian king, Olav Tryggveson. They came to grips at sea off the island of Svold – and the Norwegians were defeated. King Olav fell during the battle, thus giving Sweyn a free hand. He then turned to the west.

Of recent years there have been found, scattered round Denmark, a number of "Viking barracks" that in all likelihood date from the time of King Sweyn and his son Canute the Great. These give us a fresh insight into the final tremendous effort made by the Vikings of Denmark. The Viking fleets that now set sail westwards were no longer independent raiding fleets sent forth by individual peasant farmer settlements. It was the Danish King himself who now called the chieftains and peasants of the settlements to arms. The "barracks" were castles. Each consisted of a mighty rampart surrounding a number of "barrack halls", and both the rampart and the halls were built with fantastic precision and engineering efficiency. The best known of them, *Trelleborg* in Zealand, has 16 halls within the rampart and an equal number without, while *Aggersborg*, near the Limfjord, is twice the size. These "barracks" explain the success of the venture that now came to pass: behind the first conquest of England lay a brilliantly organized military machine.

Sweyn sent fleets westwards for several years running, and the unfortunate English king, *Ethelred the Unready*, could think of no better answer than to purchase peace by paying enormous sums in silver, subsequently known as "Danegeld". Sweyn promptly used the silver for fresh armaments – and Ethelred never got his peace.

Then Ethelred made the most foolish move of his whole life: on the night of St. Brice, November 13, 1002, he had "all Danes" murdered. This, however, only meant Danes outside the borders of Danelagh, broadly speaking south of Watling Street, and even though he did not succeed in having them *all* killed, the massacre was a comprehensive one. English chroniclers describe it as having been "ruthlessly gruesome". Among those murdered was King Sweyn's sister, who had married a chieftain in England.

From Danelagh, and from other Danes in England, a howl went back to Denmark demanding that the horrors of St. Brice's night be revenged. There was scarcely a nobleman's family in Denmark that had not been affected and therefore was duty-bound to take blood vengeance. And thus England's fate was sealed.

The Danes in England were not so very pleased with the prospects, which after all threatened the Danish districts too. But the matter was now decided. King Sweyn acted with cold singleness of purpose. During the years 1003 and 1004 he remained in England, ravaging and laying

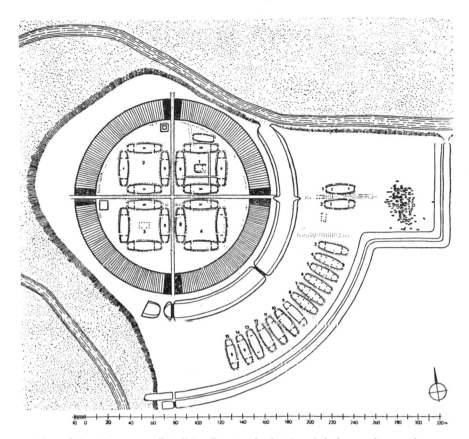

Plan of the Viking camp "Trelleborg" in Zealand. The whole lay-out has a military precision that verges on the pedantic. The square extension to the outer rampart is the graveyard. Four camps of this type have been located in Denmark to date, the largest being that of "Aggersborg", which has 48 halls within its central circular rampart.

waste far and wide throughout the defenceless land. In 1007, Ethelred had to produce Danegeld for the fourth time. Sweyn was able to sail home with 36,000 pounds of silver. Like his forefather Alfred, Ethelred tried to build ships in order to defeat the Vikings at sea. But the organization broke down, the ships' crews started fighting amongst themselves, and the fleet was withdrawn to London.

For a couple of years Sweyn stayed at home in Denmark. He sent his Jomsborg Vikings to England under the leadership of their chieftain, Torkil the Tall, and with them came Olav the Fat, a son of the Norwegian

53

King. Ethelred finally promised them a fifth payment of Danegeld, namely 45,000 pounds of silver, with which sum he brought the total he had been obliged to raise up to no less than 134,000 pounds, the equivalent in our time of a fortune worth millions. But before he managed to collect all the money from the tax-plundered English, the Vikings seized Canterbury in order to avenge St. Brice's night and slew the bishop. Most of the Vikings then sailed home again, but Torkil and Olav offered their services to the English.

The next year Sweyn returned in person. His Jomsborg Viking chieftain was in England with all the money he had managed to secure, and Sweyn was now once more the supreme warlord.

He advanced upon London, but the town managed to defend itself. So, without wasting time on a siege, he subdued all the English provinces and was promptly hailed everywhere as England's King. London was finally cut off and had to surrender without even putting up a fight. Ethelred fled to Normandy. Sweyn Forkbeard became King of Denmark and England and was thereby firmly installed as the "Caesar of the North".

But his fortune did not last. The very next year, 1014, he fell off his horse and died. The English contend that St. Edmund slew him. It is possible that he really was murdered.

Canute the Great

His son *Canute* was only eighteen. He was in England at the time of his father's death and was probably hailed as King, but the English nevertheless decided to call Ethelred home. Canute was obliged to sail back to Denmark, where his brother Harald had been proclaimed king.

Back in Denmark, Canute prepared for an expedition. In 1015 he sailed westwards with a fleet totalling 200 ships supported by a contingent of Norwegian troops under Erik Jarl. The fleet landed at Sandwich. King Ethelred was sick at the time, according to reports, so Canute ravaged the land. In contemporary chronicles an English earl named Eadrich Streon is made to play the rôle of traitor and villain, and it seems as though quite a number joined forces with Canute. Erik Jarl was installed as the Earl of York and thus the whole of Northumbria became Danish. Ethelred suddenly died and his young son, Edmund Ironside, ascended the English throne. Canute surrounded London with his men and laid siege to the town. But, not having his father's strategical talents, he succeeded in wasting time while Edmund collected an army together. On several occasions the vagabonding Danish forces were beaten. But the decisive battle between the two young Kings took place at Assandun (probably Ashingdon in Essex), and here the Danes were victorious. After the English defeat, England wanted peace. Canute and Edmund divided the country between them. Thus Canute received all the land north of Watling Street, which principally meant Danelagh, while Edmund got the south. But

Convex ornament in gold filigree dating from the Viking Age.

shortly afterwards, Edmund suddenly died too. It is claimed that he was poisoned, but nobody knows for certain. Canute was proclaimed King of all England and crowned accordingly.

He had hardly managed to consolidate his power in England when his brother in Denmark conveniently died (just of what is not quite certain) and Canute thus became King of Denmark too. Later on he became King of Norway and also reached out a tentative arm in the direction of Sweden. Canute had created his fantastic North Sea Empire and thus became *"Canute the Great"*.

One problem remained in England, namely the problem that bothers all conquerers: Canute had to make arrangements to have his army transported home again. Caesar gave his soldiers land and managed to spread them comfortably around his Roman Empire so that they constituted no danger. Canute levied Danegeld for the last time and paid off his men. They returned home to Scandinavia. On several gravestones in Sweden can still be read to this very day words to the effect that the good Swedish peasant whom the stone commemorates was in England as a young man under King Canute the Dane, and was paid Danegeld.

Canute disbanded his army, retaining only a small *corps d'élite* around him, and then set about organizing his tremendous empire.

He was fond of England and regarded it as his principle kingdom. He worked for the removal of such differences as existed between the Danes and the English. This task was perhaps not very difficult, for the countless thousands of Danes living in England were used to living side by side with the old English families, and, when all is said and done, the old Angles, who settled particularly in the Midlands and in the North of England, were themselves Northmen. So the differences in their cultures were not so very great (apart from the matter of Christianity, and the Danes in England very quickly became Christians). Several thousand place-names in England are reminders of the Scandinavian invasion. While thousands of place-names in Scandinavia bear witness to the old heathen faith, it is only in very few places in England that such heathen names are to be found.

Canute actually became an Englishman. Only once did he have to re-turn home in order to crush an attempted rising in Denmark. The Danes were displeased with the fact that their king was never at home and therefore Ulf Jarl, Canute's viceroy in Denmark, had plans (which in-volved Canute's little son) of seizing power. But Canute had Ulf Jarl murdered in Roskilde Cathedral (or in the royal courtyard) and returned once more to England. On Easter Sunday, 1027, King Canute, northern Europe's mightiest ruler, strolled up the aisle of St. Peter's in Rome beside Conrad (who that day was crowned Emperor) as his guest of honour and witness. This was the Viking pirates' greatest triumph, the culmination of the incredible Scandinavian adventure, the result of several centuries of incessant sailing and war with the west.

Canute was a good and conscientious king. There was some dissatis-faction in Norway, where he had placed one of his sons as a child-king with powerful men at his side. But Canute's happiness was relatively short-lived too. He died suddenly, no more than some thirty odd years old, in Shaftesbury, on November 11, 1035, and was buried at Win-chester.

And so the new system was established in Scandinavia, namely that of western European monarchy.

As long as the Viking fleets were "free", as long as there had been settlement chieftains to organize them on their own initiative, the Vikings continued to be a terrifying threat to western Europe. Now that a single king had assumed power after the pattern of Western Europe, the moment that king went away and omitted to leave strong men in charge behind him, or left a weak one, Scandinavia's expeditionary forces became fatally weakened.

Canute's sons, despite the fact that they were completely incompetent, were both proclaimed Kings of England. But on June 8, 1042, Canute's second son Hardicanute was the guest of the Danish chieftain Tove Prude at his fine estate on the Thames. The moment he drained his horn to the health of his host and hostess he fell down dead. Whether he was poisoned or died of a stroke was never clarified, but with his death the mighty "Danish Empire" came to an end.

The Collapse of the Danish Empire

It simply fell to pieces. England chose an English king (whose family was half Danish, but even so) and not even at home in Denmark was a Dane elected. Norway had already slipped out of Denmark's powerful clutches and war had been steadily brewing between Hardicanute and Norway's young king, *Magnus the Good*, because Hardicanute laid claim to the Norwegian throne after his father, Canute the Great. But the Danish and Norwegian nobles did not want war. They made the two young kings accept the compromise that each should rule his own country for the time being, but that the one who lived longest should subsequently take over the other's kingdom. At this time England had slipped through the fingers of her Scandinavian rulers. When Hardicanute died, the agreement was respected and King Magnus of Norway became King of Denmark.

But then a young man came into the picture. His name was Sweyn and he was the son of Canute the Great's sister Estrid. She had been married to Ulf Jarl, the one whom Canute had had murdered in Roskilde. At the time when Ulf was slain his little son was only about seven years old. He had been taken to England and had grown up at the court of Canute the Great. By the time Hardicanute died, Sweyn had grown into a mature young man, and powerful Danish circles in England gathered about him with the object of putting him on the English throne. But the English were more powerful still, and so Sweyn went home to Scandinavia. For a time he stayed with *King Anund Jacob* in Sweden. But then he came to Denmark, and Magnus made him Earl of Jutland.

Magnus' advisors warned him against doing so, but he was very young. Besides, he had many other things to attend to.

In the lands to the south of Denmark a coastal tribe known as the Wends was beginning to stir. It was partly with the object of holding them at bay that Harald Bluetooth had founded Jomsborg, but with the passing of time the powerful Viking nest had also become a danger to Denmark herself, for the Jomsborg clan regarded itself as a free, independent Viking community. Magnus now sailed down, took Jomsborg by surprise and razed the stronghold to the ground. (It had probably looked rather like the Viking encampments that have been found in Denmark). As far as the Wends were concerned, this meant that the powerful Scandinavian garrison, which had been keeping a watchful eye on them for so long, no longer existed. And so the Wends advanced northwards.

First of all Magnus had to give battle to a Wendic fleet in the Baltic, but immediately afterwards he found himself fighting on land, in Slesvig, on Lyrskov Heath, against tremendous hordes of Wends who poured northwards into Jutland. It was a broiling hot day and the battle was a bloody one. Magnus himself led the Dano-Norwegian forces and swung his father's battle-axe "Hel". For, despite the fact that Magnus' father had been a Christian and moreover had been canonized, his axe was named after the ancient heathen goddess of Death.

The 19-year old king won a decisive victory and saved Denmark from a Wendic invasion that would have changed the history of Denmark and the Danes for all time.

But Sweyn Estridson (or Sweyn Ulfson) turned against Magnus in order to win Denmark for himself, and year after year Sweyn and Magnus met in battle. As a rule it was Sweyn who was unlucky.

Magnus was allowed no peace in Norway either. His uncle, Harald Hardradi, returned home after years of compaigning and service in the

Mediterranean and demanded his share of the Norwegian monarchy. At first Magnus denied him this (though subsequently he gave in) and while ill-feeling steadily mounted between him and Harald in Norway, the friendship between Magnus and Sweyn improved proportionally, so that Magnus eventually declared Sweyn his heir to the Danish throne.

Magnus died young. It is said that just as he was preparing for an expedition to England in order to re-conquer Canute the Great's western kingdom, he fell overboard from his ship in the Sound and drowned.

"The Eider, boundary of the Roman empire". The "Eider Stone"
at Denmark's old southern border; put up in 1671, taken down in
1806, now at the Arms Museum in Copenhagen.

The news of his death duly reached England, whereupon the English king stopped the measures that were being taken to offer armed resistance against the expected invasion. Harald Hardradi became King of Norway and from now on he and Sweyn fought bitterly, year after year, for the control of Denmark. Every year Harald sailed south into Danish waters and played havoc in Viking style, and on several occasions Sweyn very nearly obtained the upper hand. But Harald managed to slip through his fingers and thus ended up the victor after all.

But then Harald suddenly made peace. He had bigger plans, for he too was now preparing for an expedition to England. This was the expedition that ended with his death at Stamford Bridge in 1066. There were rumours that Sweyn had sent the English king Danish reinforcements against Harald, for Sweyn never relinquished the dream of re-conquering his famous uncle's tremendous English kingdom. On several occasions during

59

his life he despatched fleets across the North Sea to England, for a cry was continually heard from the Danish provinces over there for help on account of William the Conqueror's suppression of the northern counties, which for the greater part were Danish. But on each occasion William succeeded in buying the Danish fleet off by means of the old method, i.e. payment of Danegeld – or what one might with greater accuracy call bribery. After all, it was really the commanders of the fleets who permitted themselves to be "bought off", i.e. persuaded into sailing home again.

In Denmark the Viking Age came to an end too. Or one might put it this way: the "domestic Vikings" who had been living by plundering the nearest settlements and by attacking merchant vessels in Danish waters, gradually decreased in number. Denmark became united under one King, and the country never reverted to what it had been before. The Danes had learnt something during the centuries of Viking influence. European culture now imposed itself gradually upon the old, independent, civilized, Scandinavian kingdom. Once more it must be remembered that all cultural currents from the south have invariably reached Scandinavia as repercussions, indirectly. No Celtic invasion ever penetrated Denmark and no Roman military forces ever marched up through Jutland. The country was never to see the building of Roman towns, no Roman roads ever wound their way through the green countryside, no Roman viaducts ever spanned the rivers, no Roman temples ever imposed Roman gods and Roman philosophy upon the Danes or upon any of the other Scandinavian peoples. This is the main reason, as mentioned earlier on, for the difference in the fate of the British Isles and that of Scandinavia. For although thousands of Scandinavian Angles and countless thousands of Danes moved west and took lands or became town-dwellers in England before and during the Viking Age, they never made England a Scandinavian country. They encountered a state of culture that merged well enough with what they had brought with them from home, but Christianity, combined with the culture that still existed in the land of the west from former times, proved so strong that the two northern European cultural spheres, i.e. the British Isles and Scandinavia, developed in an entirely different manner.

III. THE EARLY MIDDLE AGES

The Viking Age came to a close in Denmark during the time of Sweyn Estridson. The end was less noticeable than one might expect, for those who set out seldom returned. This is the reason why English chronicles and legends abound with Viking lore to a far greater extent than those of Scandinavia.

There are not many reminders left to us today on ancient Danish soil of the great westward Viking adventure. We have the occasional thing that has come to Denmark either by way of trade or as booty. Homecoming noblemen sometimes brought things with them and later took them with them to their graves. Sometimes objects were sacrificed in bogs and marshes. But all in all it is strikingly little. However, a number of Danish runic stones have tales to tell of those strange, bygone centuries. King Sweyn erected a tombstone in Slesvig over the body of his man Skarde "that sallied forth westward, but now is dead at Hedeby", and a Danish runic stone in Scania sombrely records that "Toke found death in the West".

There is no denying the terror let loose by the Vikings in England, France, Friesland and other countries that suffered from the Viking expeditions and conquests. Thousands of Western Europeans were killed or forced into slavery, for during the Viking Age Denmark's primary source of well-being was neither her maritime trade, her fishing, nor her agriculture, but quite simply her slave trade. But naturally the bloodthirsty expeditions claimed thousands of Danish lives, either slain or drowned, and despite the fact that the dead had nobody to blame but themselves, the events, seen from Denmark, i.e. the operational base, were often dismal enough. Thousands of widows all over Europe had occasion to curse the Vikings of Scandinavia, but there were widows in Denmark too, standing along the beaches every autumn, staring vainly out to sea as the ships returned home. It may be difficult for English people to see things from a Scandinavian viewpoint. Kipling managed to do so in his "Harp Song of the Dane Women":

> *What is a woman that you forsake her,*
> *And the hearth-fire and the home-acre,*
> *To go with the old grey Widow-maker?*

And the Valleborg Stone in Scania, one of the many tombstones raised in memory of those who never came back, provides a sober, contemporary record devoid of any attempt at literary romanticism:

> *Sven and Thorgot raised these stones*
> *in memory of Manne and Svenne,*
> *God will help their souls well,*
> *but they are lying over in London.*

Christianity

The greatest repercussion produced in the Danish homeland was the fact that the Vikings brought Christianity back with them from western Europe. They had plundered the churches thoroughly. Although Harald Bluetooth might well have "made the Danes Christians", it was not until the reign of Sweyn Estridson that the fact became really noticeable. Canute the Great admittedly sent some English monks to Denmark, but difficulties were experienced in organizing a Church in Denmark, even greater ones in Norway, and in Sweden there was simply nothing to be done at all. There they dangled in the trees of the sacred heathen grove at Uppsala, human beings who had been sacrificed; and cauldrons of sacred horseflesh continued to steam for many a generation after Denmark and Norway largely had become converted to the new faith.

Under Sweyn Estridson the Danish bishoprics became more firmly established. The churches were still built of wood, but they were already extraordinarily numerous. There were, incredible as it may sound, almost as many as there are today, for Denmark was already, even at this early stage, divided up into ecclesiastical parishes, and the division made in Sweyn Estridson's day corresponds more or less to that still existing.

The difficulty with which the young Danish Church was faced was that it had been placed under the jurisdiction of the Archbishop of Bremen. Canute the Great had expressed the wish that the Danish Church be incorporated under Canterbury, but firstly he did not get his way, and secondly it would have been pointless, as relationships between Denmark and England had been severed. Bremen was nearer. Sweyn Estridson was a friend of the Church and a smooth diplomat. He was something else too: rash in affairs of the heart. He left a whole string of sons behind him which he had sired with a number of different women and girls, a bequest which threatened to split up the newly united kingdom.

Adam of Bremen, the northern German chronicler who tells us about Denmark at the time of King Sweyn (and who had met the King personally) held him in high esteem, but was deeply shocked at his morals. However, it should be regarded in a different light today. The attitude held by the Christian Church towards the relationship between a man and a woman was something unheard of in Scandinavia. The concept of *sin* just did not exist in a Scandinavian mind. The woman was highly respected as such (in fact much more highly than in the rest of Europe) and morals were strict – there just happened to be different rules. And during and after the Viking Age, Denmark, as a result of the thousands of men who emigrated, the thousands of Vikings who were slain or drowned, had a surplus of women, including noblewomen, who were unable to marry. For a nobleman or a king to have the odd mistress was the most natural thing in the world.

So natural indeed, that upon the death of Sweyn Estridson, no fewer than *five* of his sons ascended the throne one after the other, and *not one of them* was the son of any of his lawful wives, of whom he had three or four in succession.

These sons were *Harald Hén, Canute the Holy, Oluf Hunger, Eric Egode,* and *Niels.*

Harald's reign was fairly short. "Hén" means "a soft grindstone". He was peaceable and a friend of the Church.

63

Canute the Holy

In his brother, Canute the Holy, the Danes once more had a Viking on their throne. Canute had spent his youth taking part in raiding expeditions, particularly in the Baltic (from all accounts), and everybody expected Viking traditions to be revived during his reign. However, when he became King he altered his ways. He was just as strong, ironwilled and determined as ever, but he now defended the legal system, clarified taxation, and in particular introduced a tax for the benefit of the Church, the so-called "tithe", or 10 per cent of all harvested corn. He worked to bring about the liberation of all slaves, and he sent to England for relics of St. Alban – with a distinct purpose in mind: he was arming for an expedition against England, firmly resolved that Canute the Great's heritage must now be recovered. William was to be thrown out of England, and he himself crowned as England's King. Danish refugees were continually streaming home from England and they told how desperately everyone was longing for a liberator to come.

Canute mustered his fleet in the Limfjord. The Norwegian king, Olav Kyrre, also wanted to come along, and so did Canute's brother-in-law, the Count of Flanders, with the result that Canute was able to get together a fleet of 1,660 ships. (When it is borne in mind that Canute the Great conquered England with a fleet of only a couple of hundred vessels, it will be appreciated that Canute the Holy's naval expedition must have been in deadly earnest, and that William had the most serious of grounds for taking the defensive precautions that he did).

The naval forces taking part were divided as follows: 60 Norwegian vessels, 600 Flemish, and 1,200 Danish. The Danish "naval combat force" during all these seafaring centuries had always consisted of about 1,200 ships. The Norwegian counterpart had been established as 310 ships, although a Norwegian force of such strength never actually put to sea. Despite the difference in size of the two countries, there were twice as many inhabitants in Denmark as in Norway, and in the Danish island kingdom a far greater part of the population lived near the sea.

The fleet gathered at the old naval base of Aggersborg. But Canute had to go down to the border of Slesvig, for as soon as news of the great westward-bound expedition seeped through, the peoples south of the

St. Michael and the Dragon, granite relief in Starup Church in Jutland.

Granite baptismal font in Nørre Alslev Church on the island of Funen. Almost 2,000 granite baptismal fonts dating from the Early Middle Ages are still to be found on old Danish territory.

Altar of oak covered with beaten, gilded copper, at Lisbjærg Church in Jutland. Danish work.

Ivory cross once belonging to Gunhild, daughter of Sveyn Estridson.

border began to stir. From their viewpoint it seemed, just as in Harald Bluetooth's day, an excellent opportunity for an expedition against Denmark.

While Canute was trying to stabilize matters in the south, trouble started brewing in his big fleet. William the Conqueror had sent emissaries to Denmark armed with big sums to be used as bribes – and they worked. Moreover, the peasants that had been called to arms became impatient. Time was passing, and provisions were getting short. The later the fleet got away, the later it would come home again. The peasant farmers sent a message down to Slesvig demanding Canute's return. He was furious, but before he had time to put matters straight on the border his huge fleet had broken up. By the time he got back to Aggersborg only the Norwegian ships were left. These he sent home, first thanking them for their loyalty.

In England, William did not dare relax his watchfulness entirely, for Canute might well collect another fleet together the following year. But instead, Canute travelled round imposing heavy fines on the peasants for having "interfered with the King's war". It ended with a rebellion in the far north of Jutland. Canute had to flee south. He crossed over Little Belt to Funen and the town of Odense. Odense is the largest town on the island of Funen. The name, in old Danish, was "Odins Vi", meaning "Odin's Shrine", and it was here that Canute the Great had founded a convent run by English monks. It was in Odense Cathedral that Canute had placed the shrine of the English saint, St. Alban, who was to have secured the success of his expedition against England for him. Now it was up to St. Alban to help him in his hour of need, but the peasants managed to slay their King inside the very church itself.

His brother Oluf became King, but during the years that ensued, a series of bad crop failures resulted in Denmark's being struck by famine. At the same time, miracles began to take place at King Canute's grave at Odense: the blind regained their sight, the lame the use of their limbs, the hopelessly incurable became well, and the rumour spread to the effect that King Canute was a saint, that the peasants had slain "Guds Drot", (God's King), and that the failure of the crops and the famine was God's punishment on the Danes.

Oluf was King of Denmark for nine years. It was not until his death that the crops picked up again, and in the annals of Danish history he has been given the name of *Olaf Hunger*.

The Crusades – Church-building

He was succeeded by his brother Eric, whereupon the corn began to grow again. So Eric was given the name "Egode", an abbreviation of *den eneste gode* meaning "the only good [one]". It was at this time that *Pope Urban* was agitating for a crusade and all the knights of Europe were making for the Holy Land. Eric became violently taken up with the new thinking of his time, but instead of going out crusading, he went to Rome and negotiated with the Pope, partly about freeing the Danish Church from the sovereignty of Bremen, and partly about getting his brother Canute properly canonized. The Pope promised to see to both matters, whereupon Eric went home. A few years later he set out travelling again. Legend has it that one day a strange minstrel came to the King's court and began to play such weird music that King Eric threw a fit of fury and slew three of his own retainers. As a penance he promised to make a pilgrimage to Jerusalem – and thus became the first European King to do so.

He travelled via Constantinople, where he paid his respects to members of the Emperor's Scandinavian Guard, the "Varingians". From there he set sail for the Holy Land, but died *en route*, at Cyprus. His wife, Queen Bodil, continued alone, but only just managed to set eyes on the Holy City before she too departed this world, on the very Mount of Olives.

The news of the King's death did not reach Denmark until almost a year later, whereupon Eric's brother Niels (the fifth of Sweyn Estridson's sons) became King. A sixth son had tried to have himself proclaimed King, but died on the way to Viborg Thing.

Niels ruled the country for thirty years, and under his guiding hand trade and shipping prospered, peace prevailed throughout the land, and stone churches appeared everywhere. (Earlier churches, as mentioned previously, had been of wood). These new ones were not built of brick, but of granite, limestone, or sandstone, despite the fact that there are very few quarries in Denmark. Only on the island of Bornholm and in the Scanian provinces was it possible to obtain stone from the rocky surface of the ground; everywhere else it was necessary to prise out stones found lying in the clayey soil, stones that had been carried down from Norway and Sweden during the Ice Age.

The churches were austere, stern and simple, more or less like the oldest Anglo-Saxon churches in England. But, especially on the island of Funen and in Jutland, they were nevertheless ornamented with a type of primitive sculpture which, at its best, is among the most impressive created in

The oldest Danish stone churches were simple, just like the oldest English churches: church-house and chancel, no more.

Europe at the time. It was not refined, artistic art, but a more ponderous and, as yet, a rather heathen form of stone sculpture. The churches were decorated inside with splendid murals in the Byzantine style, some of which have been preserved to this day. Strangest of all are the heavy baptismal fonts of granite or sandstone; these, despite the heaviness of the style, are often impressive works of sculpture. In the old Danish lands (i.e., present-day Denmark plus South Slesvig and the Scanian provinces) nearly *two thousand* of these old mediaeval stone fonts have been preserved up until our times, constituting about the largest collection in Europe.

The Age of Chivalry – The Pretendant Feuds

It was during the reign of King Niels that the "Age of Chivalry" came to Denmark, but it did not take the same form as it did further to the south of Europe. The Danish nobles were not castle-dwelling knights, but farmers. Even the richest of them maintained close contact with the soil and with shipping. This produced a sober attitude that left little time for chivalrous romantics, and few Danes set off south through Europe to go crusading.

The Danish throne was still threatened at this time by many "pretenders", princes whose fathers had been King and who felt they had a claim to the throne. One of the most prominent was a young man named Canute Lavard, a son of Eric Egode. Niels made him "Duke" of Slesvig so that he could keep an eye on the border, and here Canute Lavard pursued an independent policy that made his cousin, King Niels' son Magnus, uneasy. Magnus himself was King beyond the borders of Denmark, for the West-goths in Sweden had hailed him as such. He had a claim to Swedish land through his mother. There was some dissatisfaction amongst many of the nobles about old King Niels, who quietly and steadily attended to his affairs of state after the manner of some ancient Scandinavian nobleman farmer. The retainers and nobles who had become wrapped up in modern ideas of chivalry found him boorish, and at this time the Germans were pressing forward with the object of grabbing a share of the Baltic trade. Canute Lavard became much influenced by German ideas and felt that the Danes should learn from the Germans. Niels apparently felt just the opposite. A party was formed in support of Canute Lavard and the situation became critical. Canute Lavard conquered, unaided, a certain amount of land to the south of the Danish border and thereby became a vassal of King Lothar. Niels thereupon had to take action, for with his own duke and guardian of the border having become "lord lieutenant" on the wrong side of that same border, the political situation was obviously untenable. Canute Lavard received his uncle, King Niels, in Slesvig. Shortly before-hand, Canute had been made King of the borderfolk, known as the Obotrites. He turned up at the feast pointedly wearing his new regal crown, in other words showing himself to be King Niels' equal. The old King said nothing, but merely summoned him to a meeting in Ribe. Canute Lavard duly appeared and it seems he realized that he had gone too far. He swore allegiance to King Niels, but no solution was found.

During Christmas, 1031, Canute Lavard was staying in Zealand as the guest of King Niels. After the Christmas feast he paid a visit to his cousin at Haraldsted, near Ringsted (also on the island of Zealand) and here King Niels' son Magnus appeared and requested an audience with him out in the woods. Canute rode out, whereupon Magnus and his men slew him.

The murder aroused great consternation, and Canute Lavard's friends demanded vengeance. King Niels had to promise that Magnus would be excluded from his court for the time being; but Magnus nevertheless returned shortly afterwards.

The party that had been supporting the dead Duke was not particularly strong. King Niels and Magnus had almost the entire Danish Church behind them, including the bishops. But Canute Lavard's brother Eric would not let the matter rest. He went to war against King Niels, partly with the help of German warriors whom he borrowed south of the border. To begin with things went badly, and King Niels was victorious. But finally Eric was fortunate enough to conquer the whole of Scania. During Whitsun, 1134, King Niels and his son landed in Scania with an expeditionary fleet with the object of re-conquering the provinces, but while disembarking at *Fodevig*, the King's army was taken by surprise by Eric and his German cavalry. The affair ended in a bitter, bloody battle. The conscripted peasants, being unused to fighting against modern armed cavalry, fled for the boats. Magnus and a little group made a violent "last stand" while the old King and almost the whole army slipped back aboard the ships. During this last fight Magnus was killed. Five of Denmark's seven bishops fell, also the bishop of Vesterås, who was Magnus' bishop in his Westgothic lands. Sixty priests likewise lost their lives. Only two of Denmark's bishops took no part in the battle. One was the Archbishop himself – but after all he was almost eighty.

King Niels went over to Jutland and thence down to Slesvig, Canute Lavard's stronghold. It was the general opinion throughout the country that the Battle of Fodevig had been an ordeal designed by God as a punishment for the murder of Canute Lavard. King Niels' son and heir had fallen and thus Niels had no descendant (according to the ancient Scandinavian way of thinking the worst fate that could befall a man). In Slesvig, King Niels, who by this time was almost 70, was slain in the street by Canute Lavard's guild-brothers, whose bounden duty it was to revenge their guild-master. Eric became King.

He was given the nickname "Emune", an abbreviation standing for "the only memorable one", but he was hard and brutal. He slew his own brother and seized his nephews, took them over to Scania and had them murdered there. He became generally loathed, and at a meeting of the *Thing* in Slesvig he was killed by a Jutlandic nobleman named Black Plough. The King's young nephew, whose name was also Eric, wanted

69

to defend the dead body, but Black Plough suggested that he take things calmly and he would find it "to his advantage". This he did, for he then became King in succession to his uncle. But he was not a strong monarch, and was therefore given the name of Eric Lamb.

The country then started to fall apart, in the sense that each peasant settlement started governing itself much the way it had done before the unification of the kingdom. In practice, the person of the King still meant so little that the settlements could easily do this. Trade and shipping continued as before.

But the seas were threatened.

The Wends were still living to the south of the Baltic, and as long as the Danish King was unable to keep the seas free of pirates there were tremendous opportunities of which the Wends were quick to take advantage, not only in order to commit acts of piracy, but also to start launching raids along the Danish coast in downright Viking style whereby the Danes were given an opportunity of tasting for themselves the treatment they had been meting out to western Europe for centuries.

But Eric Lamb did not remain entirely inactive. From the Danish settlements in England came once more a cry for help, and Eric started a call to arms preparatory to launching an expedition against England just like in the good old days. He even took horses with him, something the old Viking kings had never done – they had always "acquired" horses upon their arrival in England. The Danish fleet landed safely enough, but the army was defeated. So everything had been in vain. Eric had only been on the throne for nine years, so he now abdicated and entered a convent. Shortly afterwards he died.

There were three successors to the throne ready waiting to take his place. The eldest, *Sweyn*, became King first. But at his side appeared *Canute*. Canute was the son of King Niels' son Magnus, and Sweyn therefore could not lightly brush him aside. So they became co-regents, whereafter a third figure loomed into the picture. This was a son of the Canute Lavard who had been murdered, and his name was Valdemar, corresponding to the Russian name Vladimir (a German or Scandinavian name that travelled round via Russia). This was because Scandinavian Vikings, particularly from Sweden, had established permanent settlements in western

Russia, and it was from here that Valdemar's mother had originally come. Despite the fact that Canute was the son of the man who had slain Valdemar's father, the two joined forces against Sweyn, and the final result was the three of them appealed the whole case to the German Emperor. Back in the days when there had been trouble between Magnus and Eric Egode, the parties concerned had, in order to obtain his support in the conflict, sworn allegiance to the Emperor as their feudal overlord. The final result was that the three Kings divided the country into three parts, one for each. In other words, Denmark's unity was once more sacrificed. But a few days after the partitioning, the three kings attended a banquet at the royal castle at Roskilde. That evening, armed men forced their way into the hall and extinguished the lights. Canute was slain and Valdemar was wounded. It was immediately claimed that it must have been Sweyn trying to murder his two royal partners, and after the "Bloody Banquet of Roskilde" there was just no hope of establishing peace. Valdemar fled to Jutland, whereupon Sweyn set after him with a fleet and an army, and at Grade Heath the two armies clashed. Valdemar was victorious, and Sweyn ran, but in the course of his flight he was killed by a peasant who split his skull with an axe. Valdemar became Denmark's sole king.

The Great Period of the Valdemars

Valdemar had been born one week after the murder of his father, Canute Lavard, and grew up in the home of a Zealandic nobleman named *Asser Rig* together with the latter's two sons, *Esbern* and *Absalon*. Esbern became one of Valdemar's retainers. Absalon, who had been present at the "Bloody Banquet" and had just returned from a period of study in Paris, was made bishop of Roskilde – largely as a result of Valdemar's putting in an appearance just when the canons were about to elect a new bishop.

It had for many years been common practice for Danes to study in Paris. Theologians and noblemen alike made their way to the French capital and in due course returned home well-versed in all the ecclesiastical, medical and philosophical wisdom of their time. The Archbishop of Denmark at this time was Eskild, one of Europe's learned men. He often went south in order to visit the leaders of the Church, was in Rome on several occasions and, in the dispute about the papacy which was raging through Europe just then, Eskild and King Valdemar each supported his own candidate. In other words, the King and his Archbishop were enemies. Eskild was obliged to spend many years in exile, and in the meantime Valdemar had other matters to occupy his attention in Denmark. Although trade, agriculture and shipping had by no means collapsed, the organization of the country had been seriously weakened by the "War of the Princes", and Valdemar set to work to re-establish order. He had sworn his allegiance to the German Emperor, Frederick I, but this did not mean that the Emperor interfered in the way Denmark was ruled. The King had Absalon at his side, and the young bishop of Roskilde (who was the King's sworn brother) took on the task, together with the King, of ensuring the country's freedom from the ravages of the Wends. They both realized that if the Wends were to be subdued it meant having to strike a blow at their base, and that the old Danish expeditionary fleet must therefore once more be mustered. To begin with it was not easy. The peasants failed to appear when the call to arms went out. Gradually however, as they began to see that there was some firmness of purpose behind the call, they responded, with the result that the expeditionary force once more, as in former times, became a powerful organization of some 1,200 ships. The main attack was directed at the island of Rügen, where the Wends had their principal holy shrine (a temple to the god Svantevit) in the town of Arkona. The inhabitants of Rügen, though they had been baptized and christened several times, were still heathens.

Valdemar and Absalon conquered Arkona. The temple was destroyed, Svantevit's image was toppled and Rügen came under Danish rule.

But the wars against the Wends did not end here. Summer after summer the Danish fleet sailed south and wrought frightful havoc in the land of the Wends. Up-to-date castles were erected in a great many Danish towns, particularly in the southern part of the country and along the Danish border, which until now had been defended by the ancient border defenceworks known as *Danevirke*. Valdemar built a modern brick wall of fortresses in order to safeguard the country against surprises from the south, for after Valdemar's activity in the land of the Wends several northern German princes had become dissatisfied. During the first years Valdemar had to share the spoils he obtained from Wendland, likewise indemnifications and taxes, with a German Duke, Henrik Loeve, and it was not until some time had passed that he became powerful enough to free himself.

Old Archbishop Eskild finally renounced his office, and Valdemar and Absalon went to *Lund*, the Danish archiepiscopal see. Absalon was elected, and it seems as though the choice must have been very much against Eskild's wish. But at the election itself Absalon manoeuvred so skilfully that not only was he elected Archbishop of Denmark and thus Bishop of the Scanian provinces, but he was also permitted to retain his bishopric in Roskilde. His powers thus became very great. However, his assumption of the archbishopric in the Scanian provinces did not proceed so smoothly. The Scanians became vexed at his stern rule and his new episcopal taxes and finally he had to flee to Zealand. Valdemar was obliged to go over with an army of Jutlanders before Scania calmed down again.

And then Valdemar suddenly died, at Vordingborg Castle. He was buried at Ringsted in the big monastery chapel which he had built himself, and which still stands to this day.

Valdemar's son Canute was grown-up, but Absalon, who was now more powerful than any other man in the country, ruled for him. From the Emperor came a message that he was waiting to receive the young King's oath of fealty, but Absalon replied to the effect that if the Emperor wanted Canute's oath of fealty then he had better give him a slice of territory in northern Germany, and that in Denmark, Canute was King and therefore just as free and independent as the Emperor was in Germany. The Emperor was greatly angered, but he had so many affairs to attend to that the oath of fealty was not made and the matter was never brought up again. By taking this step Absalon put a stopper to a dangerous situation which, with time, might have developed into Denmark's becoming a vassal state of Germany for good.

The Emperor, instead of marching on Denmark himself, persuaded Duke Bugislaw to go to war. Absalon received the message from a Wendic prince who was loyal to Denmark. A call to arms was sent out, but with only a few days' warning, so that the Jutlanders did not arrive in time. From the Scanian provinces there came only very few ships.

Nevertheless, Absalon set sail and succeeded in taking Bugislaw's big fleet by surprise, scaring the sailors and seizing most of the ships. Bugislaw swore allegiance to King Canute. Thus the threat from Wendland was finally crushed, and the Emperor made no further attempts to send his vassals against Denmark.

This proved to be the aging Absalon's last naval war. He returned to dry land. Shortly afterwards he was obliged to hand over the bishopric of Roskilde and finally he retired to Soroe Abbey, even though he was still Archbishop, and here he spent his last years, but he hung on to his weapons and his coat-of-mail as mementoes of his glorious past. He was buried in front of the altar of the Soroe Abbey chapel that he had built himself, and there he lies to this day – though his grave is in reality now behind the altar, as this was moved forward during the Reformation.

Archbishop Absalon was one of the most prominent men of the early Danish Middle Ages. His interests were not so scholarly as those of his predecessor, Archbishop Eskild, nor did he devote heart and soul so fervently to the cause of the great European Church. By nature he was really much more of an old Northman, an ancient Dane. He was the son of a Zealandic nobleman and throughout his life he loved the soil. He acquired a number of estates and provided for the male representatives of his family to such an extent that by the time he died considerable areas of the Scanian provinces and Zealand were in family hands. He built the monastery chapel at Soroe, started large-scale architectural activity in the French style with the cathedral at Roskilde, and made valuable donations to churches and monasteries throughout the country. But even though he was a bishop and had studied theology in Paris, he still had the heart of a Viking. Year after year he took part in naval expeditions, and throughly enjoyed them; never did he content himself with sending a representative, but always took active command himself. He also erected what was probably the last runic stone in Denmark. Ancient Danish runes were still used alongside the new ecclesiastical writing, particularly on tombstones, and at times on baptismal fonts and elsewhere. But Absalon, together with a noble friend, built a church in Scania, and to commemorate its erection raised a runic stone in the old style, requesting the divine powers to protect the two churchbuilders, Asbjoern Mule and Archbishop Absalon.

But he left a couple of other monuments too. When Valdemar the Great covered Denmark with his string of new castles he was unable to build them all himself and therefore let a number of his trusted men build their own castles at various places. One nobleman was thus permitted to build a castle at Nyborg; Absalon's brother Esbern built one at Kalundborg; and Absalon himself built another at a little town by the shores of the Sound. It was *Havn*, meaning "harbour" or "haven", and Absalon was given the town as a gift from the King to the bishopric of Roskilde. Absalon developed the place and improved its trading facilities, for which

At Kalundborg in Zealand, Absalon's brother Esbern built a five-towered cruciform church, unique of its kind in northern Europe.

reason he is now considered as its founder, despite the fact that it had already existed several hundred years before his time. The city is today the capital of Denmark, *Copenhagen*, which in Danish is *København*, being an abbreviation of *Købmands-havn* or *Merchant's Haven*.

Despite the fact that Absalon was not very scholarly (as far as we can ascertain) it is nevertheless due to his iniative that one of our most valuable early mediaeval written records came into being: it was Absalon who set his clerk *Saxe* the task of writing Denmark's "Chronicle".

Absalon had observed in Paris how the western European countries had their pasts recorded in chronicles, and he realized that if Denmark now wished to become a European nation, then her past must be inscribed in the annals of European history too. He therefore put Saxe to work, and for the same reason saw to it that he wrote in Latin, a language few Danes at the time understood. There is a considerable difference between Denmark, on the one hand, and Norway and Iceland on the other, which, during this period and subsequently, likewise had chronicles of

75

their past histories written down. The Icelandic and Norwegian "sagas" were written in Icelandic and western Norwegian respectively, being intended for domestic consumption. Saxe's work was intended to be read in Denmark, but also in the rest of Europe. Furthermore Denmark, which of the five Scandinavian countries lay furthest to the south and thus nearest to the rest of Europe, was the first to become European, while Norway and Iceland to a greater extent continued to pursue their old cultural ideas relatively unaffected by external influences. When Saxe speaks of Canute the Great and Harald Bluetooth, he speaks of them as of characters belonging to long-forgotten, ancient history. But when Snorre, the Norwegian historian, writes about Norwegian kings of the same period, kings that had been dead for several hundred years, one gets the impression that he himself knew them and had been their contemporary.

Saxe gives a very broad account, in fluent Latin, of the history of the Danes from very ancient times. He relates all the old myths and sagas concerning Denmark's ancient history, and gradually his work becomes more and more of a truly historical account. He describes the fates of the Danish kings and has various things to say about sundry Danish nobles. Now and then he lapses into pure adventure sagas, and eventually gets round to describing his forefathers' times and finally his own, including the "War of the Princes" and the period when Valdemar and Absalon were at the height of their careers. But Absalon is the main character of the chronicle. It is Absalon whom the whole weighty codex is endeavouring to depict as the "Father of the Fatherland", and Valdemar is therefore left somewhat in the background. Saxe is thus not completely objective, but provided one bears this in mind, his accounts provide a master key to the whole of the early Danish Middle Ages. The fund of folklore he gives is of tremendous value, for the majority of his heroic myths and sagas concerning Denmark's more murky past are known to us solely through his writings. As the Icelander *Snorre* also started writing his sagas of the Norwegian kings some few decades later and in them frequently described Danish conditions as well, Denmark and Norway became astonishingly well provided with contemporary, or at least ancient, written sources of material. Sweden however, has never possessed either a Snorre or a Saxe and therefore the history of Sweden during the early Middle Ages is still wrapped in a mantle of darkness.

The Churches of Denmark

During the years under Valdemar the Great and Canute VI, Denmark made progress. One gets the impression that agriculture made new strides (for many new villages and large farms were founded at this period), that these were good times for shipping, that trade was flourishing and that Danish towns must have enjoyed a large turnover of imports and exports. That capital continued to mount up in the rural areas and settlements is proved by the fact that the building of churches continued and that even village churches could afford to be richly appointed. During the first centuries of Christianity in Denmark, Danish churches revealed English influence, just like those of Norway. In Norway this English influence continued right up through the entire Middle Ages, for Norway's most natural means of contact with Europe was by ship over to England. In Denmark, English influence was natural enough in the days of Canute the Great, but not many ecclesiastic relics exist in Denmark today dating from so far back. Later, when relationships with England were broken off, Denmark's ecclesiastical interests were directed towards the south and southwest. Danish students made their way to Paris and studied the work of French architects. The grandiose church-building activity in Germany, particularly in the region of the Rhine, also came to influence the Danish. Even so, a connecting link can still be traced between England and Denmark, despite the fact that up through the first centuries of the Middle Ages it gradually becomes less pronounced. A number of Danish churches (for example that of Vestervig at Ty, up by the Limfjord) are completely English in style. Church buildings revealing English influence are also to be found in Zealand, likewise down on the island of Moen in the Baltic; lastly, a markedly English trait reveals itself in a number of churches characterized by their round towers, today still preserved only in the ex-Danish provinces of Scania and in South Slesvig – similar churches are to be found in the old "Danish" counties of Norfolk and Suffolk. The reason for this scattered English influence on Danish church architecture is presumably due to the fact that after William the Conqueror's conquest of England, a number of Danes and descendants of Danish homes left England in order to return to the old country. Amongst them were doubtless a number of master-builders for whom there would presumably have been plenty of work to do in Denmark at this time. During the course of but a few generations, village churches shot up with such rapidity that some 1,500 to 2,000 of them must have been built during these years. The one church built in pure English style, that at Vestervig (mentioned above) was originally built as a cathedral. It is situated at the old mouth of the Limfjord into the North Sea, for it was from here that ships set forth from Denmark bound for England, from here that both Sweyn Forkbeard and Canute the Great set sail, here that Canute the Holy mustered his fleet in preparation for his expedition against England, and from here that trading vessels headed for English ports. But when the mouth of the fjord filled with sand and the fjord closed up (probably at some time during the 13th century), there was no more sailing from here, and the Bishop of Vestervig moved north to Boerglum. The church at Vestervig continued to exist as a convent church, but was never built in the form of a big episcopal cathedral and has therefore retained its pure English lines – naturally it should be borne in mind that it has not gone through all the alterations in style and extensions that have left their mark on English churches up through the centuries. The church of Vestervig stands today on an open stretch of country in West Jutland, facing west over the land towards the sea, a monument to that mixture of trade-hungry dreams of conquest, some of them fulfilled, that went to make up the great westward adventure embarked on by Denmark's ancient rulers.

Towns were still of little importance. Most of them were small, and in Denmark the whole process of town-development was governed by particular factors. Due to the geographical make-up of the country, in other words the various principal areas of land with their many fjords and inlets and five hundred adjoining islands, it was always a problem to concentrate shipping at particular key-points as harbour facilities were available everywhere, and this in turn led to the situation whereby Denmark became the country in Europe having the most towns in proportion to its area; that is why these towns have always encountered difficulty in expanding. A glaring contrast was provided a few centuries later. In the year 1600 or thereabouts, Norway had in all 10 "market-towns", while Denmark had no fewer than 81; but each of these only had a very small surrounding area of countryside. This is one of the reasons why Danish towns, despite the country's excellent strategic position, from a commercial viewpoint have never expanded in the same way as Amsterdam, Brussels and other leading trade centres of mediaeval Europe. The distance to another equally good harbour is too short, and there is no hinterland.

Canute VI died childless in 1202. Throughout his life his interests lay more in the Church than in the Crown, for Absalon had taken care of the affairs of state. Canute was succeeded by his brother Valdemar.

Valdemar the Victorious

This Valdemar – Valdemar II – was a wide-awake, strong-willed man with plenty of initiative. During his younger years he had been Duke of Slesvig, with the task of guarding the border; in other words he held the same position as his grandfather, Canute Lavard. Here he quarrelled with a relative whose name was likewise Valdemar and who in the meantime had become Bishop of Slesvig. This Bishop Valdemar felt he had a right to the Danish throne, and at any rate to the Duke's title and job. However, despite the fact that Bishop Valdemar actually was Duke of Slesvig for a time, during which he guarded the border in an exemplary fashion, he was later dismissed in favour of Prince Valdemar, a fact the Bishop could never forgive. He spent his whole life waging war against Denmark. He was forever starting rebellions along the border, stirring up discontent and joining forces with the country's enemies; finally he had himself proclaimed King. He got into conflict with the Pope, defied the Holy See and thereafter, a bitter and disappointed man, entered a convent.

Meanwhile, Valdemar II ruled Denmark. He had great plans. The concept of chivalry had gradually been gaining a firmer foothold amongst Danish nobles, but Valdemar was no knight: he was a politician. His primary concern was Denmark's southern border. This he was especially interested in safeguarding in order that the vital shipping trade of which Slesvig was the centre should not be endangered. But his politics drove him from one conquest to the next, with the final result that considerable stretches of land in Northern Germany came under the Danish crown. The Emperor, Frederick II, acknowledged the Danish King's right to these territories. All was plain sailing and Denmark started dreaming of big things. The Danish fleet was a permanent, well-organized institution and was in fact organized in the same way as in the days of the great expeditions against England. More or less the same type of ship was still in use too, in other words old open Viking ships. For commercial shipping purposes a somewhat shorter vessel had been developed. It had a deeper draught and was thus capable of taking more cargo, but even so, Scandinavian prowess in ship-building was gradually falling behind. This was largely due to the fact that, in the rural settlements, people still liked the old type of vessel, and it was the rural settlements that still constituted the prime motivating force behind such shipping activity as existed – not the towns. This meant, firstly, that it was the conservative attitude of the rural settlements that prevailed, and secondly, that it was necessary to use ships of a type that could be hauled up on to the beach and that could sail up shallow fjords and rivers.

News of Valdemar's conquests in Northern Germany spread. Everyone regarded him as invincible and as a "man of fortune", for old Scandinavian, pre-Christian concepts such as "fate" and "fortune" had not yet been forgotten. A man was saddled by his "fate" from which he could not escape and which he could do very little to alter. But a man might also be a "man of fortune", and then everybody followed him just the way the great "men of fortune" were followed during the Viking Age.

The Wendic pirates had been almost completely driven from Danish waters by this time. During the first centuries of its existence, the Danish Church had given its faithful support to the King, and the King had both supported and helped the Church. It was only during occasional periods, such as the time when Archbishop Eskild was in office, that a state of tension existed between the Crown and the Church. Priests performed their duties in their parishes. The peasants had gradually become accustomed to the Christian way of thinking in so far as it concerned the protection of life and property and the salvation of the soul in the life hereafter. As regards the fertility of the soil however, the well-being of the livestock, the way the corn grew, and the fortunes of ships at sea, old beliefs and ideas had not been discarded – there was nothing in the Bible about how to raise cattle and ensure that your fields produced crops, and thus in these matters, old customs were upheld. Cattle were blessed with fire, the powers of the old heathen sacrificial springs were believed in, offerings were made to sacred stones in the fields, old sacred trees were protected, and it seems as though the Church had no objections to make, perhaps because the Danish Church had become Danish astonishingly quickly. The parish priests were neither French nor German, but men born and bred in the country, men who therefore regarded ancient Danish customs as obvious and natural.

The stone-cutters were still working away at the granite churches. Practically speaking, all Danish churches, both large and small, had by now been decorated with wall-paintings executed in glowing colours, and golden altar-pieces of beaten, gilded copper became a Danish speciality. In all Europe there are only 17 of these old beaten copper altar-piece fronts (antemensales) still in existence and no fewer than eight of them were wrought in Denmark, in the north of Jutland.

Valdemar married rather late. This does not mean to say that he had no time at all for tender feelings. Just like the old Danish kings, he had a broad outlook on the subject of marriage. He had already had several children with various women, among others a son with the widow of Esbern Snare, Absalon's brother.

Valdemar was in his mid-thirties when he finally chose a bride, a girl aged no more than about 14. She was a daughter of the King of Bohemia and the choice exemplified a departure from the traditions of the Danish royal family. Up until and including King Niels it had been the custom, even though there were occasional exceptions, for the King to take a Scandinavian wife, but thereafter wives were sought further south. The choice made by Valdemar the Victorious however, was peculiar. The King of Bohemia had cast off his own wife, thereby obliging her to live in exile. She had sought assistance from her husband's family, from the Emperor and from the Pope, but nobody would help, so she was powerless and her daughters, politically speaking, were not considered "good matches". Nevertheless, one of them, Dragomir, became Valdemar's queen. Her difficult name was changed in Danish to Dagmar, which means "Dawn" or "The Sunrise Maiden".

About Dagmar we know more or less nothing historical. But she became a central figure in popular folk poetry, where she is depicted as an intelligent, rather sharp-minded girl. For instance, she demanded the full facts concerning Denmark's finances before accepting her suitor's hand. She came sailing up from the Elbe and landed at Denmark's biggest commercial centre of the day, the town of Ribe, after which we hear nothing about her until we find, in one of the loveliest of old Danish folk ballads, the tale of her death. She was lying ill at Ribe, and the King was in Skanderborg, in the middle of Jutland. Around her sick-bed were gathered "all the ladies that in Denmark were" but they were of no help. Dagmar realized that she was about to die, and sent for King Valdemar. Her "boy", actually her stable lad, flung himself upon a horse and rode the eighty miles to Skanderborg. Valdemar immediately had his horse

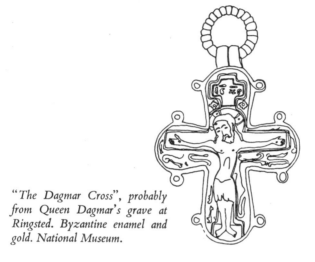

"The Dagmar Cross", probably from Queen Dagmar's grave at Ringsted. Byzantine enamel and gold. National Museum.

saddled and "with a hundred men" rode south across the Jutlandic moors. In fact so hard did he ride that "as he rode over Ribe Bridge, there rode that Sire alone". But he was too late: "Queen Dagmar died in Kirsten's arms as the King rode up the street". He strode into the death-chamber and requested all therein to pray with him that he might be allowed to take his leave of Dagmar. The miracle happened: she woke up, but "her eyes were a bloody red". She made her last request, took leave of Valdemar, and died. The poem's refrain goes: "In yonder Ringsted lies good Queen Dagmar", and it was in fact at Ringsted that she was buried. At some time during the 18th century one of the church priests had her grave cleared and put his own wife in her place. It was probably on this occasion that the beautiful little cross of gold and enamel was discovered that is still to be seen at the National Museum in Copenhagen, the "Dagmar

Cross", a copy of which thousands of little Danish girls are given as a christening present to wear round their necks.

No matter how little we really know of Dagmar beyond what the ballad tells us, the legend of her beauty and loving kindness has been sustained right up to the present day. With Dagmar Valdemar had one son, Valdemar the Younger.

A few years after the death of Dagmar, Valdemar married his second queen, a Portuguese princess named *Berengaria*, changed in Danish to *Berngerd*, meaning "The Bear's Keeper". The ballads reveal to us that although extraordinarily beautiful, she was likewise very evil. Exactly what sort of person she was is impossible to say, but when her grave was examined in 1855 by Frederik VII, who was interested in archaeology, her skeleton was intact and her skull was found to be extremely beautiful and well-formed. A lock of her hair, now withered and grey, can be seen today in Ringsted Church; once it was very thick, a rich chestnut brown.

The Conquest of Estonia

Valdemar still had big political plans, and his Danish kingdom had in the meantime won him respect. German chroniclers during these years did not date events from the birth of Christ, but from the year King Valdemar ascended the throne of Denmark. He had an eye for the opportunities that existed for Denmark, but likewise, and perhaps for that very reason, for Denmark's ancient traditions. For in the minds of all the Danish Kings of this period there still existed the old dream of a Danish Empire, a vast commercial power embracing both the Baltic and the North Sea. The old lines of trade between east and west still played an important part in the Baltic at the time, and Denmark took part in this maritime trading. Valdemar therefore became understandably concerned when he observed that the Germans were working their way into the Baltic countries at the eastern end of the sea, for this was where one of the trading bases was situated. Valdemar prepared to launch an expedition and sent out a call to arms, whereupon all the Danish villages provided their quota of ships just as in the great days of old. He held a couple of "naval exercises" and finally, in 1219, set sail eastwards with the whole Danish fleet. According to the regulations, each man had to bring his own provisions to last five weeks, likewise a sword and a shield, a crossbow and five dozen arrows. If unable to use a crossbow himself, he was obliged to provide, at his own expence, a bowman to do so for him. A large Wendic force joined the expedition, for the Wendic princes had become the vassals of the Danish Crown. The expedition was headed for Estonia, and Valdemar, by obtaining the Pope's blessing, had secured its recognition as a genuine crusade.

The Danish army landed at Lyndanisse, in Estonia, whereupon the Estonians sent their leaders to the Danish camp bearing gifts and promises of surrender. In reality these were scouts, and on the night of June 19, 1219, great hordes descended upon the Danish camp. The Danes had no chance of drawing up in battle order, and the situation was perilous. The Wendic camp was some distance away from that of the Danes, so the Wends were able to form up their troops and march their reinforcements to the scene of battle. The fight became violent and extremely bloody, and the story is told that the Danish Archbishop, Anders Suneson, fell on his knees on a hill during the battle and prayed for victory, just the way Moses had done. If he wearied and lowered his arms, then the Danes would have to retreat. But fortunately two canons supported his hands at the crucial moment – and so the Danes were victorious.

The Battle of Lyndanisse decided the fate of Estonia, which thereupon became Danish. It was in the course of this battle, according to legend, that a blood-red flag bearing a white cross floated down from heaven, a "sign from God". The flag was given the name "Dannebrog", literally meaning "the Danes' piece of cloth". The word brog can mean both cloth and clothing (actually trousers) but also a flag or banner. It is believed that on this occasion the Danish forces flew for the first time the flag which later was to become the Danish banner, and that it was sent by the Pope for the Estonian Crusade. The same flag is the banner of the Knights of Malta. If this is correct, then the flag has been the banner of the Danes for more than 700 years. Several things however, coins for instance, would indicate that the Danes had begun to use a crossed flag even earlier.

The flag did not become the Danish flag straight away. However, during periods when the Danes, like other nations, used gaudy military flags adorned with all sorts of badges and symbols, Danish flags were often marked in one corner with a little "Dannebrog" sign. The oldest Danish cross flag (dating from 1427) preserved until our times hung in St. Mary's Church in Lübeck until it was destroyed by Allied bombs during the last world war.

At approximately the same time, Denmark acquired her national coat-of-arms: three blue lions on a gold background surrounded by nine red hearts. This however, is a subsequent interpretation. Originally there were nine blue leopards and the "hearts" were in reality water-lily leaves intended as a symbol of the sea. The leopard coat-of-arms may date from

Water-jugs cast in bronze, for use in churches. Armed heavy peasant rider and knight with barrel helmet.

before Valdemar's time, but this cannot be stated definitely. It is also the coat-of-arms of the Norman dukes, in which connection it has been pointed out that these were of Danish extraction. But whether there can be such an ancient link between the Danish lion (originally leopard) coat-of-arms, and the Norman, which today is found incorporated in the British coat-of-arms, is completely uncertain.

Valdemar experienced some difficulty in retaining his distant conquest. The Russians in particular became nervous about the new Scandinavian power, because they were afraid of a western European push being made towards the Russian trade centre of Novgorod, and therefore Danish garrisons were attacked on several occasions by very large forces. In Estonia, the town of Reval or Tallinn (Danish-town) was founded, and to this day it has the three Danish lions in its coat-of-arms.

Ingeborg of Denmark

During the reign of Valdemar II an international affair which had caused extreme embarrassment to the Danish royal house was brought to a conclusion. During Canute VI's reign, the King of France, *Philip*

August, had sought the hand in marriage of Canute's sister, the 18-year old Princess Ingeborg. Philip August was a King possessed of initiative, but he was not a charming husband. He had threatened to cast off his first wife. She was now dead, and the widower was desirous of arranging a marriage with the Danish princess because he had great plans of a war against England. He requested somewhat blatantly that her dowry should include the making over to him of the claims of the Danish royal house to the English throne, likewise the right to borrow Denmark's naval expeditionary force and army for one year. To this Canute gave him a blunt refusal – the Danish royal house may possibly have had no plans against England at this time, but it was not ready to relinquish the dream for good either. The amount of the dowry was agreed at 10,000 silver marks. The marriage took place in Amiens on August 14, 1193, but during the coronation the following day the French King behaved in a most extraordinary fashion, was "pale and trembling" and straight after the ceremony demanded an immediate divorce. He affirmed that his young bride – who is described as having been very beautiful, charming and good-natured – had bewitched him. He wanted to send her back to Denmark forthwith, and when the representatives of the Danish court refused to agree to this, he expelled them from the country. He tried to obtain a divorce by means of a forged genealogical tree which he used to prove that Ingeborg was too closely related to his first wife. The French arch-bishop declared the marriage null and void. Ingeborg did not understand French, but when the judgment was read out to her she cried, weeping: "Mala Francia! Roma! Roma!" whereupon she appealed her case to the Pope. She was then sent to a convent and treated wretchedly. The Pope declared the dissolution of the marriage as having no validity, but otherwise did not dare to offend Philip August. The Pope died, and his successor, Innocent III, took up the unfortunate princess's case vigorously. Meanwhile the Danish court exerted pressure on the papal court to have her set at liberty. Philip August became infuriated and threw her into prison. The Pope placed France under an interdict, whereupon Philip promised to treat Ingeborg as a Queen and a wife, and the interdict was lifted. But instead of being set free, Ingeborg was merely transferred to another prison. Priests and physicians were denied access to her, and she was prevented from corresponding with Denmark.

But in 1213, 20 years after the unfortunate wedding, the situation began to improve for her, and once again England was behind it all. The Pope had confiscated the English throne from John Lackland and assigned Philip August the task of seeing that his judgment was carried out. Philip once more wished to take advantage of Ingeborg's Danish claim to the English throne, so she was permitted to come out of prison and was accorded a state of dignity as befitted a queen; but she was never treated as a proper wife.

For ten years she now lived peacefully (although at a considerable distance from the King) in various towns and won a reputation for kind deeds. Philip August died in 1223, and being his widow, Ingeborg was on good terms with the French kings that succeeded him, Philip's son and grandson. She sent a large sum of money home when Valdemar the Victorious had to be ransomed out of captivity, and she died, highly esteemed, in either 1237 or 1238. For England her "claim" to the throne was never to prove of any importance.

Under Valdemar II's rule, relations with the other Scandinavian countries were good, and there was lasting peace in the North. Only once was it disturbed, but this was only by a "private" war. A Danish prince laid claim to his right to the throne of Sweden, and the final result was that the Swedish King fled to Denmark and asked for help. He had relatives amongst powerful Danish families, and in 1209 an army of knights advanced up through Sweden. But the Danish knights suffered a terrible defeat at Lena, when the auxiliary force was completely wiped out. The little we know about the battle has come down to us in a folk ballad. The defeat and the mourning at home in Denmark are described in an extremely vivid final stanza:

> The ladies stood in Highloft,
> Their lords' return to see,
> But every steed with gore was red
> And empty each saddle-tree.
> The knights bore out their shields, and then must many weep.

Collapse

And then, just when Valdemar and his Danish Empire were having a spell of good fortune and the country was richer than it had ever been since the days of Canute the Great, everything collapsed.

One day King Valdemar was out hunting with his son on the little island of Lyoe, to the south of Funen. Here they were visited by *Heinrich von Schwerin*, the *Black Count*. He sailed over to the island and he and King Valdemar exchanged gifts. But actually they were enemies, for Count Heinrich claimed that Valdemar had taken liberties with territories belonging to Schwerin while he, Heinrich, had been away travelling in the south. That evening the King gave a banquet on the island for his guest, and Valdemar and his young son (who had been crowned his co-regent) got rather drunk. During the night Heinrich and his men crept from their ship back on to the island, slew the King's bodyguard, seized the King and his son, trussed them up, carried them aboard and sailed off with them to Schwerin. So Denmark was without a King.

The news of the downfall of the great Scandinavian King spread like wildfire throughout Scandinavia and Germany, whereupon the North German princes saw their chance to recover all the German provinces once more. Frederick II had admittedly guaranteed Valdemar at the time his title to these territories in writing, but he now asserted that Valdemar had seized German lands to which he had no right. To begin with, the demand was made that all land south of the Danish border should be returned, and secondly, that a tremendous fine be paid. Danish nobles went to Germany to negotiate, but the demands were so ridiculous that they came home again without having achieved anything. Despite the fact that the country was still without a king, the legal system and local administration in the rural settlements were so firmly established that the organization of the country did not collapse. Everybody merely regarded the affair as a dreadful catastrophe, largely because the ancient Scandinavian outlook still prevailed whereby the King was regarded as the country's "fortune". It is said that when King Valdemar rode through the countryside in northern Germany the wives of the peasants came to him with their children that he might touch them and bless them, and the peasants themselves asked the King to ride over their fields in order to increase the fertility of the soil.

The King was kept a prisoner for three and a half years. A Danish army was mobilized under the command of one of his vassal rulers in northern Germany, who had good luck to begin with but was subsequently defeated. Once more it became necessary to bargain, and in the end the King agreed to pay an enormous sum in ready cash. His sons were to be imprisoned as hostages and set at liberty one by one over a period of ten years. Finally, Valdemar had to promise that he would not take revenge and that he would make no attempt to re-conquer the German provinces in the future.

Valdemar returned home and wrote to the Pope saying that his promise had been extracted from him by force. The Pope released him from his word, whereupon he took up arms and marched south to make good his losses. But nobody had faith in his invincibility any more. After a couple of lucky battles the Danish army was defeated at Bornhoeved – partly, so it is claimed, because the Frisian auxiliaries had been bribed and turned round in the middle of the battle and fought the Danes instead. Valdemar himself fought like one possessed and lost an eye in the process, but all to no avail. The Danes were obliged to retreat north behind the protective line of Danevirke.

Valdemar had the good sense to realize he had lost the game. But no part of Denmark had been sacrificed. His final years he spent at home and it was during this sombre period of his reign that his (and Dagmar's) son, Valdemar the Younger, was killed by a stray arrow whilst out hunting in much the same way as William Rufus in England. Valdemar the Younger died exactly three months after his young wife. She died in August, he on the same date in November. All that remained to old King Valdemar was to put his kingdom in good order for his successor to take over.

The Jutlandic Law

Up until this time Denmark had had no written laws. The various rural settlements of the country still used the ancient decrees which had been handed down and which a "lawman" knew by heart. At the *Thing* meetings the "lawman" was used like a Statute Book – for he knew what the law said. But the rules and regulations in the various settlements were not all alike, so when the King and his administrators travelled round the country with the object of passing judgment they encountered difficulties. It was still no use trying to issue a comprehensive Statute Book applicable to the whole of Denmark, for the differences in legal viewpoints in the various settlements were too great. By way of a start, Valdemar made a law that was to apply to Jutland, Slesvig, and Funen. His intention was possibly that with time it would come to apply throughout Denmark. (Shortly before this a Zealandic Law had been introduced, followed by a Scanian Law). The Jutlandic Law was a splendid legal document for its day, very sober, humane, and concisely formulated. Broadly speaking it contains no trace of superstition and no Draconic forms of punishment, in fact in the original version there is not even a single paragraph against witchcraft. Witchcraft existed, but played no important part in jurisprudence. The Jutlandic Law was enacted at Vordingborg in 1241. Just how advanced it was for its times can be judged by the fact that it remained in force in Jutland and Funen until 1683, and was not repealed in Slesvig until 1900.

On Maunday Thursday, 1241, a few days after having put his Jutlandic Law into force, Valdemar died. Posterity has given him the name of Valdemar the Victorious, and a German chronicler wrote: "With his death the crown tumbled off the heads of the Danes".

The period ending with the death of Valdemar the Victorious is known in Danish history as the *Valdemar Period*, or as the *Great Period of the Valdemars*. Just as with Canute the Great's Empire, or whenever events have appeared to be leading up to something great in Danish history, the adventure proved to be short-lived. The country was too small; she had neither a large enough population, nor the basic essentials for such ambitious adventures involving conquests far from home, nor the ability to consolidate and retain such positions once acquired.

Under the Valdemars, the Danes became deeply influenced by European culture. Even so, everything that came to Denmark became influenced in turn by Danish culture, adapted to suit Danish conditions, made less violent, less extreme. We know little about such building as was carried on at the time apart from churches and convents. The many castles have long since disappeared, partly because Denmark has always suffered from a shortage of good building stone. Buildings that fell into disuse were merely pulled down and their stones used for new buildings. Even so, one forms the impression that a very sober, knowledgeable type of architectural art must have existed, one that only unfolded itself in all its glory in the form of big cathedrals, just as was the case elsewhere in Europe. Small, compact manor-churches are still to be found in many places in Denmark. Of the more than 1,700 parish churches existing in

Denmark today, roughly 1,500 date from the Valdemar Period or earlier. Most of them have since been modified somewhat. The Danish "round churches" built during the 12th and 13th centuries do not look very European; their heavy, massive walls possess no architectonic grace, only a crude strength whose soul cannot have been inspired by the architects of the Rhineland.

In present-day Denmark there are still seven round churches, a combination of church and castle. There were once many more. Ol's Church on Bornholm is one of the youngest.

We know very little about daily life and customs in Denmark during the Valdemar Period, but this loss is partly compensated by a wealth of folk poetry, a cultural treasure-trove that reveals much concerning contemporary thoughts and feelings. A considerable number of these poems and ballads date from this period, and even though the troubadour songs of Europe helped transform the ancient Scandinavian epic lay into gentler folk poems, these Scandinavian verses contain a poetic strength, convey a personal mood and an appreciation of the beauties of Nature that are not just an expression of romanticism. At the same time they tell of a nobleman's world that had become Europeanized, but from which the Church still had not managed to eradicate ancient thinking about matters concerning Nature. Mermaids and water spirits are still to be found in these verses, the dead return to haunt the living, maidens fly to their lovers in "a suit of feathers", i.e. transformed into birds, men have a "raven spell" cast upon them and fly by night, fairies dance in the meadows and dwell in ancient grave-mounds, and if they invite a young swain to come to them and he decides to flee, they take the most fearful revenge. Passion played an important part in these old verses, but "fate" an even greater one. "Fate" was something from which nobody could escape, and one cannot help reflecting upon the blending of modern Christianity and ancient peasant settlement traditions revealed in a poem that starts:

> *There is dancing in the churchyard,*
> *Dancing girls with flowing hair.*

Valdemar's Sons

After Valdemar there was once again a whole string of heirs lined up in readiness, just as at the death of Sweyn Estridson. Berngerd had presented Valdemar with three sons, and all three were to become King in turn. Once more the same old game started – with one disappointed claimant after the next.

The three sons were Eric, Abel and Christopher.

Eric had already been crowned King during his father's lifetime, and his brother Abel was made Duke of Slesvig, just as his father had been before him. But Abel regarded himself as the independent owner of the Slesvig territories, an attitude which resulted in a regular war starting up between the brothers. Abel marched north into Jutland and thence across to Funen. Ribe and Odense were plundered and burnt. Eric was unable to save his kingdom, for Abel worked methodically, winning first his younger brother Christopher over on to his side and then persuading the town of Lübeck to join him in his war against Denmark. Lübeck was interested in seeing Denmark's foreign trade weakened as much as possible; in 1248 Copenhagen was seized and burnt, and Absalon's castle was razed to the ground. At this time Eric was dreaming of launching an expedition against Estonia in order to consolidate and expand Denmark's possessions there and to convert the heathens, both within the borders of Estonia and beyond, to Christianity. As far as is known he set forth in due course on his expedition, but little came of it. Meanwhile troubles at home increased steadily. Eric's nickname of "Ploughpenny" originated from his having introduced a plough tax. He had studied in Paris, but even so his attitude towards the Church was the worst imaginable. The Bishop of Roskilde had to go into exile because the King wanted to take Copenhagen away from him. Copenhagen, as already mentioned, had been given to Absalon and the bishopric of Roskilde by Valdemar the Great. Finally, Eric advanced into Slesvig, whereupon Abel was obliged to surrender and acknowledge his brother's sovereignty. But shortly after their meeting in Slesvig, Abel had his brother seized and taken by boat at dead of night out into Slien Fjord, where his head was promptly lopped off by a Danish nobleman named Lave Gudmonsson. The execution naturally solved the dispute, and curiously enough the Archbishop of Denmark declared that nobody was to be suspected of having committed the assassination. Abel became King – this was in 1250.

However, despite his swearing a solemn oath as to his innocence, the rumour persisted that he had been guilty of fratricide. Miracles began to occur at Eric's grave in Slesvig. In other respects Abel was a strong and efficient King, but he was not destined to rule the country for more than two years. He lost his life during an expedition against the Frisians and thus became the only Danish king since Harald Bluetooth to have died in battle.

Christopher, the third of Valdemar's sons, then inherited the kingdom; but he also inherited some very strained relationships with the Church. Absalon's family was still in control of the Danish Church, but the former spirit of collaboration between Church and Crown no longer existed.

Crown versus Church

Abel's son became Duke of Slesvig, but he too was bitter at not having been able to succeed to the throne after his father. Thus for centuries afterwards the border country of Slesvig became one of the most difficult problems with which the Danish kings had to contend. For, despite the fact that the Dukes of Slesvig acted, so to speak, as the King's "lord lieutenant" in the province, they nevertheless considered themselves as being independent. They were in continual opposition to the King and allied themselves time and again with Denmark's enemies. It must be remembered that the name *Slesvig* covers two things: 1) the town on the Sli, successor to the old town of Hedeby, and 2) the Duchy of Slesvig, of which the town was the capital. The duchy is also known as *Sønderjylland*, meaning *South Jutland.*

Simultaneously, Christopher had his difficulties with the Church. In Lund, Jacob Erlandsen, a highly gifted, authoritative, but at the same time domineering and stubborn man, was elected Archbishop by the canons very much against Christopher's wishes. Further to the south of Europe the struggle for power between Church and Crown had been raging for many generations, and whilst in Scandinavia up until the present time the two had remained more or less at peace, the general European conflict was now extended to include Denmark. Jacob Erlandsen was a relative of Absalon and held lofty views as to the rights and powers of the Church. He wished to see the Church freed from all worldly authority, but he was unable to reach any agreement with the King. Finally Christopher threw him into prison and thereafter had him conducted, a prisoner, and with a fool's cap on his head, over to Hagenskov Castle on the island of Funen. A papal interdict was immediately placed upon Scania and Zealand, but the King had the churches opened and forced the priests to perform their duties. It appears that the parish priests were not particularly interested in the squabble anyway.

Shortly afterwards, in 1259, just after he had received Holy Communion at Ribe Church, Christopher suddenly died. Abbot Arnfast had been officiating at the altar and the rumour immediately sprang up that the altar wine the King had drunk had been poisoned. His friends thereafter called him "Christ-offer" – which in Danish is a pun on his name meaning that he was "sacrificed to Christ".

Christopher's son Eric was only 11 years old when his father died, and his mother, Queen Margaret, therefore ruled the country for him. She was an efficient and authoritative lady and was given the two nicknames, "Black Greta" and "Margaret the Prancing Charger". She immediately set Jacob Erlandsen at liberty, whereupon he left the country. For several years negotiations were conducted with the object of bringing about a compromise, and in the end he was actually on his way home to Denmark in order to reassume his duties as Archbishop of Lund when he had the ill fortune to die.

In the meantime Eric had grown up into a man. He made his peace with the Church – at least more or less. But the Danish nobles were not so tractable now as they had been previously.

The Royal Charter – Murder of the King

They considered that the time had come to curtail the King's powers. At a meeting in Nyborg in 1282, King Eric was made to sign Denmark's first Royal Charter, corresponding to England's Magna Carta of 1215. He had to promise to call a national assembly once a year and also that he would collaborate with the nobles. Nobody was to be forced into doing anything, or to be punished or imprisoned without legal sentence being passed beforehand. But there was no peace in the land.

In November 1286, King Eric was on a hunting excursion in central Jutland. The story goes that one night he had to seek shelter in a barn in the village of Finderup, just southwest of Viborg. Apart from his stable-boy and one Rane Jonsson, his "chamberlain", he was unattended. It was a terribly stormy night, and during the small hours the barn was attacked by a band of men who forced their way in and killed the King. It was said that Rane Jonsson had been in league with the regicides.

The King's body was taken to Viborg. It had 56 wounds. An inquiry was initiated and at a court-of-law in Nyborg it was decided to bring an action against nine of the country's leading men, amongst them the Lord High Constable, Stig Andersson Hvide, and Count Jacob of Halland. They were all banished from the country.

Folk ballads were soon claiming that the Lord High Constable had killed the King because the King had been offensive to his wife, but this was probably pure fiction. King Eric was given the nickname of "Clipping", inferring "a shorn sheepskin", or "a silver coin with a piece clipped (i.e. nicked) out of it".

Once more a child ascended the throne of Denmark. Eric's son, likewise named Eric, was only twelve years old. He was given the nickname of "Menved". Anglicized, this might become "Menwot" and would still be a little difficult to explain, but it possibly derives from an oath, "[By holy] men [that] wot". He was faced with the problem of the regicides, who had been obliged to leave the country and forfeit their rich lands. Count Jacob built himself a rock castle, *Varberg Castle*, in Halland, and the Lord High Constable, Stig Andersson, retired to the little island of *Hjelm* in the Kattegat. Here he lived, like an ancient Viking king, by piracy and by raiding the Danish coast. He set up his own mint on the island and counterfeited King Eric's money. The regicides were also afforded shelter and protection by the King of Norway, and thus for many long, troubled years King Eric had to fight them until compromises were found or, one by one, they eventually died. A couple of them were imprisoned and executed.

But whilst the fight against the regicides was going on, *Jens Grand* (another relative of Absalon) was elected Archbishop of Lund, whereupon the conflict between Church and Crown started all over again. The King sent his brother Christopher to Lund. Christopher arrested the Archbishop and took him to Soeborg in North Zealand, where the Archbishop was promptly thrown into a dismal dungeon and chained to a block of stone. The King offered to make peace with him and arrange a compromise, but the Archbishop said he would rather have every bone in his body shattered on the wheel than relax his demands one iota. Finally the Archbishop managed to escape from prison (a scullery-lad helped him) and although very weak from his confinement he succeeded in reaching the coast, where he clambered aboard a ship and sailed to Bornholm. Here the Archbishop had a stronghold named Hammershus. From thence he proceeded to Rome. Pope Bonifacius was firmly resolved to take up his case, but just at that moment he was having difficulties with *Philip the Handsome* of France. So when Eric commenced negotiations, the Pope relented and decreed that the Archbishop was to relinquish his office, but receive compensation in the form of a large indemnification in ready cash. Jens Grand subsequently died at the Papal Court in Avignon, and Eric made his peace with the Church.

It was at this time that Eric became seized by the wave of romanticism that became so popular during the latter part of the Age of Chivalry. As he did not find sufficient opportunity for indulging in pomp and splendour in Denmark, he went to northern Germany. On several occasions he gave sumptuous performances (in particular a tremendous tournament at Rostock) and everywhere he was hailed as the royal knight of all knights. But such lavish festivity was expensive, and King Eric had no money. He therefore had to borrow in order to pay for all the sumptuous feasts and splendid prizes and awards. Back in Denmark no particular pleasure was manifested at his theatrical triumphs, despite the fact that his behaviour in Germany probably secured him more than empty glory.

Mural painting in Sæby Church in Zealand.
Older Danish wall-paintings are in Byzantine style.

During the Middle Ages numerous churches had ceiling arches built in, and later Danish murals are lively and narrative. The pictures on the walls, partly hidden by the arches, are older. Keldby Church, Møn.

Amongst other things it was said that he obtained quite considerable political advantages. It just so happened that they were untenable. Finally he began to pledge part of Denmark in order to raise money to meet his expenses.

In his private life he was not happy. His wife Ingeborg bore him a great number of children, but they all died young. Her last son looked as though he were going to live, but she accidentally dropped him out of her carriage when holding him up before the crowds – and he died as a result of the fall. After this she went into a convent. In 1319 Eric Menved died.

Dissolution of the Realm

His brother Christopher II became King, but nobody trusted him. It was he who had imprisoned Archbishop Jens Grand in his time, but since then he had been involved in an uprising against his brother, and nobody had faith in anything he said. The country's finances were on the verge of collapse, the country itself seemed to be facing dissolution, and all inward peace had been destroyed. The nobles therefore started negotiations with *Count Gert* (or *Gerhard*) of Holstein, who was regarded as a highly talented and efficient prince. He took immediate action and had his nephew, Duke Valdemar (who was a member of Abel's family) elected King of Denmark. In reality it was Count Gert who ruled the country for him.

But Christopher did not give up his throne without a murmur. He too commenced negotiations, and in return for pledging Funen and most of northern Jutland to Count Gert as security for large sums of money, and Scania and Zealand to Count Gert's cousin, *Count John the Mild*, he officially recovered his crown. After all, he had merely pledged his lands, not given any of them away. But he did not have the remotest prospect of ever being able to raise the enormous sum required to redeem those parts of the country which he had pledged, and finally not one single square foot of land remained in his possession.

Denmark was actually without a King for eight years. Count Gert and Count John controlled all the Danish territories with the exception of North Slesvig, which was still ruled by Duke Valdemar. Denmark's German masters built castles all over the kingdom and levied severe taxes.

Furthermore, they vouchsafed a complete lack of understanding of Danish ways and customs and of the privileges of the peasants in the rural settlements. Everywhere they went they behaved the way they were accustomed to behaving in Germany. Crippling taxes were imposed and regiments of soldiers were sent out to round up the money. They did so without compassion.

And so the Scanian provinces backed out. They submitted to the rule of the King of Sweden, Magnus Smek ("smek" means "a caress") on condition that they should not be obliged to become Swedes, but that Magnus should recognize their independence. He was to be King of Sweden *and* of the Scanian provinces – but separately.

Finally, Christopher's eldest son, Junker Otto, took arms and marched with an army against the oppressors. But he was defeated at the Battle of Tap Hede and taken prisoner. And then, in the midst of his own misery, practically unnoticed, deserted and improverished, Christopher died.

Murder of Count Gert

By 1340 the situation was desperate. Rebellion was seething throughout the land, and the country's position appeared hopeless. Count Gert marched up into Jutland with an army of 11,000 men with the object of quelling the trouble at its source. But on the night of April 1, a Jutlandic squire named Niels Ebbesen forced his way into Count Gert's headquarters and slew him in his bedchamber. The news of the great man's death sped all round Jutland, rebellion began to stir everywhere, and the Count's army retreated south without fighting. The Count's sons' courage failed them, with the result that they dared not follow up their father's plans. Niels Ebbesen died during the siege of Skanderborg while the Count's sons were negotiating with Christopher's youngest son, Valdemar.

Valdemar Atterdag

Valdemar had spent his youth in Germany. He had been brought up at the Imperial German Court as a European man of fashion, for his sister had married the Emperor's son. He had already called himself in his seal the "true heir to the throne of Denmark". He was now acknowledged

King of Denmark by Count Gert's sons, by Count John the Mild, and by the Duke of Slesvig, because they all realized that if peace were to be established in the country at all there would have to be a Danish King on the throne. Moreover they probably imagined that the young Prince would be easy to manage. When the agreement was drawn up, Valdemar promised that he would allow the Counts to retain their land mortgages until such time as he was able to redeem them. Having married Helvig however, who was a princess of Slesvig, he was granted a small portion of North Jutland straight away as a dowry.

None of the mortgagees could have been expected to guess that, in choosing Valdemar, they were placing a robust, cunning, determined, bold, and highly talented politician on the Danish throne. He immediately set about the task of reconstruction. He imposed severe taxes in the small part of the country that was his, sold Estonia to the German nobles, redeemed land here, conquered land there, and laid siege to several of the German-occupied Danish castles. Bit by bit, he consolidated the country. He had no scruples about the methods he employed as long as they were effective. He won little affection in Denmark (in fact he was known as Valdemar the Evil) but on the other hand he did not spare himself, working and toiling ceaselessly until, at the end of nine years of war and complicated political manoeuvering, he had succeeded in uniting and liberating practically the whole of Denmark.

And then, the terrible bubonic plague which had been ravaging the whole of Europe at this time, finally reached Denmark. It was known as the Black Death and it claimed almost half the Danish population. During these years Valdemar carried on methodically, using his authority, confiscating large areas of land whenever these found themselves, thanks to the plague, without 'a master', and in particular worked to re-establish law and order in the land after all the years of lawless dissolution. He put down a rising of the nobility, and, after negotiating with their Jutlandic leaders, sent them home again. On their way, in the town of Middelfart, three of them were murdered. The King swore he knew nothing about the affair, and nothing more was done about it either – beyond the fact that right up until the year 1872 Middelfart was obliged to pay a yearly fine.

The Scanian provinces were still under the Swedish King, and Valdemar gave Magnus Smek a written promise to the effect that he might retain these lands. But at the same time he succeeded in betrothing one of his daughters, Margaret (who was only six) to Magnus' son Hakon, who was King of Norway. He then invaded Scania, seized the provinces from Magnus and incorporated them once more under the Danish Crown. Magnus was most disappointed.

The Conquest of Gotland

Valdemar then fitted out a fleet. The old method of raising a naval expedition was no longer practicable. Instead, merchant vessels had to be requisitioned or borrowed and then manned with troops. The fleet sailed south through the Sound and nobody knew what the plan of action was. But the King then set an easterly course and made for the rich Swedish island of Gotland. Valdemar had not forgotten Denmark's old commercial position in the Baltic. In many ways his politics reveal an intimate knowledge of the outlook prevailing during the old Valdemar Period. Gotland was (or had been) one of the most important trading centres in the Baltic, and *Visby*, the rich capital of the island, was almost entirely in the hands of the German Hanseatic League. Valdemar landed on Gotland and marched towards Visby. Outside the walls of the city there was a frightful battle during which the primitively armed Goth peasants fought for the freedom of their island whilst the citizens of Visby, mostly foreign merchants, looked on passively from the tops of the walls – for their one concern was to remain on good terms with the victors.

Valdemar's troops had modern weapons and the fight developed into an extremely bloody one lasting practically the whole day in the burning July heat. It was the Danish cavalry that finally decided the outcome. With the battle over and the Danes victorious, some 1,800 Goth peasants lay dead, thus constituting a terrible blow to the whole peasant settlement.

A few years ago the graves of these warriors were subjected to archaeological research. The skeletons excavated revealed that the massacre must have been of an extraordinarily macabre nature, sheer butchery in fact, for the fallen had been horribly maimed. Over the graves where they lay buried there still stands a cross erected at the time and bearing an inscription to the effect that "on 27 July 1361 these Goths fell at the hands of the Danes before the gates of Visby. Here they lie. Pray for them".

The citizens of Visby immediately threw open their gates, but Valdemar disdainfully declared that they were to tear out a wide breach in their city wall so that he could march in eleven abreast in the approved style. The breach in the wall can still be seen today. A tax was levied on the town, but Valdemar has been incorrectly accused of having destroyed the town's commercial prosperity. Valdemar conquered Gotland because he had sold Estonia and because he wanted to re-establish Denmark's commercial position in the Baltic. But by this time the old east-west Baltic trade was very much on the decline. Gotland's old commercial wealth had already become, even in Valdemar's time, as much legend as it was fact, and year by year it had been deteriorating. Trade was seeking other routes and navigating skill had improved so much that intermediate stations were no longer necessary.

From that day onwards the Danish King called himself "King of the Goths", just as ever since the conquest of Wendland during the Valdemar Period he had called himself "King of the Wends". These titles are still used by the King of Denmark to this day.

The Swedish nobles were furious at Valdemar's act of usurpation. They called off the betrothal between his daughter Margaret and King Magnus' son Hakon, and they succeeded in betrothing Hakon to a Holstein princess. But just as this Holstein princess was on her way to Sweden, her ship had the ill fortune to run aground on the Scanian coast. Valdemar had her interned in the most dignified manner possible, sent for Magnus and Hakon, and married Hakon to Margaret in Copenhagen.

This was too much for the Swedish nobles. They declared Magnus a traitor, chased him out and proclaimed *Albrecht of Mecklenburg* King of Sweden.

So far, Valdemar had had success wherever he turned. Denmark had undergone reconstruction, the Scanian provinces had returned to the Danish Crown, Gotland had been conquered and Valdemar had prospects of obtaining control of the Baltic trade. But his conquest of Visby had made him some powerful enemies. The tremendous trading organization known as the Hanseatic League was a union comprising a great many northern European commercial towns, and what with Visby's being a Hanseatic town, the League's commercial and economic authority had been affronted. The Hanseatic League already constituted a grave threat to the Scandinavian countries as it was, for it managed to force its way in wherever there appeared to be opportunities of trade and good profits. Bergen, Norway's most important commercial centre, was dominated by immigrant German businessmen. In Sweden, German merchants in Stockholm were so powerful that although the city was not actually a Hanseatic town, i.e. not a member of the League, the German inhabitants constituted the most powerful factor in the government of the city. Denmark's towns were not threatened quite so much, partly because there were so many of them that trade never became focussed so much on one particular, dominating point. On the other hand Denmark possessed a financial centre of considerable importance in northern European trading circles. This was what was known as the Scanian Fair.

Fishing in the waters of the Sound (and in Danish waters generally) had been famous ever since the early Middle Ages, and the most incredible quantities of herring had been caught. Fishing was concentrated principally off the southwestern corner of Scania, i.e. the peninsular with the two small towns of Skanoer and Falsterbo. Most of the year the peninsula was practically uninhabited, but as soon as the fishing season started in autumn, people flocked there from the whole of northern Europe in order to take part in the herring fishing. Herring catches were brought ashore, cleaned, salted, packed in casks and exported to markets throughout Europe. So famous did "Scanian herring" become that in the fish market in Paris the law stated that fishmongers *not* selling Scanian herring must fly a red flag. At the same time as the fishermen, salters and "gill-girls" took possession of the deserted littoral marshes, merchants came surging in from all quarters and put up their tents and stalls. Tented taverns did a brisk business, for this was an international trade fair and there was plenty of activity on the little tongue of land. While the boats pulled for the shore with their hauls of fish, and carts lurched along the narrow sandy tracks with herring-casks both full and empty, money passed quickly from hand to hand. Sometimes more than 70,000 people gathered on the peninsular during the hectic months of the herring season. The whole area was carefully divided up into "plots" so that each fishing company and each town had its own little piece of land where salting was carried out. Danish fishermen occupied the "front" plots – i.e. the best ones, while behind them towns like Stettin, Danzig, Stralsund and Lübeck had their appointed places. At Falsterbo and Skanoer there were two small castles where the Danish King's representatives kept an eye on the fishing generally and collected rights and dues on behalf of the Danish Crown. The Hanseatic towns took considerable part in the fishing and paid a fixed amount in tax. The Scanian fishing grounds were not the only fishing grounds Denmark possessed. Fishing was also carried on from the harbours and coastline of Zealand and from the islands to the south. The Crown had its own salting-house on the island of Amager, and fishing in the Limfjord was also plentiful. The Hanseatic towns were deeply involved in the lucrative Scanian fishing industry and were therefore interested in keeping the peace with the King of Denmark. But having now conquered their fine town of Visby, the Hanseatic towns realized that Valdemar constituted a threat to their existence, and they sent a fleet against him. Unfortunately for them it was met in the Sound by the King's fleet and completely destroyed.

The Coalition against Valdemar Atterdag

For a whole year the Hanseatic League remained quiet, but then its members gathered for a conference at Cologne. Representatives from 77 Hanseatic towns took part and decided to send King Valdemar an official challenge. He received it calmly and scoffed at them, whereupon his other enemies allied themselves with the Hanseatic League. He could not stand up against a conspiracy of the whole of northern Europe. With Holstein and Albrecht of Sweden allied together, Denmark was threatened by a pincer movement. Once again, however, Valdemar astonished his enemies. He left Henning Podebusk in charge of the country and went off to Germany in person. To no small extent the conspiracy had been formed against him personally, and when he was no longer present, the solidarity between the conspirators weakened. The Danish government concluded peace while Valdemar continued working on the conspirators abroad one by one, and even though the peace looked serious enough, the situation nevertheless was more or less saved. The Hanseatic League was the most dangerous opponent. It was accorded the Scanian coast in the form of security for a 15-year period and moreover complete freedom to trade as it wished in Denmark. On the other hand the remaining conspirators got nothing at all. Valdemar came home.

Only one part of Denmark was now still beyond Valdemar's control and it seemed as though there might even be a chance of recovering this too. Slesvig had belonged to Abel's family ever since Abel's death in 1252. The family now died out, and Valdemar therefore wanted to confiscate Slesvig. He had started to do so when, at Gurre Castle and only 55 years old, he suddenly died "of an unfortunate remedy for curing gout".

He was one of the most noteworthy of Danish Kings: a dynamic personality, cold and calculating, energetic and restless, consumed by one overriding thought, that of re-constructing the land which his grandfather and father had abandoned almost to the point of extinction. He worked hard throughout his life and had no scruples about the methods he used to attain his ends. What he managed to achieve was little short of miraculous: not only was Denmark once more free, united and re-established, but furthermore stronger and richer than at any time since Valdemar the Victorious. He was not very religious (it is said that he regularly mocked at both the Church and Our Lord) but nevertheless he co-operated willingly with the Church. He was full of surprises. After he had been working on the reconstruction of the country for the first nine years of his reign he suddenly called a national assembly, to whom he presented an exact statement of account concerning the economics of his reconstruction programme: this had cost so much, so much had been raised by taxation, so much had come from his own pocket – the whole budget was detailed down to the last farthing. In the middle of all his incredible labours he nevertheless found the time to ride down through Europe (he departed suddenly and without warning) to Jerusalem, where he had himself knighted a *Knight of the Holy Sepulchre*. He found himself in difficulties with the Pope, who claimed that he had had no right to do such a thing without papal permission, but this did not worry Valdemar, who of all Europe's monarchs became "the first amongst equals". For years the name he left behind him was somewhat murky. His taxes were severe, his methods cruel, and he gradually slid into becoming part of ancient heathen superstition. From before the advent of Christianity there had existed the belief in Scandinavia that whenever a storm suddenly burst upon a district accompanied by thunder and lightning, it must mean that Odin and his warriors were riding across the heavens into battle. In Denmark this belief was slightly altered. It was no longer Odin, but 'King Volmer' riding

"The Kalmar Letter", the document that formed the basis of the Kalmar Union
between Denmark, Norway and Sweden in 1397.

Count Christopher, son of Valdemar Atterdag, died before his father and was buried in Roskilde Cathedral.

through the night with his hunting hounds mounted on a coal-black charger as an everlasting punishment in return for his heathen lack of Christianity. He was given the nickname of Valdemar Atterdag, literally meaning "Again-a-day"; for Denmark, thanks to him and according to popular belief, "once again had her day". Others contend that the name was taken from a Low German expression, "ter tage", meaning more or less "what times we live in!"

Upon his death in 1375 the situation was serious, for Valdemar only had one son, and he died before his father. Valdemar's daughters had been married abroad, and if a King were to be found from amongst the members of the old royal family, it would mean finding a son of one of those daughters. Moreover the Hanseatic town of Lübeck had inserted a clause in the peace treaty to the effect that it was to be consulted when a King of Denmark was elected after Valdemar's death.

Queen Margaret

It is not quite clear how the negotiations were really conducted. The best claim to the throne was held by one of Valdemar's grandchildren, the son of his daughter Ingeborg. Ingeborg had married the Duke of Mecklenburg and the Duke, naturally enough, was keen on getting his son on to the Danish throne. But from Norway came Valdemar's younger daughter, Margaret, aged 22, together with her little 5-year old son, Oluf. It appears that Margaret managed to push her elder sister's son out of the picture. She diplomatically renounced her own claim to the throne – in favour of her son. She recognized the assembly's complete freedom to choose whomsoever it wished – and succeeded in getting her own son elected. She obviously must have acquired some powerful men friends. The Mecklenburgs were very angry, and it led to many complications in the future, but the decision nevertheless remained final.

Possibly it was assumed that a 5-year old boy and his 22-year old mother would be easy to sway, whereby the Church, the nobility, and other authorities would be able to enjoy free play. But if this was the case, there was a miscalculation. Even before her father died young Margaret had proved herself to be a girl with her wits about her. In Norway, where she was the wife of King Hakon, she had worked determinedly, administering her estates herself. She was extremely talented and now offered to rule Denmark on behalf of her little son. From that day on she became Denmark's uncrowned Queen. Five years later her husband, King Hakon of Norway, died. So she took over the rule of Norway as well, by this time still only 27 years of age.

She carried on where her father had left off. The coast of Scania, together with all the western Scanian castles, had been handed over to the Hanseatic League for a 15-year period dating from the conclusion of peace in 1370. Margaret's character was different to her father's. She was intelligent and shrewd, but never violent. Upon the expiration of the 15-year period the Hanseatic League was disinclined to hand back the castles, so she made her little son Oluf write them a very indignant letter. Immediately afterwards they received a letter from her in which she explained that she would endeavour to speak to her son in order to smooth matters out. At about this same time pirates began to be active in the Baltic, and it was the vessels of the Hanseatic League that suffered most from their attentions. The League complained to Margaret, claiming that it was the duty of the Danish Crown to keep Danish waters free of pirates. Margaret answered and agreed that they were right, but regretted her inability to do anything unless she had control of her Scanian castles. Finally, when the Hanseatic League realized that the only way it could keep the castles would be by going to war, they gave up – and so Margaret got her way. At the same time she gave her attention to Denmark's eternal headache, the question of Slesvig. She got the Holstein nobles to recognize the Danish King's suzerainty over Slesvig, but further than this she dared not go for the moment. In the meantime she continued working on other fronts. Her late husband, King Hakon of Norway, was the son of Magnus Smek of Sweden, and now, in order to "challenge" Albrecht, she had her son Oluf call himself the "true heir to Sweden".

And then, quite suddenly, young King Oluf died at Skanoer Castle.

For Margaret the situation was a politically tricky one, for she herself had renounced all claims to the Danish throne. She had no rights in Norway either (for she had ruled both countries "on behalf of her son") and in Sweden she simply had no business whatsoever. However, the knot loosened itself with astonishing rapidity. The nobles of Norway and Denmark hailed her, not as their Queen, but as "Dame of our Kingdoms,

Master of our House, Mighty Guardian". She continued her negotiations with various aristocratic circles in Sweden. She avoided war as long as possible, but finally there was no other way out. At a battle fought at Falkoebing in Sweden, Albrecht's army was defeated. He himself was captured by the Danes. The whole of Sweden agreed to submit to Margaret's rule with the exception of the city of Stockholm. Here the Germans wielded considerable authority and succeeded in terrorizing the Swedish inhabitants, partly by having a large number of Swedish citizens burnt to death. In the meantime Margaret kept Albrecht in prison until such time as he should become more malleable. Finally he was set at liberty on condition that he relinquish his demands and that his party surrender Stockholm.

The Scandinavian Union

The programme of reconstruction which her father had commenced in Denmark in 1340 had so far, half a century later, culminated in the unification of the three Scandinavian kingdoms under the Danish Crown. But Margaret was neither usurper nor conqueror. Her authority in Norway had been acquired through negotiation, and her action in Sweden had taken place only after consultation with Swedish nobles. She continued her policy determinedly.

She had lost her son. She now made provision for a successor by adopting her sister's grandson, who had been born in Pomerania and given a Slav name. She diplomatically renamed him Eric, a name already acceptable as a king's name in Denmark, Norway and Sweden. She travelled round the three kingdoms with him and had him proclaimed King. Then she summoned the famous convention of Kalmar in 1397. Here were gathered nobles from all three kingdoms and here Eric was duly crowned King of Scandinavia. From now on the three kingdoms were to be united under one King, to be elected jointly. The Kalmar Union lasted, with intervals, until 1523 – in other words for 126 years. Then Sweden finally broke away. But between Denmark and Norway the union established by Margaret lasted from 1380, when her husband King Hakon died, until 1814, when it was disrupted by England. Denmark and Norway were united for 434 years.

The Kalmar Union between the Scandinavian kingdoms was intended to ensure peace in Scandinavia, and with the three kingdoms united under one Crown a basis was provided for the creation of a Great Power in the North. The three countries were supposed to be equals in the union, in other words no single country was to be allowed to dominate the others. But perhaps Margaret's private intentions were not quite so idealistic. She probably regarded Denmark as the "senior" country, and, contrary

On Margaret's sarcophagus in Roskilde lies an idealized figure of the Queen in alabaster.

to the spirit of the Union, very soon placed Danish and German nobles in Sweden's royal castles.

Despite everything we now know about Margaret, she remains one of the great enigmas in Scandinavian history. What was she really like, this strange woman who, after the death of her husband, the King of Norway, never married again but nevertheless obliged all men, even the most violent and primitive of the Scandinavian nobles, to obey her and submit to her will? She was a friend of the Church and its officers and achieved all her ends by means of shrewdness. She knew how to wait, knew the right moment at which to act, and succeeded in putting everything in good order. She travelled round her kingdoms ensuring the proper administration of justice – something which had suffered from corruption during the troubled years. She put a stop to attempts by certain noblemen to behave as "local kings", and confiscated, calmly and resolutely, every square foot of land whenever the owners failed to produce legally valid title deeds, by the simple expedient of declaring such lands to be the property of the Crown. She donated lavish sums to churches and convents and was methodical in her upbringing of her young adopted son. She sent him travelling round his kingdoms but requested him to leave all the more weighty decisions to her. One problem remained unsolved for her, just as it had done for Valdemar Atterdag when his royal labours were practically over, and that was the question of Slesvig. The Holstein count who had been installed in Slesvig as a Danish Duke died, whereupon Margaret endeavoured, little by little, to confiscate the territory. The Holstein leaders saw the danger approaching and trouble started. Margaret went down in order to arrange matters with her customary diplomacy, but just outside Flensburg she died aboard her ship – or possibly it was on one of the islands in Flensburg Fjord.

Margaret was never given a nickname. She has simply gone down in history as "Queen Margaret", although in reality she was only Queen of Norway. But royal nicknames were not being used so much any more. Her father, Valdemar Atterdag, was the last King to have one. Eric, her adopted son, was known as Eric of Pomerania, but this was a heraldic name, like that of his successor, and hereafter the practice stopped and Kings were given numbers instead. Thus an ancient form of familiar intimacy came to an end.

The Union after the Death of Queen Margaret

On the death of his foster-mother in 1412, Eric was 30 years old. He felt himself a Dane, despite the fact that his father had been a Pomeranian nobleman – from all accounts a "great robber". From 1401 onwards, when he officially came of age, he had been Margaret's co-regent. Thus by this time he was not only a mature man but moreover very familiar with conditions throughout his three mighty (albeit somewhat thinly populated) kingdoms. He is described as having been a handsome man with "a beautiful physique, golden-yellow hair, a ruddy complexion, and a long, slender neck which he covered with a linen cloth fastened by a golden brooch. He would leap into the saddle alone and unaided without the help of stirrups, and all women were drawn to him, especially the Empress, with passionate yearning."

He pursued his foster-mother's Union policy, which was to rule the three kingdoms equally but let Denmark be the "senior" kingdom. Just as she had done, he refrained from filling the highest posts in Norway and Sweden and instead ruled the two countries with the assistance of

German and Danish bailiffs. He immediately took up the matter of Slesvig, but where Margaret had endeavoured to incorporate the province gradually without revealing her ultimate objective, he came straight to the point, declared Slesvig to be Danish and finally even got Emperor Sigismund to affirm that the territory had never really been a hereditary fief. For twenty years he fought to incorporate Slesvig naturally into the kingdom of Denmark. But he never succeeded. Furthermore the endless feuds in Slesvig cost money. Eric levied severe taxes in Norway and Sweden, whereupon discontent grew.

The Sound Dues

On one point Eric antagonized all the seafaring nations of Europe, and this was by introducing Sound Dues. At this time the Sound and the Belts

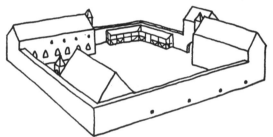

Krogen at Elsinore, the original "Kronborg", was a strictly quadrangular castle, very modern in its day.

were exclusively Danish territorial waters, for the Scanian provinces still belonged to Denmark. The Danish King therefore controlled the entrance to the Baltic, and the Sound was one of Europe's busiest channels. Ever since ancient times the Danish King had maintained proprietary rights on the waters surrounding Denmark, and Eric now decreed that all who passed through the Danish King's waters were to pay toll. In order to make sure that these dues were paid he built a number of castles on both sides of the Sound (those at Malmö and Landskrona for instance) and it was probably he (though possibly Valdemar Atterdag before him) who built the solid tower called *Kernen* that still stands at Hälsingborg. Just opposite (it is here that the Sound is narrowest) he built a very modern, square castle called *Krogen*. This is now Kronborg Castle, at Elsinore. At first the toll exacted was only one rose-noble per ship, but it was soon raised and became very complicated. For 428 years the ships of all nations were obliged to dip their flags and strike their topsails when passing Elsinore, and pay Sound Dues. These produced immense sums of money for the country, but at the same time immense political difficulties, so that in the end they proved fatal.

While still quite a young man Eric had married Philippa, the daughter of Henry IV of England. One might well assume that Margaret, in arranging this marriage, had Denmark's ancient dream of dominion in the west in mind. However, it appears that she herself had been dubious about the match. Philippa was wedded to him in Lund Cathedral in 1406 and

Opposite Krogen lay Kernen, in Hälsingborg. The entrance to the Sound was well guarded on account of the Sound Dues.

proved a good and faithful queen. During the fighting over Slesvig Eric found himself obliged to wage a naval war. In this he was for the most part fortunate, but on one occasion Copenhagen was besieged during his absence. Having been entrusted with "the keys of the Palace", Philippa, in her capacity as the highest authority both in the palace and in the city, held the enemy at bay. Copenhagen did not fall.

In Sweden, a peasant uprising led by Engelbrecht Engelbrechtson proved decisive. The Swedish nobles at first regarded the revolt with extreme displeasure, but soon realized the advantages to be obtained in giving it their support. The unrest spread to Norway, whereupon the nobles in all three countries saw a chance of putting an end to the somewhat autocratic rule which had been introduced by Margaret and continued by Eric. Eric did not possess Margaret's canniness and shrewdness, and was therefore more or less powerless to combat the interests of the nobility and the national risings. When the nobles finally felt they had him where they wanted him he decided to abdicate, removing his crown with the words:

Queen Philippa's gravestone at Vadstena, showing her English coat of arms.

"I do not intend to be your yes-master". He hied himself to Gotland and pensioned himself off as a pirate after having attempted, for 24 years, to master the virtually impossible art of ruling the three kingdoms as one. By this time his wife, Philippa, had died. She was buried in the Birgittine Church at Vadstena in Sweden, where her tombstone can be seen to this day. Eric tried to get the members of the Scandinavian *Rigsraads* (assemblies of noblemen and high churchmen) to proclaim his cousin, Bugislaw of Pomerania, as his successor, but they upheld their right to elect whomsoever they wished and instead decided upon his nephew, *Christopher of Bavaria.*

After various difficulties Christopher was duly proclaimed King in all three countries. The Union was thus once again in force. Christopher was a King who represented the interests of the aristocracy, having been called upon and proclaimed by the nobles of all three kingdoms. Servile obedience on their part was thus a thing of the past. From now on they wished to have a say in all matters. At the same time the lot of the individual peasant became far severer, particularly in Denmark. The nobles tried to introduce suppression of the peasants in the form that had been common in many European countries ever since ancient times. The peasants had already been deprived of their old *Thing* freedom and privileges, and the nobles now wished to subjugate them entirely. A peasant revolt in northern Jutland showed signs of becoming very serious indeed. In fact it was not quelled finally until Christopher arrived in person at the head of an army and inflicted a bloody defeat.

Christopher had trouble winning respect. He reigned only nine years and died suddenly, in 1448.

IV. THE LATE MIDDLE AGES

Once again the Scandinavian kingdoms were not only without a king but furthermore without a king's son who could succeed to the throne. In other words the situation was the same as at the death of Valdemar Atterdag, or when Eric of Pomerania abdicated. The health of the newly formed Union was naturally going to be endangered unless the succession could be settled smoothly and without endless discussion.

The Danes were interested in having a Holstein prince (for this would provide a peaceful solution to the Slesvig question) but they finally settled for *Count Christian of Oldenburg*. This young man was, granted, only distantly related to the ancient royal Danish house, but it was considered most important to continue the line somehow or other. During the 1,000 year period during which we can account for the Kings of Denmark, the Danish crown, whilst admittedly having passed on several occasions to the distaff side whenever the direct line came to an end, has never once passed over into the hands of a completely new house – and this despite the fact that there is no word in any of the laws enacted during the Middle Ages concerning the royal succession. In fact nowhere is it stated that the crown can be inherited at all. The monarchy was to be decided by election.

The Oldenburgers

Count Christian was 22 years of age, somewhat untried, and not very well off. One of the conditions governing his election was that he should marry his predecessor's, Christopher of Bavaria's, widow, in order that she might thus be provided for. But despite the fact that she was a widow, she was still only eighteen and a gifted girl, so her widowhood can hardly have proved much of a deterrent. Christian had to agree to share his powers with the Rigsraad, in other words the leading group of nobles. He was also granted royal powers in Norway, but the Swedes decided to elect a Swedish nobleman named Karl Knutsson as their King, thereby disrupting Margaret's Union for the first time. But Christian did not intend to give up Sweden without a struggle. He went to war and for a time really managed to have Sweden under his control. Karl Knutsson's reign was an extremely unsettled one and when he died in 1470, no Swedish King was elected to take his place. Instead, a young Swedish nobleman named *Sten Sture* was made regent. Christian then sailed to Stockholm with his army, but on Brunke Hill (in those days just outside the city) the Danish army was beaten by Sten Sture's troops and suffered a crushing defeat. Christian himself was badly wounded, whereafter for many years Denmark renounced her claims on Sweden. It is said that as the armies advanced upon one another, both prayed to St. George to help them, but as Sir Sten prayed in Latin and Christian was only able to do so in German, the Swedes won the day. The Swedes sang the hymn of St. George and it is therefore now played daily on the carillon in Stockholm's City Hall in memory of the victory. In Stockholm's biggest church, Storkyrkan, there is a magnificent carving of the St. George and the Dragon which was carved by a German woodcarver named Bernt Notke (he also worked in Denmark) in commemoration of the battle. The carving was a gift to the church from Sten Sture and intended as a thankoffering to St. George for the victory.

On the other hand Christian had better luck in the everlasting matter of Slesvig.

It will be remembered that Count Adolf of Holstein was also Duke of Slesvig. He died childless. Once again the opportunity presented itself, and this time it was seized. In 1460 King Christian was elected as his successor in both Holstein and Slesvig. Thus the two provinces became united under the Danish Crown. In Slesvig, Christian was "his own Duke" so to speak, for as King of Denmark he held suzerainty. In Holstein, which was German, he was admittedly only a feudal lord, but in practice the two provinces were ruled by the same man, and that man was the King of Denmark. Thus Slesvig was by this means recovered, and in order to make sure of retaining Holstein (and likewise in order to pacify such Holstein nobles as owned estates in Slesvig) he had a clause inserted in the document sealing the agreement which stated that the two provinces were never to be separated. They were to be "up ewig ungedeelt", in other words "for ever undivided". The regrettable result of the arrangement, namely that the Danish province of Slesvig became indissolubly linked to the German province of Holstein, was something Christian did not foresee. But then he could hardly have been expected to at the time.

Christian possessed no sense of economy. As a Count who had been promoted to a throne he was fond of demonstrating his royal dignity. He maintained a large court and behaved generally in a lavish manner. Once he set off on a journey down through Europe to Rome. On the way he carried on in more than royal fashion (despite the fact that he was supposed to be a humble pilgrim) and showered magnificent gifts about him. Unfortunately he had no money with which to pay for them, so he had to borrow en route. An old soldier and *condottiere* by the name of Colleoni received him as his guest at his palace of Malpaga, where a number of frescoes exist to this day to tell us something of the visit. In Milan he was magnificently received by Duke Galeazzo Maria, and in Rome, Pope Sixtus IV welcomed him splendidly. The King presented the Pope with "Scandinavian gifts" (a consignment of herring, some furs, and dried cod) and the Pope handed Christian "The Golden Rose". One result of the visit was papal permission to found a university in Copenhagen. Christian was most anxious that Danish students should be in a position to obtain an education at home, and furthermore Sweden had founded a university at Uppsala a few years previously, and Denmark could not lag behind.

Christian's daughter Margaret was married off to King James III of Scotland at the age of 13. Christian as usual had no money, so he had to give King James the Norwegian islands of Shetland and Orkney by way of security for a dowry which he promised to pay later. The pledge was however, never redeemed, and thus the ancient Scandinavian island groups became Scottish.

By the time King Christian died, in 1481, his son Johannes, or *Hans*, had already been elected as his successor and therefore became King of Denmark and Norway. In both Slesvig and Holstein he was supposed to follow (according to the new arrangement) in his father's footsteps, but the situation in the border lands straightaway became hopelessly mixed up – largely, it is said, because his mother interfered in the matter. He had to share his power down here with his brother *Frederick*, and as the two provinces were to remain "for ever undivided" the partitioning was done in such a muddled fashion that both were given large, unconnected tracts of land in both provinces. On ascending the throne Hans was made to sign a strictly formulated agreement which gave the nobles great powers.

In Sweden quite a strong party wished to have Hans as King of Sweden too, so the Union was renewed – partly because the Swedish nobles saw the advantage in having a King who spent most of his time in another country. But Sten Sture saw to it that negotiations were made to drag on from year to year. Several conferences were held, but as a rule the Swedish negotiators were not in possession of sufficient authority to make decisions – or else new questions cropped up necessitating the postponement of the meetings. Hans lost patience and marched upon Stockholm at the head of an army. After a siege the city surrendered Hans rode into Stockholm at Sten Sture's side and was duly crowned King of Sweden. Once again the Scandinavian Union was established.

Defeat in the Ditmarshes

But then King Hans, who was otherwise an extremely steady-going and peaceable man, was tempted into embarking upon an adventurous little spree. The nobles of Holstein had long wanted to conquer the Ditmarshes, which was a small peasant free state situated in the fertile marsh region at the root of the Jutlandic peninsula, facing on to the North Sea. The peasants who lived in these marshes were neither German nor Danish, but Frisians. They spoke Frisian, had their own culture, and ever since ancient times had enjoyed a peasant autonomy like that which formerly existed in Scandinavia. Thanks to their cattle trading they were very rich. Duke Frederick, Hans' brother, now decided that he would launch an expedition against them and invited King Hans to join him. It was as the Duke of Slesvig, holding a share in the Holstein territories, that King Hans took part, but quite a number of Danish noblemen tagged on to the expedition voluntarily. It was presumed that it would be a simple matter to beat the leaderless and boorish marsh peasants, but even so the army that finally gathered was quite a sizeable one and included mercenary troops, namely the "Saxony Guards" commanded by Junker Schlentz.

The expedition was regarded by those taking part more or less as a delightful opportunity for recreation. The knights took silver tableware and magnificent tents with them, plenty of servants and every conceivable form of luxury. By February it was felt advisable to start moving in order to get out on to the soft marshlands while the ground was still hardened by frost. But a thaw set in unexpectedly. The roads became bottomless seas of mud and the tremendous army was slowed down by the hundreds of carts carrying all the baggage and luxurious equipment and which were meant to be loaded up with the anticipated booty. The knights and their mounts were weighed down by armour, the rain lashed over the marshes in torrents, and laboriously the army struggled along the dike road, on either side of which there were deep ditches. The Ditmarshers had prepared themselves for battle. In fact, in accordance with ancient custom, they had "consecrated a maiden to God". This did not actually involve a human sacrifice except to the extent that the girl was obliged to lead a pure and unmarried life for the rest of her days and thus constituted a symbolic sacrifice which would secure them God's assistance during the battle.

They had barred the way by means of an entrenchment and a couple of guns. The army was obliged to halt, whereupon the Frisians attacked from the marshes. The tremendous army was paralysed on the narrow, muddy track, but the Frisians leapt across canals and ditches using their pikes as jumping-poles and fell upon the helpless army from both sides. Shots rang out from muskets and crossbows, horses became panic-stricken, the rain poured down and then the Frisians even opened the sea-dike so that the waves washed in over the marshes. The army was trapped on the road, everything was sheer chaos and defence was impossible. The heavily armoured knights were helpless and unable to use their weapons, their horses stumbled into the ditches, and both riders and soldiers trampled each other underfoot. To the rear the road was blocked by the tremendous train of vehicles, which in the meantime had sunk into the mud up to their axles. The story goes that King Hans and Duke Frederick saved their own skins by jumping from cart to cart the whole way back along the train, where all the servants and screaming camp-girls merely added to the wild and general confusion.

The Frisians' booty was enormous. They got the war-chest, all the personal property of the nobles and their royal masters, cartloads of silver-ware and colossal quantities of armour and weapons. For the Holstein

"The King of the Danes", title-page to the 1514 edition of Saxo's chronicle. The coat of arms includes Denmark, Sweden, Norway, Wendland, Slesvig, Holsten, Stormarn and Oldenburg. The pennant is the Dannebrog badge.

nobles the defeat was a catastrophe, for not one single nobleman's family failed to share in the loss of that day. Not many Danish noblemen lost their lives.

That day the old "Dannebrog" flag, which had been preserved ever since Valdemar the Victorious' expedition against Estonia, was lost. It had been the banner of the Danish kings for almost three hundred years and therefore must have been a little fragile. It was hung up in a church in the Ditmarshes, and not until many years later, when the Ditmarshes were finally conquered, was it taken to Slesvig Cathedral, where it is said to have remained until its last shreds disintegrated.

The defeat was utter and complete. The famous (and notorious) Saxony Guards had been crushed. Their commander, Junker Schlentz, was killed in the battle. It is said that the Frisians knocked the helpless, iron-clad man off his horse with a pole, beat in his neck with a club, hammered a pickaxe through his armour into his back, toppled him into a ditch filled with water and finally tipped his horse in on top of him. A suit of armour has been preserved at the Arms & Uniforms Museum in Copenhagen. It is badly dented at the neck and has three holes in one of the shoulder plates. In other respects it is a magnificent suit of armour for a hefty, big-muscled warrior, and according to popular tradition it once belonged to Junker Schlentz.

For King Hans the defeat in the Ditmarshes, despite his personal losses, did not constitute a catastrophe in itself but was more of an incident to be ashamed of. Holstein had suffered far worse and after all the affair was, strictly speaking, no concern of Denmark. Nevertheless, King Hans was to suffer the consequences, for people did not regard his two offices – that of King and that of Duke – as being distinct from one another. The news that the peasants of the marshlands had crushed the powerful army of knights, including a professional mercenary regiment, went all round Europe. In Sweden and Norway, the news was not without its consequences.

Rebellion in the North

The Swedish peasants, having now learnt that even peasants had been able to defeat King Hans, rose in rebellion. At first the Swedish nobles were once more contemptuous of the peasants for trying to take the law into their own hands, but subsequently they began to realize the advantages to be obtained by supporting the uprising. King Hans went to Stockholm in January 1501. He departed from the city in August in the company of his mistress, Adele Ironbeard by name, and left Stockholm Palace in the hands of his wife, Queen Christina. In September a siege was launched and just like Philippa (Eric of Pomerania's Queen, the English princess who defended Copenhagen Palace for her husband) Christina too held out doggedly in Stockholm Palace until only 70 men were left out of a garrison of 1,000. The rest had been killed or died of hunger and disease, and the last 70 were scarcely able to stand upright. Christina was still waiting for King Hans, who was supposed to be coming with a fleet to relieve her. Finally, on May 6, 1502, she was obliged to surrender. Sten Sture granted her the right to depart freely and return home, but he broke his word and interned her instead. Two days after the Danish flag had been struck from Stockholm Palace's principal tower, called the "Three Crowns", King Hans and the Danish fleet arrived at Stockholm.

Christian I setting forth from Malpaga, a castle belonging to the Italian condottiere Colleoni, during his journey in 1474. Fresco of slightly later date at Malpaga.

St. George and the Dragon, monument in Stockholm's Storkyrka to commemorate the Swedish victory at Brunkeberg, October 10, 1471.

King Hans built Europe's first state fleet. The ships were roughly of the same type as on this tapestry of a slightly later date.

Saints on Claus Berg's altar-piece in Odense Cathedral.

But he was too late. Sten Sture did not release Queen Christina until October. The Union was shattered and Sten Sture was once more the regent of Sweden. King Hans fought to recover his Swedish crown for many years, but never succeeded. There was trouble in Norway too, but here the Union stood firm. The Hanseatic town of Lübeck allied itself with Sweden but was defeated by the Danes at sea. It was during these years that King Hans built Europe's first proper navy. Up until this time it had been considered sufficient to arm merchant vessels, but now King Hans had ships built specially for war. He also founded a permanent naval base at Copenhagen.

The Church of the Late Gothic Era

During the Late Middle Ages the position of the Danish Church was in many respects altered. The old conflict between Church and Crown was over, partly because it had now become a tradition to award all the highest ecclesiastical posts to Danish noblemen, and in view of the power enjoyed by the nobility there existed neither the motivation nor the opportunity for indulging in ecclesiastical controversy on matters of principle. The Danish Church and its aristocratic leaders were not particularly interested in subtle theological and philosophical problems, nor in maintaining strictly ecclesiastical viewpoints. What bishops and abbots were interested in was *land*, and the Church was very rich. Land fell into the hands of the churches and convents in the form of gifts in return for requiems, and in the course of interminable exchanges of real estate. In fact the chief activity performed by the churches and convents was more in the nature of grandiose estate management rather than strictly ecclesiastical work.

Even though secular viewpoints were thus not subdued, the Church worked well enough. In the market towns the newer style of red-brick church was frequently to be seen and there were many convents spread throughout the three kingdoms. The monasteries were rich, excellent, well-organized and under serious leadership. The convent hospitals functioned diligently, attendance at church schools was good, and the St. George Institution took such effective care of lepers, isolating the sick with help of Draconic laws, that Denmark was able to lay claim to being the first country in Europe to have eradicated the disease – and this was before the close of the Middle Ages.

The wealth of the Church resulted in sumptuous ornamentation and the Scandinavian countries obtained particular triumphs with their *al secco* murals. Most parish churches had been decorated with murals during the Romanesque Period, but during the Gothic Period the pictures took on a different character. They were no longer flat paintings completely filled out with colour, but became more by way of being light, coloured drawings on a chalk-white background, alive and festive, as expressive

During the Late Middle Ages the old stone churches had armouries and towers added, and were given Gothic stepped gables.

and naive as contemporary woodcuts, but nevertheless well-executed and emanating an artistic freshness. In short, it was a distinctive art that imitated neither the Italian nor the German schools of painting, but pursued its own course. The murals of the Late Middle Ages can still be seen and admired in hundreds of churches. Denmark and Sweden possess the two largest collections in the world, and the reason they have been so fantastically well preserved is that during the 15th and 16th centuries they were white-washed over and have only been brought to light again during recent times, thus re-appearing as fresh as when they were first painted. Even the smallest parish church was able to afford to have its walls and vaulted ceiling decorated with these colourful pictures so delightfully replete with action from Bible scenes. Such action is at times so drastically portrayed that, once photographed for museum archive purposes, it has unfortunately been necessary to whitewash them over again.

Several woodcarvers of European standing were active in Denmark during these years. In Husum, a little town in Slesvig, there lived a woodcarver named *Hans Brüggemann*, a serious, deeply religious artist who was responsible for the magnificent altar-piece commissioned for the

Danish nobleman and family at table. Tempera wall-painting.

convent chapel at Bordesholm and today Slesvig Cathedral's most treasured relic. The altar-piece is of unpainted oak with countless figures appearing in small scenes from the Bible. In this work Hans Brüggemann used typical marshland characters, horse-dealers and mercenaries, citizens and their wives, depicting them with a naturalism extending beyond the Middle Ages towards that spirit of renascence which had still not yet reached Scandinavia. Almost at the same time, another woodcarver named *Claus Berg* was working at his workshop at Odense, in Denmark, where he was a supplier to the Royal Court – the latter wished to create a chapel for itself in one of the convent churches of the town. He was the sculptor responsible for King Hans' magnificent tombstone, which has since been transferred to Odense Cathedral together with the most beautiful altar-piece in Denmark, Claus Berg's celestial scene depicting Christ on the Cross surrounded by all the saints. Claus Berg had an eye for female beauty and some of his saints in the altar-piece resemble ladies of the Court of Copenhagen more than classical female martyrs. At the same time numerous Danish churches could afford to import ecclesiastical art from the workshops of northern Germany and thus Danish churches of the time were really lavishly decorated.

Peasants and Townsfolk

But behind it all, the peasant settlements continued to pursue their own lives. Christianity was no longer a new thing on the farms, but older beliefs had not died out completely. Pilgrimages were still made to holy springs that in some cases still bore such heathen names as Balder's Well and Thor's Spring. Relics of ancient heathen cults were still to be observed at spring and harvest festivals and parish life bore the mark of ancient peasant-settlement beliefs that refused to disappear. Rome was far away. On "wakeful nights" the young men and girls of the village went to the church taking their beer-casks with them and danced and made merry. Night life in the church was thus not exactly Christian. In order to avoid offending the images of the pious saints on such nights however, their pictures were turned with their faces to the walls.

In Denmark, just as throughout northern Europe, a gap began to appear between the Church and its congregation. In the convents and at the universities thoughts involving Christian theology and philosophy were forced up into dizzy heights and took on a delicious aura of fanaticism into which no attempt was made to drag ordinary mortals. This is one of the reasons why village life became more intense and here, as elsewhere, the Church's hold upon the population slackened, so that witchcraft and other "uncontrolled tendencies" gained ground. In Denmark such tendencies never became really wild or hectic, for the Danes, then as now, were a stolid, earth-bound people. Even so, a certain unrest with regard to ecclesiastical matters was felt. The broad population was perhaps unaware of it, for people still went to Mass and attended to their religious duties, but somehow the Church and the people were no longer one.

Just as in Central Europe, life in Danish towns had begun to pursue regular channels. The old trading habits of the peasant settlements had to a certain extent become paralysed. The towns had acquired privileges in regard to all trade, thereby obliging the peasants to take their wares to the town market. It was thus here that the country's commercial activity became concentrated, here that most artisans had gradually settled down, and here that the Church had invested its money most solidly.

Christian II

During King Hans' latter years his son Christian had been "governor", or vice-regent, in Norway, having his headquarters in Norway's rich trading centre of Bergen. While still a young prince, Christian had revealed himself to be a determined and efficient youth, but likewise somewhat ruthless whenever anybody happened to cause him annoyance. He had received a bourgeois upbringing, for his father, King Hans, had been very interested in developing conditions in the towns. This was partly because he saw the importance of ensuring that his citizens lived in sufficient comfort to be able to pursue their commercial activities successfully, and partly because the King had need of a solid counterweight in his dealings with his self-willed nobility. Throughout his life Christian remained in opposition to the nobles, and when he met the object of his dreams in Bergen it was not in aristocratic circles either. At a feast at Bergenhus he started dancing with a young Dutch girl named *Dyveke* (Little Dove) and promptly fell in love with her. He took her as his mistress and at the same time made the acquaintance of her mother, *Sigbritt Willumsdatter*. "Mother Sigbritt", as she subsequently came to be known, was a middle-class Dutchwoman, the widow of an otherwise unknown gentleman by the name of Nicolaus who had lived in Amsterdam. In Bergen, Mother Sigbritt sold sticky cakes to sailors and must have been in fairly modest straits. Prince Christian installed both mother and daughter in his household, took them with him to Oslo and built a house for them in the middle of the town. When Christian's father, King Hans, died, and he was obliged to return to Copenhagen, he took them both with him, and from that day on Mother Sigbritt played a rôle in Denmark's history the like of which it is probably difficult to find in the history of any other country. She is described as having been incredibly ugly, but she was extremely talented and had a deep insight into the problems of commerce and organization. She became young King Christian's adviser in all economic matters, in reality a sort of unofficial chancellor of the exchequer, and the nobles were furious at having to negotiate with the lady, who was anything but pleasant and hated the entire nobility from the bottom of her heart.

It was possibly through her that Christian II became interested in conditions in the Netherlands. He was full of plans for the future of his kingdoms and he looked upon Holland as a model of perfection. What the Dutch had succeeded in doing in Amsterdam and other towns, in other words the building up of trade relations on an international basis, must also, he felt, be possible in Scandinavia – therefore all that was needed was to get the Danes and the Norwegians to understand how it was to be done. He and Sigbritt conscripted Dutch peasants and settled them on the island of Amager to the south of Copenhagen so that they could teach the Danes how to grow vegetables. Furthermore both Sigbritt and the King worked energetically to improve conditions in the towns, and in the course of his reign King Christian enacted a number of quite revolutionary laws that in reality were far ahead of their time. They were aimed at benefitting the peasants and curbing the powers of the nobles, whose horizons as a rule were limited to the furthermost boundary lines of their estates. They maintained the viewpoint that cattle-raising and their own privileges were the only subjects of any importance to the country at all.

Despite King Christian's sympathies with the middle classes, Dyveke could not become Queen. He therefore requested the hand in marriage of a daughter of the house of Habsburg, *Elisabeth*, whose brother subsequently became Emperor Charles V. Elisabeth came to Denmark, a mere child of fourteen, on two conditions: firstly that King Christian would send Dyveke away, and secondly that he would shave off his big red beard. He welcomed his child bride with much warmth and pomp and splendour – but nonetheless retained both beard and Dyveke.

Young though Elisabeth was, it was surprising how quickly she learnt to assert herself at her husband's side. The Court of Habsburg made one attempt after another to have Dyveke removed and had the most pointed of threats delivered to King Christian. But Elisabeth stood by him and insisted that the matter was none of her family's business and concerned nobody but her husband and herself.

Christian had not been on the throne more than three years when he entrusted Mother Sigbritt with the administration of the Sound Dues and all other toll revenues in the two kingdoms. He made mother and daughter a present of a fine estate in Copenhagen not far from the Palace, and the situation in general appeared to be stable. But then Dyveke suddenly died, and there was a rumour that she had been poisoned. The chief steward at Copenhagen Palace, Master Torben Oxe, was suspected of having sent her a basketful of poisoned cherries, and it was revealed that during a ball

Christian's and Elisabeth's signatures. Christian II. Woodcut by Lucas Cranach.

at the Palace, when Master Torben had got rather drunk, he had made advances towards Dyveke, who likewise had been present at the ball.

Christian was furious and had Master Torben brought before a court of law. He was not accused of murder, but merely charged with having irregularities in his accounts and a few other matters. As Christian encountered difficulties in getting Master Torben legally convicted, he refrained from passing judgment himself (not possible anyway according to Danish law) but instead fell back on an ancient legal practice. He called in twelve peasants from a village just outside Copenhagen and had them pass judgment according to ancient Nordic custom. They conveniently condemned Master Torben to death with the words: "Not we, but his deeds do judge him," whereafter Master Torben had his head chopped off.

How much Master Torben had to do with Dyveke's death we do not know. Maybe she died a natural death, maybe the Court of the Netherlands was behind it, perhaps it was instigated by completely different forces, but whatever the true facts of the case one thing remained, and that was that Master Torben's execution produced an irreparable breach between King Christian and the Danish aristocracy.

Subjugation of Sweden

In the meantime, King Christian had not forgotten the claim of the Danish kings to the Swedish throne, and it so happened that a comparatively strong party in Sweden still wanted the Danish King back. The Swedes themselves provided an excuse for action. *Sten Sture the Younger* was ruling Sweden as regent, and between him and Archbishop Gustav Trolle in Uppsala there existed very strained relations, amongst other reasons because the Archbishop was pro-Danish and wanted to see the Union re-established. The Union had not actually been dissolved – it was merely "not in force". Sten Sture the Younger finally resorted, at a national assembly, to the daring step of deposing the Archbishop and throwing him into prison. The members of the assembly then formed a secret conspiracy and were incautious enough to draw up a sealed document to the effect that they were prepared to fight whomsoever gave support to the Archbishop, even the Holy Father in Rome himself.

The Archbishop's imprisonment constituted a direct offence against the Holy Church, and in his capacity as claimant to the Swedish throne Christian took up the Archbishop's case in the name of the Church. In 1520 a strong Danish army marched up through Sweden armed with a papal bull against Sten Sture the Younger and the text of the bull was spiked up on every church door in every village through which the Danes passed.

Sten Sture headed an army against the Danes, but was defeated and himself fell in the battle. The Danes took the whole of Sweden by force of arms. In the meantime King Christian had blockaded Stockholm with the Danish fleet. The city surrendered, and the keys were handed over to King Christian. He made his formal entrance and was crowned by Archbishop Gustav Trolle as Sweden's *hereditary king*, a title he was unable to claim in Denmark. Big feasts and celebrations were commenced at the palace in Stockholm and during the process a number of nobles were knighted. But the Swedes noticed that there was not a single Swede amongst all the newly created knights. On the other hand King Christian had promised that past deeds should be forgiven: the Union was to be re-established and the three kingdoms were to live in peace, side by side, just as in the days of Queen Margaret.

But on the fourth day of the celebrations Archbishop Trolle stepped

As propaganda against Christian II, Gustav Vasa had copperplate pictures of the Stockholm Bloodbath printed. Here: the executions, the corpses being taken away, and Sten Sture's grave being opened.

forward and demanded revenge and compensation for all the wrongs he had suffered at the hands of his enemies. He named a number of names. Sten Sture's widow then stepped forward in turn and declared that if the case were going to be brought up at all there were several others who were just as guilty. In her hand she held the famous conspiratorial document bearing all the signatures and seals. The King intervened and withdrew all the pardons he had promised – after all, this constituted a revolt against the Holy Church and in the case of an event of such magnitude he was not in a position to grant pardons. The King's secretary, a sinister German by the name of Didrick Slagheck, probably played quite an important part in the negotiations that followed. The doors of the palace were closed and all the coronation guests locked in for the night. Not until the following morning, that of November 9, 1520, were a few of them

129

led out. They had been condemned as *heretics* and were executed on Stockholm's main public square, Stortorv. The burgomaster and city councillors met the same fate because they too had signed the conspiratorial letter and the number of accused persons grew steadily. Exactly how many were executed has never been determined, but on the first day the toll of victims is said to have reached 82 and executions went on during the days that followed. Sten Sture's body was dug up from its grave and burnt, and later all those who had been executed were likewise burnt on a bonfire. In other words, according to the conception of things at the time, not only did they lose their lives but also all hope of salvation. These mass executions are remembered in Scandinavia as the *Stockholm Bloodbath*. The affair constituted a turning point in Christian II's life.

King Christian's victory in Sweden had been complete. The Swedish aristocracy had been paralysed and crushed, the country cowed. King Christian himself returned with all speed to Denmark. His German mercenaries followed after him and made the general situation far worse by terrorizing the countryside and plundering and murdering in the convents. This action was the height of folly in view of the fact that the country was now under Christian's rule, and it is hardly likely that he can have been responsible.

The Nobility in Rebellion

At home in Denmark once more, Christian dedicated himself to the business of law-making. He likewise endeavoured to clamp down on Lübeck's commercial activity so that Copenhagen could take over the rôle as the leading trade centre of the Baltic. Contrary to the terms of his coronation charter he installed commoners in many of the important posts in the Union. His rule displayed great singleness of purpose, foresight and efficiency. But in the middle of everything he suddenly left Copenhagen, on horseback and virtually unattended, and made his way down through Germany to Holland in order to see for himself the commercial empire the Netherlands had succeeded in building up. He was deeply interested in art and paid personal visits to both Claus Berg and Hans Brüggemann. In the Netherlands he bought up works of art and spoke to outstanding people such as Albrecht Dürer, who painted his portrait (the sketch is in the British Museum), and Erasmus of Rotterdam. The Royal Print Collection in Copenhagen contains an almost complete collection of Albrecht Dürer's engravings, presented, it is said, to King Christian by Dürer himself. The King returned to Denmark and on this occasion the palace in Copenhagen was enriched by a brand new Dutch altarpiece for the chapel. His wife, Elisabeth, who by now took just as much part in the ruling of the country as Mother Sigbritt, had attended

In 1499, on the day after St. Valborg's Day, the Danish admiral Jens Holgerson Ulfstand ("Wolf-denth") laid the foundation stone of his Castle Glimminge in Scania, a solid stone fortress that still stands.

to the throne's business in his absence and everything promised fair. A dynamic, violent King, but at the same time a man who displayed imagination, singleness of purpose, and a sincere interest in the spirit of the Renaissance, he was in the process of building up a commercial empire on the foundation of three re-united kingdoms, and he had succeeded in crushing all opposition.

Nearly all. A young Swedish nobleman named Gustav Vasa was Christian's parole prisoner at Kaloe Castle, in Jutland. But the young Swede broke his word, travelled south disguised as a cattledrover, negotiated with Lübeck for support and returned to Sweden just at the moment when the bloodbath was in the process of decimating the Swedish aristocracy – and incidentally the Vasa family, for Gustav Vasa's father had been executed. Gustav went to Dalarna to rouse the peasants there to rebellion, but they told him it made no difference to them whether a few nobles had had their heads chopped off in Stockholm. In fact they said the more the better. Gustav was already on his way fleeing across the mountains on skis in order to reach Norway and escape from Christian's clutches when the peasants of Dalarna chased after him, brought him back and hailed him as their leader – the trouble being that they had heard a rumour in the meantime that the Swedish peasants were about to be deprived of their weapons. The rumour was purely fictitious, but it proved fateful to Danish rule in Sweden. Within a couple of years Gustav Vasa had obtained control of the whole of Sweden and permitted himself, despite the fact that up to then there had been no kings in his family, to be crowned King of Sweden. The Union between Denmark and Sweden was hereby finally disrupted.

Christian had no time to launch a counterattack and simultaneously the Danish nobles rose against him. He was supposed to negotiate with them at a meeting in Jutland, but instead the nobles sent him a letter in which they formally withdrew their "allegiance and support". A Danish nobleman named *Mogens Munk* brought this letter to King Christian but did not dare hand it over openly. Instead, he "forgot" his glove with the letter inside and promptly left for Gottorp Castle near Slesvig in order to see Christian's uncle, Duke Frederick, and offer him the throne of Denmark.

Then a strange thing came to pass: despite the fact that Christian actually had a large part of the country behind him, in other words both the inhabitants of the towns and the rural population, he suddenly lost heart. The story goes that he had himself rowed back and forth across Little Belt from Jutland to Funen that night, time and again, without being able to make up his mind whether to stay in Jutland and fight, or return east.

He chose the latter course. He went to Copenhagen, begged the city to hold out and then sailed from the capital together with his wife Elisabeth and their children. He intended to go and seek help in Holland. Amongst other things he hoped to obtain payment of the dowry which Emperor Charles V had been too miserly to part with. Christian had constantly tried to make him pay up. Mother Sigbritt was also on board with him. That evening the entire population of Copenhagen was gathered along the harbour mole. People clambered up on to the rooftops or perched themselves in the riggings of the ships, and everywhere complete silence reigned. Not a sound was heard as King Christian, Elisabeth, and the children slowly sailed out of the harbour. A contemporary folk ballad reveals something of the emotions that gripped the ordinary Danish citizen on the day King Christian left the shores of Denmark behind him:

> *With all his young that Eagle King*
> *Did forth from forest fare,*
> *And wildly fluttered the lesser fowl*
> *With none to counsel there.*
>
> *God pity the eagle old and grey*
> *That flies o'er the weary waste!*
> *No rock he finds nor sheltered bower*
> *Where he may build his nest.*

The people of Copenhagen ran northwards along the shore trying to keep the ship in sight as long as possible. But by that time Duke Frederick had already been proclaimed King at Viborg Thing, and King Christian's laws had been burnt by the executioner as being "harmful" – to the nobility.

V. FROM THE REFORMATION UNTIL THE DEATH OF CHRISTIAN IV

Duke Frederick, who had scrupulously divided Holstein and North Slesvig between himself and his brother, old King Hans, was now at long last King of Denmark himself. But he was not a Dane, and never became one. He preferred to spend his time at Gottorp Castle and his retainers were Holsteiners or Germans. On being proclaimed King he had to sign a very strictly formulated coronation charter, and as he was in complete favour of the nobility he allowed the Rigsraad to rule the country more or less as it pleased. He held one trump card however, which he could play whenever he wanted his own way: he could threaten to abdicate and thereby oblige the Danes to take Christian II back again. Whenever he did this the nobles immediately became tractable.

He had to contend with two difficult problems during his period on the Danish throne. Firstly, King Christian in exile constituted a permanent threat. Secondly, the doctrines of Martin Luther were beginning to make themselves felt in Denmark.

King Christian had had bad luck in Holland. He did not get his dowry, was thoroughly depressed, and he and his family lived in extremely modest straits in "Het Hof van Dennemark" ("The Court of Denmark") in Lier. His thoughts were constantly occupied with plans for the re-conquest of his kingdom. He was in contact with friends in Denmark and was moreover aware that thousands of people in both the towns and the country districts would rejoice at his return. But he had no money. And then, only 26 years old, Elisabeth died. During the last years of her young life she had developed into a polished diplomat. When she was about to leave Denmark together with King Christian, Duke Frederick had offered her free asylum and royal maintenance in Denmark, but she replied with the words: "Where my King is, there is my Kingdom" and accompanied her husband. During their exile she had to go and see her brother, Emperor Charles V, and later negotiate with Henry VIII of England. (Christian had carried on quite a lot of correspondence with Henry in the course of his reign on the subject of Icelandic fishing rights. It appeared that English fishermen had been consistently trading in an illegal manner and moreover indulging in acts of piracy. Christian tried to get Henry VIII to do something about it. Henry wrote back charming letters full of promises that he would see what he could do, but no more came of it. English fishing captains continued to fish in Icelandic waters just as much as they pleased.) At times Christian worked methodically and even published leaflets in modern style. In Denmark, Frederick caused a treatise to be prepared against Christian in which he even accused him of having murdered his own mother. This never saw publication in book form, but the manuscript has been preserved. At the same time Christian became much affected by Luther's teachings and for a time lived in a house very near Luther's – with the result that his Catholic brother-in-law, Charles V, then had every reason to refuse payment of the dowry, claiming that Christian had offended his religion. Christian reverted to Catholicism.

In Denmark, Frederick had virtually been obliged to assume power by force of arms. Copenhagen was besieged, and surrendered. Finally, in 1531, Christian succeeded in raising cash, ships and troops, and with a good fleet he sailed northwards for Norway. Unfortunately the fleet ran into a storm, and many men and much equipment went to the bottom of the North Sea. But Christian landed in Norway, where he was well received, and began to lay siege to Akershus Castle near Oslo. Frederick sent a fleet north under the command of Knud Gyldenstierne, a bishop of the nobility, who started negotiations with Christian. As a result of these negotiations Christian agreed to come south and meet his uncle. Apparently he was no longer in possession of his former strength and confidence, for his chances of taking Akershus and winning power in Norway were by no means small. So now he sailed down south towards the Sound on the strength of a formally sworn assurance of safe conduct. On the beaches of Elsinore the Danes crowded to catch a glimpse of him sailing past, but by the time his ship had reached as far south as Copenhagen he received a message that Frederick had in the meantime sailed for Flensborg and that the meeting was to take place there instead. Christian sailed on, but it was not until his ship swung in towards Als Sound that he realized he had been tricked. The promise of safe conduct was broken and he was taken to Soenderborg Castle. He was seized with a fit of fury. The palace steward tugged his beard for him and the chain of the Order of the Golden Fleece was wrenched from about his neck. He was a prisoner.

Gravestone in Soenderborg Church over the Danish nobleman Ditlev Brochdorff, Christian II's prison-warder at the castle.

He was allotted a large room in a tower of the castle and granted the right to use several other rooms. He was allowed to walk freely under observation and was provided with suitable servants and attendance. Approximately at the same time as he was imprisoned, his son Hans, heir to the three Scandinavian kingdoms, died in Germany. Christian II was to spend 17 years as a prisoner at Soenderborg, continually being put off with half-promises of negotiations regarding his freedom.

Unrest in the Church

A young student named Hans Tavsen, a native of Funen, came home to Denmark from Wittenberg. He had heard Luther preach, and he himself now began to preach the Reformation in Viborg. People listened

HAC TABVLA ADORNATA FVIT CONSILIO D IOANNIS IACOBI PASTORIS HVIVS ECCLESIÆ ANNO DNI ॰C∙1561∘6

Frontispiece of an altar-table, showing the new reformed church service
with a sermon, baptism and the
Lutheran communion. 1561.

Catholic altar goblet of silver, dating from about 1475.

Blissful scene in Renaissance Denmark. From a tapestry woven for Kronborg Castle.

Chain of the Order of the Garter and St. George, presented to Frederick II by Queen Elisabeth. At Rosenborg.

to him, and despite the protests of the bishop, Hans Tavsen obtained the King's permission to continue preaching. Others began to follow his example in other Danish towns, with the result that the stir caused by the Reformation began to spread in the form of a market-town movement. Hans Tavsen went to Copenhagen and won many supporters. Each time the Church protested, King Frederick, with a display of extraordinary shrewdness, managed to protect him in some way without ever actually revealing his hand. The new religious thinking thus seeped into Denmark without the Church's being given an opportunity of strangling it. One day St. Mary's Church in Copenhagen, long the stronghold of Catholicism, was stormed by a mob of citizens who began tearing down the altars and images of the saints. Their leader was *Ambrosius Bookbinder*, the burgomaster of Copenhagen, but Hans Tavsen himself appeared in the church and begged them to spare the big golden high altar. He declared that there was no point in destroying it, and the mob agreed with him.

The whole business was not achieved without incident. There was a feeling of resentment against the mendicant friars who exercised such control over trade in the towns that in many instances there were only very few wares with which the citizens were permitted to trade freely. In many places mendicant friars were driven out of their convents and the trade privileges considered as abolished. Otherwise the manner in which the Reformation passed over Denmark was one of the most curious in European history. Danish monasteries were, broadly speaking, spared. Even though it was claimed (just as in Germany for instance) that the friars were fornicators and overfed drunkards, discipline in the monasteries as a rule was good. Had life in these institutions really been so pleasant there would doubtless have been many more monks, but Denmark's largest monastery only housed some forty-five. Matters had been worse in the nunneries, for these had been abused, largely as a result of the Church's aristocratic leadership. Families belonging to the nobility had used the nunneries more or less as "approved schools" to which they could send their daughters for life. It was cheaper to send a girl to a nunnery at the age of ten or twelve and let her have a watermill or a couple of farms by way of an entrance gift than to have to produce a whole dowry in land and gold in the event of her being permitted to grow up in freedom and get married. The nunneries were therefore full of light-hearted young damsels who had never asked anybody to lock them in, and who found themselves growing up to face a meaningless existence. They were, as the Catholic Church expressed it, "true to the faith, but unsuitable for convent life." They jumped out of the windows at night or invited young men into their dormitories to take part in uproarious feasts. Thus in many instances the nunneries were somewhat peculiar institutions. Now and again a bishop re-established discipline in a nunnery by placing a strict prioress or abbess in charge, but it only helped matters for a short while. It was quite simply impossible to turn such exuberantly youthful specimens into useful nuns.

A spiritual controversy existed, but it was only mild. The only Catholic personality really worth mentioning was Poul Helgesen, who whilst admitting that the Church was in need of certain reforms, nevertheless wanted to retain the Holy Catholic European Church under the leadership of Rome. The spiritual leaders on both sides were few in number, and in the meantime Luther's doctrines spread in the form of a popular movement through the towns. The transition to the new Church had not been *legally* completed by the end of Frederick I's reign. He died in 1533. The ecclesiastical controversy did not become apparent until the time came to elect his successor. The Lutheran members of the Rigsraad and all the lesser nobility wanted to crown his eldest son, Duke Christian, who had long before introduced Lutheran services in the town of Haderslev in Slesvig. Duke Christian had been present in person at the Diet of Worms and heard Luther defending his opinions, from which day onwards the Duke had been a firm "Lutherite". However, a solidly Catholic party amongst the nobility, likewise the aristocratic members of the clergy, were very much against having such a blatantly Lutheran King. And trouble started in the towns, whose citizens wanted Christian II released from prison and reinstated upon the throne.

Curiously enough this clamouring for Christian II on the part of the Danish provincial towns was supported by Christian's old enemy, the town of Lübeck. The Hanseatic towns had begun to feel the effects of the commercial slump which resulted from the great voyages of discovery. The Mediterranean and the Baltic were no longer the rich trading seas. What counted now was the Atlantic, the trade routes to America and

138

round the Cape. It was countries such as Holland and England, Spain and France, for whom prosperous times now lay ahead, partly because they were placed nearest the big oceans. The old trading nations nearest the two "inland seas" were now more or less in the rear and had correspondingly poorer chances. Lübeck's violent burgomaster, Jürgen Wullen-

Heads from gravestones of Danish noblemen. Renaissance.

wever, hoped that if he helped to set Christian II free and reinstate him on the Danish throne, it would procure such power for Lübeck in Scandinavia that it would mean a revival of the town's commercial prosperity.

The Count's War

One reason why the Reformation proceeded more or less peacefully in Denmark was that the country had other things to think about. The accession to the throne was far from peaceful. A large army from Lübeck landed in Zealand under Count Christopher of Oldenburg, who obtained control of Zealand and the Scanian provinces because he came in the name of the captive Christian II. This remarkable and bloody internal war in Denmark has since been known as the *Count's War*. The two most important towns in Denmark at the time, Copenhagen and Malmö, swore allegiance to the Count in the name of Christian II. After all, the whole object of the war was to liberate the beloved monarch. The nobility in eastern Denmark supported the Count too, reckoning that the game was lost anyway. The Count obtained control of Funen in the same way and then sent his right-hand man, *Captain Clement*, to Jutland. Under the leadership of this seafaring gentleman the peasants of northern Jutland rose in open rebellion against Duke Christian, so that when the Jutlandic nobles sent a well-armed army of knights against the peasants, the latter inflicted a crushing and bloody defeat. The revolt spread down through Jutland. Manor houses and castles were stormed and set ablaze. For a while it looked as though the rest of Jutland, and thereby the whole of Denmark, were about to fall into the Count's hands so that the rebels would be enabled to fetch Christian II out of Soenderborg Castle and

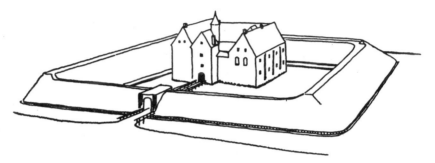

Castle Spoettrup in Salling was destroyed during the Count's War and thereafter rebuilt with ramparts and double moats – the thought of another peasant storming was not relished. The drawing shows how the stronghold looks today.

give him back his old privileges once more. What weakened the Count's opponents was the fact that they were unable to agree on which King they wanted, due to the conflict of interests existing between the Catholics and Lutherans within their own ranks. But a Lutheran member of the Rigsraad named *Mogens Gøye* (Magnus Cuckoo) summoned a meeting of Jutlandic nobles in Ry Church in central Jutland. Though quite a big church, it could not hold them all and the lesser nobles had to remain outside in the churchyard. Inside the church the aristocratic Catholic bishops still opposed the election of Duke Christian, but after a while the lesser nobles lost patience. They broke into the church noisily shouting that they wanted Duke Christian as their King. The bishops were obliged to give in, realizing that in so doing they were virtually signing the death warrant of the Catholic Church in Denmark.

Duke Christian therefore came up to Jutland and was proclaimed King in Horsens – for the old coronation town of Viborg was situated too far north in the rebellious districts. He had brought his Holstein general with him, *Johan Rantzau*. Rantzau marched against the peasants and took the town of Aalborg, Captain Clement's permanent key position, by storm. The inhabitants of the town plus 2,000 peasants were slaughtered in the streets and the town itself was plundered. Very soon the whole of northern Jutland was subdued, the peasants either being executed or deprived of their freeman privileges. Captain Clement himself managed to slip away from Aalborg, but a couple of informers betrayed the badly wounded peasant leader. He was imprisoned and subsequently executed.

The next year Rantzau led his forces against the Lübeckers and inflicted a crushing defeat. In the Scanian provinces, whole peasant armies were slaughtered in the course of frightful blood baths. It was at this time that Duke Christian's high-born admiral, Peter Skram, defeated the Lübeck fleet in a naval battle off Svendborg.

But Copenhagen remained consistently faithful to Christian II. For more than a year Duke Christian laid siege to the city. Finally famine overtook the inhabitants. People ate every cat and rat and even chewed and swallowed the grass growing on the city ramparts. The dead piled up in the streets and in the houses. At last the city surrendered and Count Christopher and the city councillors went out to the Duke's camp. The Duke – in reality now king Christian III – pardoned them. But Christian II's old personal friend, Burgomaster Ambrosius Bookbinder, went home and hanged himself.

Throughout the war Christian II had been subjected to stricter discipline at Soenderborg. There were orders to kill him if the castle should be stormed by the Count's men. After the fall of Copenhagen at the end of the Count's War he was treated quite well again, but negotiations between him and his cousin, King Christian III, proceeded very slowly.

The Fall of the Catholic Church

When the Count's War was over, Christian III summoned a national assembly in Copenhagen, whereupon he had all Catholic bishops imprisoned at one swoop. They were only released on condition that they give up all resistance to the Lutheran Reformation. At a big open-air meeting at Gammeltorv (the "Old Square" in Copenhagen) the King persuaded the nobility, the citizenry and the peasantry all to vote for the abolishment of the old Church organization. Thus the Reformation became law.

Denmark and Norway had passed through troubled times. In Denmark especially, the Count's War had involved tremendous bitterness and bloodshed. It had been a peasants' revolt combined in the first place with political tactics connected with the election of a successor to the throne; and in the second, with the struggle on the part of the nobles for ecclesiastical plums in the way of lucrative bishoprics and abbotcies. The war had not been a religious war and the ecclesiastical controversy had faded into the background.

The way the Reformation took place in Denmark, i. e. the actual transition from Catholicism to Lutheranism, was very uneventful compared with other European countries. The reasons were many, but one of them was the existence of a cool sobriety in spiritual matters. Fanaticism and mass excitement are fairly unknown factors in Denmark's history. The actual exchange of faith took place with incredible smoothness. In England Bloody Mary's axe went crashing to the block, in the annals of France shines the dark red stain of St. Bartholomew's Eve, Germany was ravaged by massacres in the convents and the sadistic maltreatment of monks, nuns and priests, sectarian excesses were driven to the point of sheer madness, such as "King" Johann and his "ministers", Krechting's and Knipperdollinck's ecstatic, colourful and lecherous "thousand-year kingdom" in Münster, and in Switzerland Calvin apparently had few qualms about using an axe against his opponents. Everywhere the religious conflict and fanaticism cost blood, blood, blood. The annals of the Danish Reformation reveal only very few cases of death. Everything, in fact, bore the stamp of level-headed, almost passive soberness. At the start there was some unrest in the towns, but the acts of violence were relatively few in number. Monks and nuns were thrown out of their convents in the towns and a few saint figures were destroyed. And that was that – or rather, the whole picture was then reversed. The Reformation carried with it the liberation of enormous areas of *church land*.

After the meeting in Copenhagen, Christian III promptly confiscated all church property, and whereas prior to the Reformation Crown property in Denmark represented one sixth of the total area of the country, after the confiscation of church lands it grew to *much more than half*.

Which shows how much land had been grasped by the Church. Land was something tangible, and in the Danish Reformation it played an important part. A certain amount of church land passed to the nobility as a result of the sale and exchange of real estate, but the actual change-over from the old Church to the new was conducted with a degree of quiet moderation and common sense not experienced anywhere else in Europe. The Catholic Church had been crushed, but no resentment was borne. The big convents became Crown fiefs and were taxed accordingly, but they were permitted to *continue functioning as convents*, permitted to hold Catholic services in their churches and chapels precisely as before, even permitted to run schools for children provided that the Lord's Prayer and the Creed were taught in Danish. Basically there were only two important changes: firstly, convents and churches were no longer allowed to accept land as 'frankalmoin', and secondly the convents were not permitted to take on new monks or nuns. Brethren and sisters already in convents at the commencement of the Reformation were allowed to choose freely between returning to a normal life in society, emigrating to southern Europe in order to join fellow believers down there, or else remaining in their Danish convents until the end of their days, in which case, as their numbers gradually dwindled, they would be consolidated in single convents. This explains the exceptional state of afffairs whereby Catholic convents with their monks and nuns, Catholic rites, abbots and abbesses, all continued to function in Denmark for more than thirty years after the Reformation; and whereby fief-holders from amongst the nobility, who to a certain extent took over the administration of the convents, were bound by contract to take care of aging brethren and sisters. As regards Denmark's thousands of Catholic parish priests it is no longer possible to account for what happened to all of them, but it was apparently not infrequent that a Catholic priest learnt the new ritual, went over to Luther, and quietly remained in office. However, this did not apply to all of them, for we know that there was a great shortage of Lutheran priests during the first few decades. Some Catholic abbots became Lutheran parish priests in their old age.

Christian III had to do something about administering his new, re-formed Church and called in Germans to advise him. He himself was thoroughly informed about German matters and kept many members of the German nobility around him. He felt it justifiable to introduce German church services not only in Holstein (which after all was German) but also in most of Slesvig (which was Danish). The new Church was given, like the old, seven leaders, and they were given new titles. They were called *Superintendants*. But this soon proved too complicated, so they reverted to their old title of Bishop. There was one important difference between the new bishops and the old ones: they were now 'public servants'. No longer did they have, as their predecessors, a seat in the Rigsraad. All they were required to do was perform their functions and keep their noses out of things. This increased the King's power considerably – though Rigsraad members belonging to the aristocracy naturally still remained in office.

Norway and Slesvig

In yet another important question did Christian reveal that he had been brought up further south: he changed Norway's status. The position of the nobility had been weakened much more in Norway than in Denmark. It was not easy to travel around in the vast, mountainous country. It was sparsely populated, and there were comparatively few towns. Norwegians therefore found it difficult to agree unanimously on anything, with the result that the country fell apart into a number of separate rural settlements. Christian III introduced the Reformation into Norway by law, decreeing that Norway was no longer to be a kingdom like Denmark, but instead was to be ruled as a Danish province – just like Zealand, Scania, or any one of the other Danish provinces.

This was a flagrant violation of the terms of the Union, but the Norwegians were too weak to protest effectively.

Lastly, he succeeded in making an even greater mess of the unhappy question of Slesvig. The Danish Royal Family regarded the two duchies – both the German one of Holstein and the Danish one of Slesvig – more or less as private Crown property, and therefore Christian felt himself justified in appointing his brothers as co-regents over them, just the way things had been under King Hans and Duke Frederick. His brother, Duke Adolph, was duly installed at Gottorp Castle – a position from which the Gottorpian Dukes were not only inclined to become very independent, but furthermore often ready to ally themselves with Denmark's enemies. This of course was rather unfortunate and at the same time produced a very dangerous situation, but in most instances it was dictated by Holstein's continual fear of being swallowed up by Denmark.

A decision was finally reached concerning the aging prisoner of Soenderborg. Christian II was given permission to move to Kalundborg, where, though still not allowed to travel, he was otherwise treated once more as a royal person. But even here he was kept under observation – for he was still a man to be feared.

Christian III died in 1559. Barely three weeks later Christian II died too, 78 years of age, at Kalundborg.

The Renaissance

Ever since time immemorial a change of kings in Denmark had provoked a serious state of affairs, but finally, on this occasion, Christian III's son experienced no difficulty whatsoever in becoming Frederick II. He was to prove Denmark's "Renaissance King" *par excellence*. Unfortunately his education had been appalling. His father had not taken the trouble to have him taught anything at all. He had some difficulty in wielding a pen and as his upbringing had been half German, his Danish was only broken.

He had a number of lofty ideas about the dignity of kings, his dream was to re-conquer Sweden, and furthermore he was young, ambitious, and a romantic. Gustav Vasa of Sweden, by this time an old man, died the year after Frederick's accession to the Dano-Norwegian throne. Gustav Vasa's son, who then became Eric XIV of Sweden, was likewise young, ambitious, and a romantic. Frederick, as an indication of his ambitions, inserted the "Three Crowns" symbol in the Danish coat of arms. Eric countered by using it himself as a demonstration of Sweden's claim to rule the "Nordic Union", i.e. the three Scandinavian kingdoms, for Eric regarded Frederick as a German usurper of the Danish throne. Frederick, for his part, regarded Eric as an aristocratic farmer's boy who had somehow managed to get himself on to the throne of Sweden. Philip II of Spain was interested in the Scandinavian kingdoms, declaring that he held a hereditary claim to them through his father's sister, Elisabeth, who had been Christian II's Queen. At a certain stage an agreement was

145

actually reached between Sweden and Spain with regard to the conquest and division of Denmark, the idea being to deport the Danes, every man jack of them, to Spain or America. However, Philip II soon had other things to think about, with the result that this extraordinary plan collapsed together with the Invincible Armada.

Seven Years' War about the Scandinavian Coats of Arms

Frederick's first kingly action was to restore the honour of the Danish Royal House by avenging the defeat of King Hans in 1500. This time the Ditmarshes were conquered without much difficulty, whereupon Frederick, disregarding sound advice from all sides, attacked Sweden. This was intended to be a "quick war", but lasted seven years. It was very much a nobleman's war, all officer ranks being filled from amongst the aristocracy. The Danish fleet enjoyed supremacy at sea, but on land the two countries were equally matched. The war was conducted with much determination and much bloodshed, with endless ravaging expeditions across the borders of the Danish provinces in Scania up into Sweden, and from Sweden down into Scania. On both sides the war was waged with a complete lack of mercy. Famous is the order of the day issued by Eric XIV just before the massacre carried out in the Danish town of Ronneby, in Blekinge: "Take no Dane prisoner, but slay everybody and everything as God's grace permits". The war led nowhere at all. Both young kings continued to use the "Three Crowns" in their coats of arms as a demonstration of their claim to rule all three kingdoms. This question has never been properly solved yet. To this day Sweden uses the three Scandinavian crowns as her national coat of arms, and to this day the same three crowns are found in the Danish coat of arms.

The war weakened both countries tremendously. As far as Frederick was concerned he very nearly lost the two crowns he had, in fact on one occasion he actually abdicated, but the Rigsraad persuaded him to change his mind. His minister of finance was the violent but none the less efficient *Peder Oxe*, who for a long period was obliged to live in exile, where he remained in close contact with the heirs of Christian II and in a state of deadly animosity towards the Danish Royal House. But Peder Oxe displayed incredible efficiency at the task of straightening out Denmark's war-torn finances. Manipulating the Sound Dues proved the most dangerous game of all. Each time the state coffers became empty it was tempting to solve the problem by merely jacking up the Elsinore toll tariffs a few extra notches, but each time this was done the maritime nations of Europe let out a howl of indignation. However, there was little they could do about it, for the Sound was narrow and guarded by solid fortresses. Frederick promised that "from now on" the tariffs would not be increased,

The Scandinavian "Seven Years' War" caused a commotion throughout the Baltic countries. This is the title picture to a Low German ballad about the naval battle off Øland.

but he did not keep his word. It was to cost Denmark dear less than a hundred years hence.

In order to show that Denmark not only held power, but likewise occupied a position of importance in Europe, Frederick decided to build, on Elsinore's outermost low stoney tongue of land, a fortress that in due course became more of a sumptuous fortified palace. His idea to start with was to modernize Eric of Pomerania's mediaeval stronghold, "Krogen", but in the end it had to be completely rebuilt, or rather overbuilt, for strangely enough Eric's old castle had been constructed so well and with such precision that its walls still stand, to this very day, within Frederick II's new castle – which was then given the name of *Kronborg*. It was an offence to use the old name, in fact those who forgot themselves were fined 'one good ox'. Kronborg Castle did not cost the kingdoms of

Denmark and Norway a single penny, for the outlay involved was met by Sound Dues. It was first built of red brick and thereafter completely enclosed in sandstone, thus becoming one of the most splendid European castles of its time. It was sumptuously appointed both inside and out, in fact sculptors, woodcarvers, carpenters, tapestry-weavers, silversmiths and artisans of every kind worked for years equipping the fortress, whose situation (with the sea on two sides) was unequalled in Europe. The bastions were well studded with good brass guns so that the ships of all

Chancellor Johan Friis built the manor of Hesselager on the island of Funen.
From an old picture. The main building still stands.

nations might see that the Dano–Norwegian monarch was capable of guarding his territorial waters.

At this same time the Danish nobility commenced building too, partly because so many old aristocratic homes had been destroyed during the Count's War, and partly because there was a demand for newer, more modern manor houses. Denmark was furthermore enjoying a period of prosperity after the Seven Years' War. The country was earning enormous sums by its shipping, commerce and agriculture, and throughout the two kingdoms new country homes in Renaissance style rose up. In the middle of North Zealand Frederick II built himself a delightful little country seat and thereafter started buying up as much of the surrounding land as he could, so that in the end he acquired tremendous hunting-grounds.

Intellectual Life

Frederick also supported the sciences. He was no scholar himself, but the times were scholarly. Aristocratic ladies started collecting old mediaeval folk poetry from all over the country and copying the poems into books. It is from such books that we now know these ballads and poems. Learned men started publishing books on the history of Denmark, and, as an extra gift to a rich country already enjoying a period of prosperity and stability, there appeared, out of obscurity, a young, hitherto unknown

On the island of Hven in the Sound, Tycho Brahe built his renowned observatory and scientific institute "Uranieborg", a well-equipped little luxury palace with "all modern conveniences".

Danish nobleman by the name of *Tycho Brahe*. He produced a little book about "a new star". Frederick gave him his support and eventually Tycho Brahe was given the island of *Hven* (in the middle of the Sound) as a fief. Here the learned Master Tycho built his observatory, or rather, two observatories. The first was *Uranieborg*, which served both as a country seat and a scientific research centre, and the second, later on, was an underground affair, *Stjerneborg*, where all his delicately adjusted instruments could be installed without fear of vibration. He had his own laboratories, a museum, a valuable library, his own printing-press and his own paper-mill on the island, and young scholars from all over Europe flocked to him. Even King James VI of Scotland paid him a visit. Thus for twenty years one of the most progressive European scientific institutes of the day continued its activities on this green little island in the middle of the Sound under the leadership of the scholarly but truculent, somewhat difficult Master Tycho, who, despite the fact that the telescope had still not been invented, managed to work out the first reliable star catalogue the world had ever known.

"His Royal Majesty's Seas"

On one point Frederick II showed a far greater understanding of the needs of his Scandinavian kingdoms than his predecessors. He maintained that the Danish King held sovereignty over all the seas lapping at the shores of Denmark, Norway and Holstein. At this time Denmark felt her Sound Dues to be threatened by the fact that several countries, England, France and Holland among them, were beginning to let their ships sail round to the north of Norway, down into the White Sea, and trade via this route with Russia and Finmark. Frederick II considered this to be a violation of the rights of the Dano–Norwegian Crown, and he actually succeeded in getting both England and France to recognize his surpremacy over "His Royal Majesty's Seas". In return for the Sound Dues she received, Denmark undertook to build lighthouses at specific strategic points in Danish waters, likewise to keep Dano–Norwegian territorial waters free of pirates. Frederick persuaded England to pay an annual fee in return for his allowing the "Russian or Moscovy Company" to send its ships to Archangelsk. He dispatched expeditions to "rediscover" the old Norwegian land of Greenland (in which England by this time was beginning to show interest) and finally crowned his labours to establish the importance of the sea in the lives of his countrymen by producing his "Marine Law" of 1561, a splendid legal document. For Frederick II realized that "The Power of Our Kingdoms lieth mainly Yonder in the Seas."

Frederick II remained unmarried for a long time. He made an attempt to woo Elisabeth of England, but all he got out of it was a refusal and the order of the Garter. He fell in love with the daughter of a Danish nobleman, but finally had to give up and marry *Sophia of Mecklenburg*.

He was of a gay and cheerful disposition, but also had spells of melancholic bitterness. He loved building, he loved hunting, but above all he loved wine. He drank heavily, but then so did everybody. Ever since early mediaeval days the Danes had been known for their tremendous thirst and appetite all over Europe. Frederick II won a great reputation as a wine-drinker. In fact a foreign ambassador once wrote home: "At Koldinghus Frederick II taught me how to drink wine. For such a King would I lay down my life!" Wine consumption generally was considerable. In circles where expense was of no consequence the average quantity consumed was probably about ten or twelve pints per person per day – more, of course, on festive occasions. At Frederick II's burial service the court priest officiating permitted himself the observation that "... had the King drunk a little less he might have lived many a day yet."

Christian IV

King Frederick's son Christian was no more than a child when his father died. A regency composed of members of the Rigsraad therefore ruled the country for him. Upon Frederick II's death the two kingdoms were enjoying a greater state of prosperity than they had done for years. The state coffers were full, everything was going well and prospects generally were bright.

However, let no mistake be made. The two Scandinavian countries, Denmark and Norway, were on the outer edge of Europe and therefore the tide of Renaissance splendour which washed in over Denmark – late perhaps, but none the less forcefully for that – never reached as far north as the tremendous, rugged land of Norway. Few Renaissance buildings rose in those mountainous regions, and despite the fact that there were many solidly established, aristocratic landowners in the Norwegian valleys, as a whole the vast, unwieldy land was poor. There was a thriving fishing industry, but it was not sufficient to make the country rich. The forests produced timber, and there was a certain amount of farming in the valleys, but the roads were long and in a deplorable state and the country moreover was very thinly populated. In Denmark, the power was in the hands of the nobility (or at any rate a part of it), and Danish noblemen lived in fine modern manor-houses, but Danish manor-houses were small by comparison with the manor-houses of other European countries. The towns pursued their commercial activities satisfactorily, but there was still such an extraordinary large number of them that none was ever given a real chance of expanding – the land surrounding them, or their hinterlands, were too restricted. Agriculture was prospering, but in large parts of the land the old Danish "free" peasants had gradually fallen into a state of dependence. They rented their farms and land from a nobleman or from the Crown. This in itself was not too bad an arrangement, but the power their aristocratic masters wielded over them was considerable. Admittedly they never sank quite so low as the peasants of Central Europe. Denmark was comparatively thinly populated too and Danish roads were likewise in terrible condition. Large tracts of country had become useless for the purpose of growing crops as heather had started spreading like a thick blanket over the old peasant settlements of Jutland. This was not really due to inefficiency, for the peasants of the time simply knew no method of preventing this wholesale destruction of their arable land. They simply did not possess the knowledge of later generations concerning the chemistry and biology of the soil. Thus, in large areas of the country where the soil was lighter (i.e. sandy) the disaster that overtook the country was much the same as that which on a far greater scale befell the old Roman cornlands in North Africa, the ancient Babylonian wheat plains, and which today is destroying vast tracts of country in North America. What happens is that when the light soil is left bare for six months of the year, the top soil is blown away, leaving behind nothing but sand and stones. Denmark was rich, but her wealth lay more or less on the surface; its foundations were not particularly solid.

When Prince Christian reached the age of 19 – in 1596 – he was duly crowned as Christian IV, whereafter he became Denmark's most renowned King – the one all Danes know best.

He inherited two quite good kingdoms, likewise his father's ambitious dream of building up the two Scandinavian kingdoms into a Holland of the North with ships sailing on all the seven seas. He also inherited a dream of conquering Sweden. In the meantime Sweden's history was developing along Shakespearian lines. King Eric XIV was a dreamer, a dynamic, fiery soul, but unfortunately quite mad. He did the strangest things. He treated his nobles in the most remarkable fashion, and then fell in love with a dragoon's daughter who sold fruit on the market square and raised her to queenly dignity. Finally he had a number of leading aristocrats thrown into prison, whereupon it became a fixation in his mind that they would have to die. He charged down into their cells in order to murder a couple of them in person. He then murdered his old tutor as well, raved around in a delirium and finally begged his brother, between sobs, to take over not only his throne but likewise the responsibility for all that had occurred. At last he himself was imprisoned.

Christian IV on horseback. Painting by the court painter, van Mandern.

Monument at Kringen in Gudbrandsdalen in Norway, where peasants defeated Scottish mercenaries on August 26, 1612.

Room during Christian IV's time (ceiling slightly later). Dutch paintings on walls. Rosenborg.
Christian IV's ship's lantern, compass and night-light, all of silver. Rosenborg.

His brother assumed power and Eric died in prison – from all accounts at his brother's hand. A third brother later became King of Sweden (after a Polish intermezzo) and was, by the time young Christian ascended the throne of Denmark, an elderly man. Christian wanted to establish a reputation for himself and therefore embarked upon the *Kalmar War*. Having conquered Kalmar Castle he discovered that war was not the great illustrious adventure he had dreamed about. The young Swedish Crown Prince, Gustavus Adolphus, marched south and began ravaging Scania. Plague broke out in the Danish camp, and the old Swedish King, Charles, sent Christian a letter in which he proposed their fighting a personal duel instead of wasting the lives of so many men. This duel was then to decide the outcome of the war. For a number of reasons Christian had his misgivings – one of them being that fighting a duel (it was to be with side-arms) with the old and feeble Swedish King would not bring him much glory, no matter who won. He therefore dispatched a letter of refusal couched in the coarsest and most vulgar terms. The war produced no real results – except that of engendering deep Swedish resentment against Denmark.

At one period some Scottish names were involved in the Kalmar War. Sweden had hired a regiment of Scottish mercenaries, of whom 800 men under Colonel Mönnichhofen sailed over to Norway and started ravaging and laying waste. The rest of the force, 300 men under a certain Colonel Alexander Ramsay, wrought havoc down through Romsdalen. Apparently the Scots behaved in a manner fairly typical for mercenaries of the day. At all events the Norwegian peasants decided to take their revenge. At *Kringen*, in *Gudbrandsdalen*, the Norwegians prepared an ambush and succeeded in waylaying the Scots. The battle was brief and bloody, a clear Norwegian victory. We are told that 134 Scots survived, but that on the following day these too were shot, all except some eighteen "for with these same eighteen his Majesty would have quite enough to feed." Of these, three officers were sent south to Copenhagen. Others entered into Dano–Norwegian service, and a few settled amongst the peasants of Gudbrandsdalen. One of them was shot by his master because he started passing comments about the battle. Two others were shot as soon as the harvest had been gathered in "because the peasants saw no point in supporting them all through the winter."

Behind this bloodthirsty Scottish–Norwegian drama lay a desire on the part of the Norwegians to avenge the massacre by the Swedes of three hundred Norwegian soldiers earlier that spring.

The Great Builder

Christian set to work in his two kingdoms: renewing, replenishing, and above all, building. He founded towns from one end of his realms to the other – although strictly speaking there were quite enough already. He was particularly interested in solidly fortified towns along his borders, and he was likewise interested in trade and shipping. But his favourite interest lay in the navy. He built Europe's largest and most modern *naval arsenal* at Copenhagen – perhaps rivalled only by the arsenal at Venice. He built a new *Stock Exchange* along a mole in Copenhagen harbour, anticipating that within a few years Copenhagen would become the Amsterdam of the North. He even built homes for the seamen of his fleet. In short, he was active throughout his kingdoms, vouchsafing a particular interest in Norway, to which country he made frequent visits. He went down south to Holstein, through the Baltic to Gotland, and even sailed north round Norway in order to inspect problems there for himself – both those involving trade and shipping, and those involving the border. He was a jovial monarch with an excellent capacity for food and drink. His court was particularly gay. His young wife, Anna Cathrina, died young, whereafter, as a young widower, his private life became somewhat rash. As a result he eventually fathered quite a number of illegitimate children. At the age of about 40 he finally married again. His new bride was only 17. This marriage lasted ten years – somewhat stormy ones.

He pulled down his father's little country seat, Frederiksborg, and re-built it. The new version was much larger and much more magnificent. He built a residential college for university students in Copenhagen, likewise a church for them, and in conjunction therewith his "Round Tower". This last venture possibly had something to do with the fact that Christian IV, being of a somewhat lively temperament, had not been able to agree with Denmark's renowned son on the island of Hven, the learned Master Tycho Brahe. It ended with a clash and the King behaved rather meanly.

He took Master Tycho's island of Hven away from him and forbade his making astronomical observations in Copenhagen. Tycho Brahe emigrated to Prague. This proved a disappointment, despite the fact that he was helped by one of his learned pupils, Keppler by name, and some few years later Master Tycho died, a deeply disappointed man. His

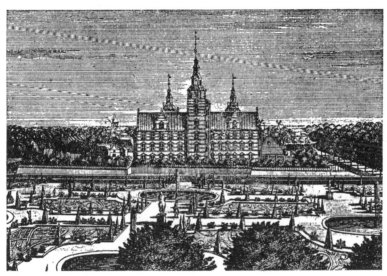

Just outside Copenhagen (today in the middle of the city) Christian IV built his "pleasure palace" of Rosenborg. From an old engraving (Danske Vitruvius).

fairy-tale world on the island of Hven had been literally obliterated and within a few years not a single stone was left standing. But the affair was by no means a credit to King Christian, and it probably nagged at his conscience. At all events he built his "Round Tower" in Copenhagen as an observatory in order to show his interest in astronomy.

He tore down Copenhagen's old defence bastions and expanded the city to twice its former size. He worked and he gave orders. More than 3,000 letters originating from his own hand have been preserved. He was indefatigable. Nothing escaped his attention and he poked his nose into everything. He ruled his two kingdoms rather in the manner of a careful country squire, and completed one building after another in the manner of an efficient building contractor. He personally checked timber measurements when ships were under construction, personally bought up the stone and timber required for his castles, personally completed both rough sketches and finished architectural drawings, personally tested the mortar used at building sites and criticized it, conducted negotiations with foreign ambassadors, wrote and spoke several languages, loved good music and was the founder of a distinguished era in Danish organ-building and the demands made upon Danish organists.

His outlook was a broad one. He sent Admiral Gjedde southwards round the Cape to Ceylon, whereafter the Admiral came home and announced that he had founded Danish "colonies" in India – the trading post of Tranquebar. He sent several expeditions to Greenland (among them one under the guidance of the English navigator James Hall) and he attempted to find a Northwest passage round the north of America leading to China and India. On this mission he dispatched *Jens Munk*, a trustworthy sea-captain and the son of a Danish nobleman, with two ships. Jens Munk was forced to spend the winter in Baffin Bay and the bold expedition ended in disaster. During the winter his two crews died of scurvy and when spring came only Jens Munk and two other men were still alive. They scuttled one of the ships (guns marked C4 have been found at the mouth of the Churchill River in modern times) and the three men brought the other ship across the Atlantic to the safety of a Norwegian port.

Christian IV's sister had married King James I of England. On two occasions Christian sailed over to London to pay her a visit. He was received with due pomp and circumstance and was personally delighted. Wealthy England overwhelmed her Danish guests with hospitality. Her guests, in return, demonstrated their ability to floor their hosts completely in certain spheres of activity such as that of drinking wine. The English hosts found themselves obliged to record one complete fiasco: knowing that the Dano–Norwegian monarch loved hunting, the Earl of Salisbury carefully arranged a splendid day's outing. But the Scandinavian king departed from the field showing visible signs of disgust and revulsion after twelve horses had been ridden to death. Christian IV planned a tremendous fireworks display as a little surprise when the English King came on board to inspect the splendid Danish ships, but unfortunately (thanks to the whimsicality of the English tide) it had to be held in broad daylight. But otherwise everything was joyous and Christian was invested with the Order of the Garter.

On July 20, 1639, a curious incident took place in Denmark. Down in the province of Slesvig a young peasant girl stumbled over a horn sticking up out of the ground. At first she thought it was a hunting horn, but a goldsmith told her it was pure gold. It ended up in the hands of

Map of Denmark by John Speed, an Englishman, 1626.

the King, who presented it to his son with the advice that he should get it melted down and made into a decent drinking cup "in memory of your old ancestors". A learned doctor named Ole Worm managed to prevent this being done and thus, on this occasion, the horn was spared. A hundred years later a farmer found another gold horn at approximately the same place. The two horns eventually found their way to the royal "treasure chamber" and represent – or represented – the greatest treasures ever to be found in Denmark. They dated from about 500 A.D. – in other words more or less the time when the Angles emigrated from Slesvig in order to occupy Celtic Britain and give the country its new name: Angleland.

The Fatal Turning Point

Meanwhile Christian IV had set his mind on doing greater deeds and on acquiring a mightier reputation amongst Europe's rulers. He decided to take part in the Thirty Years' War, despite the warnings of the members of his Rigsraad, who clutched their heads in despair and begged him to keep out of it. It was difficult for him to go to war without the support of his Rigsraad, so he chose instead to secure himself the title of "District Colonel of Lower Saxony". He duly went to war – as "Colonel Christian" – because the Protestants of northern Germany were in difficulties and had asked the renowned Scandinavian monarch for his assistance. Christian's army was defeated by Tilly at *Lutter am Barenberg*. His defeat was complete and utter, and thus Christian's part in the Thirty Years' War came to an end. He retreated northwards, but his cunning did not help him very much. His war concerned neither Denmark nor Norway in any way at all, but nevertheless German troops moved up into Jutland – for nobody saw why Christian should be permitted to swop titles at the border.

Jutland was terribly ravaged. Its towns were destroyed and its manor-houses plundered, but the foreign invaders did not succeed in crossing the sea to Funen and Zealand.

Although the peace treaty Christian was made to sign was fairly lenient, the country had nevertheless suffered badly, and Christian himself felt deep disappointment and bitterness. He continued with his work, but his rather unhappy private life did not help to make things brighter.

The Protestants of northern Germany then turned to the Swedish King, Gustavus Adolphus, asking for his help. Gustavus Adolphus was willing – and suggested to Christian that if Sweden and Denmark were to enter into an alliance it would enable them to take part in the Thirty Years' War together. Christian refused – thereby committing the most foolish error of his reign. But he found the situation too bitter and was moreover afraid that after his defeat, the Swedish King would end up dominating the scene. Not only did he refuse the offer of an alliance: he also refused to promise to keep the peace with Sweden as long as the Swedish action in Germany was in progress. Thus nothing came of the meeting between the two kings beyond the fact that the King of Sweden saw his wise, magnanimous offer rejected merely because of Christian's envy and personal small-mindedness. That Gustavus Adolphus should subsequently reveal himself in Germany to be one of Europe's greatest military geniuses did not in any way mollify Christian's feelings in the matter. The Swedish army succeeded in changing the course of the Thirty Years' War, going from victory to victory until at last the imperial crown seemed to be within the grasp of the Swedish King. No doubt when the news of Gustavus Adolphus' death at *Lützen* reached Christian IV he must have felt enormously relieved. But the political manoeuvres of the Danes behind the backs of their would-be Swedish allies could only end by causing irritation to the members of the Swedish Rigsraad. The result was that a Swedish army under Torstensson marched up into Jutland. Simultaneously, Swedish troops swept down into the Scanian provinces, ravaging

Rigsadmiral Claus Daa built Holmegaard in Zealand in 1635. Several Danish manors have half-timbering.

and laying waste as so often in the past. Denmark was in difficulties. The Danish fleet managed to keep the Swedes off the main Danish islands, but Jutland and the Scanian provinces once more suffered terribly – Jutland for the second time within only a few years. Christian himself, although by now an old man, was at sea with his fleet. Even though the Swedish naval forces were by no means inconsiderable, the Danish fleet was the stronger. Christian IV was badly wounded at a naval battle off *Kolberg Roads* – and in fact lost an eye.

When "Torstensson's War" was finally over, Christian was obliged to sign a humiliating peace treaty near the Swedish border. This was the Treaty of *Broemsebro*, in 1645. Gotland, the island which Valdemar Atterdag had conquered in 1361, and another island named Oesel, were surrended to Sweden, and Norway had to surrender the two large provinces of *Härjedal* and *Jämtland*. In order to guarantee the peace, the Scanian province of Halland was to be Swedish for thirty years.

Christian IV lived for three more years. He was now 70, tired, deeply disappointed, and so impoverished that he hardly knew how to pay for a load of coal to feed his fireplace at Frederiksborg. His magnificent palace had been stripped of all its silverware and silver-plated banisters. Somehow practically all his projects had dwindled to nothing. In Norway he had begun working copper mines at Roeros and silver mines at Kongsberg. He kept hoping against hope that riches would suddenly start streaming forth from these mines, but they barely produced enough to cover running expenses. His far-reaching, complicated plans had nearly all collapsed. Even his father's splendid stronghold, Kronborg Castle, had been destroyed by fire. He succeeded in rebuilding it, but never in re-equipping it inside. His lovely arsenal in Copenhagen, "Toejhuset", had also burned down. The many building projects he had launched came to a standstill. His friends failed him, or merely died round him. The Danish nobility took no further notice of him. He was divorced from his second wife and spent his last years with her chambermaid, *Vibeke Kruuse*, who looked after the old man affectionately and even presented him with two children. His many children took sides "according to mothers" in everlasting squabbles and he had endless trouble with his sons-in-law. He had become a lonely, bitter old man. He represented the Danish Renaissance during the baroque period like a relic from the past – happy days that had long since vanished. One grey February day in 1648, when the snow lay thin and a slushy thaw was setting in, he was driven by sledge for the last time from Frederiksborg to his beloved little Rosenborg Palace. Here, a week later, he died – peacefully, and practically forgotten by everyone.

VI. THE WARS AGAINST SWEDEN &
THE ABSOLUTE MONARCHY

Christian IV's eldest son, likewise named Christian, died of drink a few years before his father. Christian IV's second son had been christened Frederick and ascended the throne as *Frederick III*. He had been Bishop of Bremen, was a scholarly man and had a "treasure-chamber" at the palace. He bore little resemblance to his full-blooded father. He was silent and reserved, a difficult man to fathom. He took over two impoverished, ravaged countries, many of whose towns lay in ruins, many of whose farms had been razed to the ground, and whose populations were being stricken by the plague. In spite of all this Denmark demonstrated once more one of her most remarkable abilities: that of being able to get back on to an even keel within an astonishingly short space of time and in an almost inexplicable fashion. It is something that just seems to happen. Frederick really succeeded in putting the torn land more or less back in to shape again. But there was no shortage of serious problems, one of them being Sweden's strength, which was a continual threat. It was now *King Charles X* of Sweden, a professional soldier, who started leading the Swedish army through Europe, ravaging and laying waste wherever he came. Though fully engaged in the business of wiping out Poland, he made no secret of the fact that it would be Denmark's turn next. Frederick decided to act and declared war on Sweden. He assumed that as Charles was so heavily committed in Poland, Denmark should stand a good chance. But Charles seized upon Frederick's declaration of war as an excuse to extricate himself from his Polish affairs – which were becoming a little too complicated. He marched through Germany, up into Jutland, and finally, towards the end of the summer, came to a halt at Little Belt.

This was where the new fortress of Fredericia was being built, but it was only half finished. Charles stormed it. After half a day's bitter fighting and much bloodshed he succeeded in overpowering it. Before declaring war Frederick had naturally done his best to secure himself some allies amongst the German princes, but Charles' surprise action was launched long before any help could be mustered – and when it did come it was worse than nothing. The foreign hired mercenaries plundered the land just as badly as the Swedish troops and into the bargain brought the plague with them. So the whole of southern Jutland was paralysed and very nearly depopulated.

Charles was unable to cross Little Belt because the Danish fleet was superior to the Swedish fleet. But the winter that followed was exceptionally severe. At the beginning of January Little Belt had frozen hard and Charles decided to lead his troops over to the island of Funen. He marched across the ice and met with practically no opposition, for his crossing of the Belt was completely unexpected. So there he was in Funen, and considering the instability of the Danish climate his position might well have proved dangerous. Frederick proposed negotiations, but Charles rejected the very thought. On the contrary, he decided he would march across Great Belt too, over to Zealand. This sounded like complete madness. It is extraordinarily seldom that the waters of Great Belt freeze over solidly enough to walk across. The current is very strong and there is nearly always a wind blowing, so that even during winters when it freezes severely the ice is never permitted to lie calm for many hours.

But Charles succeeded. He marched across to the island of Lolland and from Falster over to Zealand. Frederick had no troops worth mentioning in Zealand, having reckoned on the island's being sufficiently protected by the surrounding sea. Members of the Danish Council of State met in Taastrup to negotiate terms with Charles. This became known as the "panicky peace" of Roskilde. For Frederick's position was not all that hopeless. Charles' forces in Zealand amounted only to some 5,000 men and Frederick would have been able to mobilize more. His excellent cavalry was in fine fighting trim and he was advised by many to give battle. But something like mental paralysis in the face of the unexpectedness of Charles' action got the upper hand. In Roskilde Denmark signed the most expensive peace treaty in the entire history of the country. The provinces of Halland, Scania and Blekinge, likewise the island of Bornholm, were handed over to Sweden – in other words, all the old Danish territories east of the Sound (or a third of all Denmark) and furthermore considerable territories in Norway.

In return, Charles naturally promised to withdraw his troops from Denmark. But this he did not do. In fact early in the autumn of that same year he fell upon the Danes by surprise once again. He regretted

Charles X crossing Great Belt. Print in Pufendof's book on the wars of Charles X.

not having seized the whole of Denmark while he was at it and therefore broke his word (and the peace treaty) and landed in Zealand. A fleet transported his army from Kiel to Korsoer. He immediately marched on Copenhagen and brushed aside any talk of negotiations. It was to be now or never, for he knew that the defence bastions of Copenhagen were unprepared and that they only boasted six guns.

But as he approached the city he found the suburbs in flames and realized that Copenhagen's citizens were clearing the terrain so that they might the better be able to defend the city. Despite the fact that practically the whole of the rest of Denmark was in Swedish hands, the people of Copenhagen had decided to fight. Charles started to lay siege to the city and in Copenhagen everybody got to work on the defence ramparts.

Women and children, university students and citizens alike, all worked shoulder to shoulder. Regular shifts were organized for both work and guard duty. King Frederick was in the city and had his tent pitched up on the very rampart itself. Within a short time the defence bastions had been repaired. Then an auxiliary fleet came from Holland under *Admiral Opdam.* The Dutch did not wish to see Denmark obliterated, for it would only mean that the Swedes would obtain complete control of the Sound. The Swedish fleet tried to blockade the entrance to the Sound, but after a violent naval battle (which Opdam directed from an armchair on deck as he was suffering terribly from gout) the Dutch fleet arrived at the besieged city bringing both provisions and reinforcements.

Although the siege had commenced in August, it was not until after New Year that Charles got ready to take the city by storm. He had established a well-defended camp, and the Danes moreover were forced to swallow the bitter pill of seeing Kronborg Castle surrender. Charles was thus master of the entrance to the Sound and controlled shipping. At the same time Denmark's castles and manor-houses throughout the land were destroyed and plundered. Paintings and furniture and fountains were bodily removed from the magnificent palaces of Frederiksborg and Kronborg and taken to Sweden, and valuable collections of books belonging to Danish noblemen were loaded on to carts and thereafter shipped across the Sound – and nowadays contribute to the excellence of Stockholm's fine libraries.

A rebellion started in Malmö, but it was put down and many of those implicated were executed by the Swedes. Bornholm freed itself by a *coup.* The Swedish commandant on the island was shot and a couple of men sailed across the ice-filled sea in an open boat to the besieged capital in order to hand over their island to Frederick, proposing that he should keep it as his personal property.

On the night of February 10, 1659, Copenhagen was stormed. The Danes knew the attack was coming, and every man was at his post. These were no longer the despairing inhabitants of a large city. Considerable military reinforcements had been brought in and these were deployed along the defence ramparts, well-trained civilian companies alternating with professional troops. Women and other forms of "casual labour" were to assist with the loading of muskets, the dragging of stones and wooden beams up on to the ramparts so that they could be heaved down on to the heads of the enemy, and the boiling of water and lye to pour over them as they tried to clamber up. A limited section of the rampart to the north of the city was manned by the Dutch. The rest was held by Danes. University students were allotted the section nearest the palace. Some 300 good guns had been installed along the ramparts as well.

The attack was launched at one o'clock at night. It was directed at the

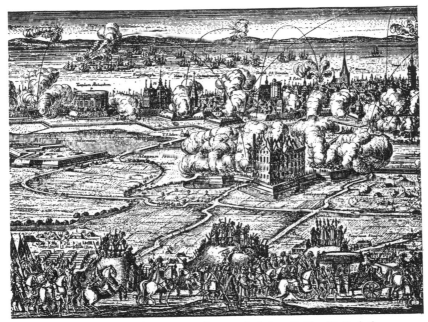

The siege of Copenhagen seen from Frederiksberg Bakke (Pufendorf).

city's weakest point, the area near the frozen harbour entrance where it was possible to go round the ramparts merely by walking out on the ice. Hour after hour the Swedish troops stormed, only to be flung back time and again. The fighting was very bitter. After several hours of hard pressure a fresh attack was made at the bastion at Christianshavn – and likewise repulsed. Finally, towards morning, an attack was directed against the northern bastion where the Dutch troops were installed, but this too proved fruitless. As dawn came, Charles was forced to call a retreat. It is estimated that more than 3,000 Swedes lost their lives that night, while Danish casualties amounted only to some 20 men.

Thus the city was saved. That morning, soldiers and citizens, their wives and children, all went to sing the Te Deum in the churches of their city – churches where the renowned organs had been silent throughout the months the siege had been kept up.

But peace did not make any great difference to the situation – for Holland suddenly turned and went over to the other side. The Dutch did not wish to see Denmark fall into the hands of the Swedes, but on the other hand they did not wish to see the Danes recover the Scanian provinces either. Denmark was now made to pay for her foolish monkeying with the Sound Dues. The other European maritime powers, especially England and France, were just as interested in the new balance of power in the Sound. The Scanian provinces were lost.

Shortly after giving up the conquest of Denmark, King Charles died of a stroke.

Absolute Monarchy

Denmark had been reduced in size and ruined economically. The prevailing mood in the country was gloomy. Everything was blamed on the nobility. Frederick seized advantage of this mood. The citizens of Copenhagen felt they had saved the country. The whole political situation was leading up to a realization of the fact that an end must be put to the old mediaeval system of government by the aristocracy. Frederick felt the time was ripe to introduce *absolute monarchy* – not by a bloody rebellion, but by negotiations conducted with (one might well say) extraordinary astuteness. All classes – the nobility, the citizenry and the peasantry alike – acknowledged him as Denmark's and Norway's *hereditary prince and absolute monarch*.

He thereupon set to work reorganizing his kingdoms, in other words what was left of Norway and Denmark. The various districts had formerly been administered by fief-holders belonging to the aristocracy, but the work was now done by salaried 'civil servants'. King Frederick nourished a deep mistrust of the old Danish nobility. In fact he was continually expecting the nobles to rise against him – they just never did. The Danish nobility was really so enfeebled that it faded into the background. Frederick and his successors permitted many Germans and other foreigners to immigrate. By elevating them to the ranks of the aristocracy a new peerage was created whose representatives owed their position to the absolute monarchs of their period and therefore could be expected to display greater loyalty.

One violent clash still remained: Frederick's half-sister, *Leonora Christina*, had married Christian IV's major-domo, *Corfitz Ulfeld*. Ulfeld had been behaving in a somewhat remarkable fashion and had in fact finally committed pure treason by entering the service of the Swedish King and acting as his representative at the signing of the humiliating peace treaty of Roskilde. Subsequently he was restored to favour, but then he broke off relations with Denmark again. Leonora's attitude could not be described as strictly Danish either. They were both imprisoned for a time and later released, but the situation gradually became so complicated that Ulfeld ended up wandering round Europe, homeless and practically an outlaw. Leonora Christina went over to see the English King (Charles II at this time) in order to obtain payment of a sum of money which he owed Ulfeld, but he decided it would be cheaper to have her arrested and sent to Denmark. She arrived in Copenhagen and was once more imprisoned. She spent the next 21 years locked up in a tower as a traitor to her country, the enemy of the Queen Mother, and the only person upon whom the Danes were able to vent their spleen because of the loss of the Scanian provinces. Leonora Christina wrote a detailed account of her prison years, giving it the title of "Jammersminde", meaning "Memories of Woe", and displayed such high literary and human qualities that the work has since become a Danish classic.

The Scanian War – Griffenfeld

Where Frederick was obliged to leave off at his death, his son Christian V took over. From all reports he was not a brilliant man, but at least he was extremely honest in his efforts to rule the country well. To assist him he had an eminently qualified and highly talented young man named Peder Schumacher, whom he subsequently raised to the nobility with the name of *Griffenfeld*. During Christian V's reign the whole country was at last given a single, comprehensive Statute Book, *Christian V's Danish Law*, which took the place of the old provincial Laws dating from the Valdemar Period. At the same time a corresponding Statute Book was drawn up for Norway.

The problem still remaining was that of the Scanian provinces. Despite Griffenfeld's warnings, Denmark and Norway once more threw themselves into a war with Sweden, the *Scanian War*, which lasted from 1675 to 1679.

The situation in the Scanian provinces was desperate. In the treaty by which the provinces were surrendered it was decreed that they should be allowed to retain their Danish laws and customs, but this clause was immediately disregarded. More than 10,000 fled to Denmark and those that remained were treated harshly. Executions were common, and the population was more or less in despair at Sweden's methods of foreign rule. So when the Danish army landed it was welcomed with open arms.

But the war was waged unsuccessfully. On December 4, 1676, the Danes lost a decisive battle at *Lund*, where the Swedish army tried to take the Danish headquarters by surprise one night because the Swedes themselves happened to be in a desperate situation. The battle started off one dark winter's morning with the cavalry forces of both armies racing against each other to occupy the strategic hilltops. The battle lasted all day. The Swedish army was in process of breaking up. The Danish King (who like the Swedish, was taking part personally) had already left the field of battle, confident that the fight was as good as over and that victory for the Danes was certain, when the Swedish King launched a desperate cavalry charge – and turned a seeming defeat into a Swedish victory. This was one of the bloodiest battles that has ever taken place in Scandinavia. That December evening, as the rain drizzled down and darkness fell, almost nine thousand Danish and Swedish corpses lay stretched in the muddy fields to the north of Lund.

Thereafter the war became a matter of senseless havoc and destruction. In those days there were no petrol dumps to blow up – so villages and farms were destroyed instead. Cornfields and well-filled barns were burnt in order to deprive the enemy of feed for his horses. As a result, the Scanian provinces were completely devastated. Thousands of Scanians fought on against the Swedes as independent guerillas, and the war dragged on. The Danish fleet held supremacy at sea and won important victories, but the final result was more or less a *status quo*. Sweden's mighty

Door from farm on island of Langeland, with shot-holes dating from the Swedish war.

The door was painted in about 1600 with a verse that relates how Swedish soldiers shot the door down, turned a pregnant woman out on to the bed-straw, and behaved very badly; but God helped, and the enemy received his just reward at the battle of Nyborg on the island of Funen. National Museum.

The four kings who started the great Scandinavian war: Frederick IV of Denmark,
Peter the Great of Russia, Charles XII of Sweden and August the Strong of Poland.

ally, France, dictated the terms of the peace: the Scanian provinces were not to be returned to Denmark. From that day onwards legend has it that Christian V had the windows of Kronborg Castle that faced the Sound blocked up – for he was unable to bear looking out across the water towards the green coastline of Scania.

During the war there were a number of domestic feuds of a political

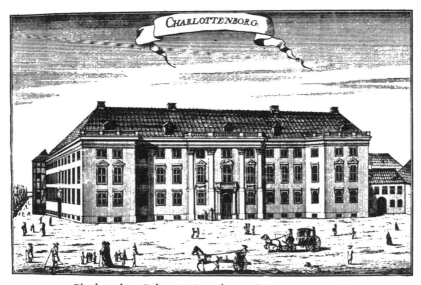

Charlottenborg Palace in Copenhagen. (Contemporary print).

nature. The final outcome of these was the fall of Griffenfeld. He was forced out of power by political intrigues, condemned to life imprisonment and sent to a prison in Norway. In Denmark all was quiet. An oppressive peace seemed to be descending over the land.

Molesworth

It was during these years that *Sir Robert Molesworth* came to Scandinavia and wrote his "An Account of Denmark as it was in the year 1692" and its companion volume, "An Account of Sweden".

The book is brilliantly malicious and is quoted in all history books in Danish schools. For, despite the fact that its political aim is very clear, it nevertheless manages to say something of importance. The book seeks to depict drastically for an English public just how bad everything can be in an absolute monarchy where the population is made apathetic and subjugated into a state of animal wretchedness. Of course in Sweden everything was different.

It is a case of the hasty traveller who knows what he wants to find beforehand, the way certain people nowadays go to countries knowing just what they must expect to find because the country in question is governed in this way or in that way. But there is much to be got out of Molesworth. That he frequently gives himself away is only a charm in itself. Even so, he has succeeded in putting his finger on some important facts: the country was poor, the peasants were not having too good a time of it (even though things were by no means as bad as they may have seemed) the towns were small and wretched, only Copenhagen was anything approaching a city by European standards (but even so seemed to have no 'push' and instead seemed somehow to be on the point of expiring) and the population as a whole was strangely apathetic. Legislation he admitted to be excellent and the administration of justice and security exemplary. But autocracy as such he nevertheless found to be calamitous. After which he noted with honesty that His Autocratic Majesty's own dwelling was just about the most wretched building in the whole city.

However, when reading Molesworth's book, it should be borne in mind that, for a member of the British Embassy in Copenhagen, he had behaved unfortunately (to put it mildly) and in the end he was practically chucked out of the country. He was deeply offended, particularly at not being presented with a parting gift by the King, and he wrote the book by way of revenge, anonymously, so that for a long time nobody had any idea who its author could be, and the case developed lengthy diplomatic consequences.

The Great Nordic War

When Christian V's son succeeded to the throne, Denmark once more had a young king – and embarked upon a new era. But while England, France, Spain and Germany were passing through dramatic times, the Scandinavian kingdoms continued to develop their own private histories.

When Frederick IV came to the throne in 1699 he was 28 years old. Peter the Great of Russia at this time was 27, and Augustus the Strong of Poland 29. The three young kings formed an alliance, for on the throne of Sweden sat a boy of no more than 17, and it seemed as though at long last Russia, Poland, and the joint kingdom of Denmark and Norway, were to have a chance of obtaining their revenge on Sweden, who during her "days of glory" had inflicted such deep wounds upon the fates and fortunes of all her neighbours. The young Swedish boy-king was notified of their declaration of war one day while he was out hunting bears, and made up his mind promptly. None of the three allies were to know that in this boy, *King Charles XII*, Sweden once more was about to launch a military genius of unusual stature into Europe's sorely tried arena.

Charles attacked Denmark straight away – which came as a shock to Frederick IV. He had kept the greater part of the Danish forces down on the borders of Holstein – firstly because he was expecting an attack from this quarter, and secondly because he was preparing to fall upon the Swedish provinces in northern Germany. In Zealand (just as in 1658) there were no troops worth mentioning. Charles XII landed at *Humlebaek* and Frederick was obliged to make peace. But the terms were cheap. He merely promised to take no further part in the war. Charles then turned his attention eastwards and at Narva the 18-year old king-general inflicted a crushing defeat on Peter the Great. It was now that Charles XII's remarkable career really began in earnest. He marched against Augustus of Poland and defeated him too. Thus he had in fact defeated all three opponents, but he did not stop. He was a soldier and a military romantic. War was his life and war was his passion. His officers and men idolized him. He conjured forth one army of Swedish peasant lads after the other and led them to victory after victory all round eastern Europe. For about ten years he kept on conquering almost incessantly, making political decisions to suit his own ends. But then things went wrong. In 1709 he was defeated by Peter the Great at *Poltava*. His army was thoroughly shaken up, and he himself was obliged to retreat southwards to Turkey. Here, curiously enough, he stayed put.

Once more Frederick IV led Denmark and Norway into war, this time because Holstein had allied itself with Sweden against Denmark. For a while the situation had been perilous, but things now changed and a very large Swedish army had to surrender to the Danes. At the same time the Danish fleet was enjoying supremacy in the Baltic and the North Sea. It was during this war that a Norwegian named *Peter Wessel* made a name for himself in Scandinavian history. He was not really a great sea-admiral type, but more of a freebooter, a Viking, above all a seaman – and his battles were incredible. Once he was bound for Bergen in a small coastguard vessel when a ship flying the English flag came bearing down on him. Wessel dipped his flag in salute, but at that moment his opponent struck his English flag and in its place hoisted the Swedish flag. It transpired that the ship was commanded by an English captain in the service of the Swedes. The two ships fired away at each other for a couple of hours until both of them were in somewhat poor shape. Then Wessel hoisted a truce flag and sent a boat over with the message that he was unable to return his enemy's fire any more because he had run out of ammunition. The Englishman answered that unfortunately he had only sufficient for his own needs, whereupon the two captains drank each other's health in Rhenish wine, tossed their glasses into the sea and sailed off in opposite directions. Wessel got into trouble with the Dano-Norwegian admiralty, who claimed that he had behaved incautiously and in an unwarlike manner. This he undeniably had, but Frederick IV gave Wessel his protection. Wessel was finally raised to the nobility with the name of *Tordenskjold*, literally meaning *Thundershield*. Some of his most adventurous escapades were his attacks on a couple of Swedish coastal fortresses and naval harbours. By the end of the war the Swedish fleet was practically destroyed.

But the war was not yet over. A Danish army landed once more in Scania, for it was felt that the time had now come to reconquer the Scanian provinces. But at a battle near Helsingborg an efficient Swedish general named *Stenbock* defeated the Danes in a murderous clash costing many thousands of lives.

Finally Charles XII came home from Turkey. With one other companion he rode all the way up through Europe to Stralsund, slipped over the Baltic to Sweden, ruled the whole of Sweden for a long time from the town of Lund and then decided to turn his attentions northwards. What he planned to do was seize Norway from Frederick IV and after that sail across to Scotland and descend upon England from the north. His schemes were quite incredible.

He reached the border fortress of Frederikshald. Here, on a moonlit November evening, he was shot clean through the head, probably by one of his own men. His life may have been fantastic, but his death was Sweden's salvation. With him, Sweden's 'golden age' came to an end. Sweden was impoverished and more or less ruined. It was Tordenskjold who sailed to Copenhagen and announced Charles' death to Frederick IV. The King had retired to bed, but Tordenskjold was admitted to the royal bedchamber. Frederick remained silent for a long time and finally said that if the news were really true then Tordenskjold would be appointed to the rank of *Schoutbynacht*, a Dutch naval rank corresponding to that of rear-admiral.

The war was still not over. Many important events took place after the death of the Swedish King and peace did not come until 1721. But once more Denmark was disappointed: the European powers would not agree to both sides of the Sound once more falling into Danish hands. Denmark was admittedly still exacting Sound Dues, but it was felt that a better hold could be kept on the situation if one side of the channel were controlled by the Swedes.

Young Tordenskjold did not live long. He became vice-admiral of the Dano-Norwegian fleet and was given leave of absence in order to go to England (partly to look up a certain Mrs. Harriet) but on the way he became involved in a duel with a Swedish colonel in Hannover and was killed.

Intellectual Life

King Frederick had been in Italy as a young man and had greatly admired the Italian style of architecture. He built a couple of palaces in Denmark, and it was during his reign that Danish rococo developed. He was somewhat careless in his private affairs. He entered into a morganatic marriage (his second) with a young lady of the aristocracy, the 17-year old Anna Sophie Reventlow, while his Queen had to live more or less in exile in the provinces.

It was also during Frederick IV's reign that intellectual life began to develop in Denmark. Scandinavia was astonishingly slow to take part in the European literary culture of the time. Art did not thrive either. Paintings were bought in the south or else artists were called in from

Germany or France – as was also the custom in England. But apart from a couple of splendid hymn-writers there was not much literary activity. During Frederick's reign the Norwegian playwright *Ludvig Holberg* wrote a number of comedies in the style of Molière for Denmark's first theatre. Whereas England by now was already able to regard Shakespeare as past history and furthermore was going through a fruitful period of dramatic and literary activity, Denmark did not acquire its first little theatre until the commencement of the 18th century. Until then she had made do with foreign theatrical companies or else let university students put on a comedy now and again. The Court itself performed a considerable number of comedies, tragedies and open-air festivals and the "opera house" was given royal support. But the theatre as such was comparatively unknown in Denmark.

It is curious to think that while Shakespeare was celebrating his triumphs in London before a theatrically-minded public, Copenhagen was having to make do with university students putting on performances for highborn royal guests. So unaccustomed to the theatre was the Danish public that sometimes peculiar situations arose. For instance, on the occasion of Christian IV's baptism in 1577, a play was acted in the courtyard of Copenhagen Palace, a drama about the conflict between the Jews and the Philistines, entitled "David's Victory Over Goliath". But the students taking the parts of the Philistines refused to give way as demanded of them in the scenario because they objected to having to surrender in the presence of their royal audience. It ended in a regular brawl. Denmark's renowned old admiral, Peter Skram, drew his rapier, leapt on to the stage and started leading God's chosen people on to a bloody victory with such aplomb that by the time the noble audience began to express its loud approval of the victory there lay several badly wounded students spread over the proscenium.

By Frederick IV's day this incident lay 150 years in the past, but even so a proper theatre was still virtually unknown in Scandinavia. It was finally created by the Norwegian poet and playwright Ludvig Holberg, who succeeded in poking fun at his own times in a number of bitingly satirical comedies. He was furthermore a professor of history and the King made him a baron.

Greenland

While Holberg was founding the Danish theatre in Copenhagen, and while Danish and Norwegian towns sent ships voyaging upon the seven seas, Greenland was at last rediscovered in earnest. During the Viking Age Norwegian and Icelandic *landnamsmen* had colonized Greenland and founded settlements that were still in existence in about 1500, when contact with Norway and Denmark was finally lost. Nobody had the slightest idea how things had been progressing in the meantime. The few ship's captains who had reached that far north and come home again told tales of deserted farmsteads and a vast, barren land inhabited by strange people, small dark men called Eskimoes. A young priest named *Hans Egede*, the son of a Zealand priest but born in Norway, evolved the theory that over the course of 200 years the ancient Greenlandic Northmen might possibly have forgotten their Christianity. He decided to go up there and find out for himself. After an 11-year struggle trying to raise funds to finance the expedition, he and his young wife, Gertrude Rask, set out for Greenland. To Hans Egede's great disappointment they found no Northmen alive – they had died out in about 1500 – but he felt that his voyage had been the result of divine intervention. And so, despite the difficulties of learning the Greenlandic tongue (which nobody knew in those days) he became a missionary to the Greenlanders. He lived up there for fifteen years and when he came home his son carried on his work. In this way contact was once more established, and before long not only Danish and Norwegian ships, but also English, French and Dutch whalers began sailing up the Greenlandic coastline.

In 1728, shortly before the death of Frederick IV, a big fire swept Copenhagen, thereby reducing a considerable area of the city to ashes. The old mediaeval church of Our Lady, with its countless relics of Denmark's past and numerous sepulchral monuments to the great sons of Denmark and Norway, was destroyed together with all that it contained.

VII. DANISH ROCOCO

Shipping and Porcelain

Frederick died in 1730 and his son, Christian VI, was a completely different man. Together with his stiffly mannered German wife he was deeply taken up with German pietism. The newly established little theatre was closed down, deep religiousness was literally enforced by law, and such intellectual life as had started was obliged to cease. Christan VI worked as energetically and methodically as a departmental manager trying to rule his kingdoms according to the precepts of enlightened despotism. He was painstaking and meticulous, but in certain respects not particularly thrifty. Amongst other things he built (at long last) a new royal palace in Copenhagen. Incredible as it may sound, Copenhagen's ancient mediaeval castle had been made to suffice until now in spite of the fact that it was no bigger than the White Tower in London – perhaps not quite as robust and sinister, but nonetheless a dank and mouldy den of a place. The King owned better palaces at various points outside the city, but the castle which had caused Molesworth to shake his head still served as the King's principal residence. Frederick IV had attempted to modernize it, but it was now pulled down and a tremendous rococo palace built in its place. In shape and design this was the same as the Christiansborg Palace standing in Copenhagen today (the old walls are still intact) but it was bigger. It was magnificently furnished with the finest French furniture that money could buy and vast sums were spent on decorating it with suitable dignity. It was a maze of galleries and chambers and halls, but it is doubtful whether it was ever really very cosy.

At the same time Christian VI worked with deliberation to improve his kingdoms and their safety. Trade was having a boom period, and the navy was reorganized so that it became one of the best in Europe. There were Danish and Norwegian ships plying the seven seas and good profits were finding their way back to the market towns.

Numerous factories were built in both kingdoms. These were not as a rule particularly large, but a demand had arisen for domestic manufacture

Copenhagen in about 1740, seen from Amager, blissfully rococo, her citizens busy fishing. In the left background Frederiksberg Castle.

instead of imported goods. In Denmark many of the attempts failed miserably due to lack of *power*. Denmark is a low-lying country; her rivers seldom originate high enough to provide sufficient pressure to drive even a reasonably hefty water-wheel, and water reserves are limited. Her ever-proximate coastlines and comparatively small inland areas prevent her from having large rivers – there are plenty of them, but they reach the sea before they can grow large enough to support an industry. And in Christian VI's time no forms of power were known other than wind, water, and horses.

After Christian VI came his son Frederick V, who was adored by his people but otherwise not very much use. He loved wine, but his standards of decadence were not comparable with those of a Louis XV. Frederick was just a delightful person who hated to be bothered. Fortunately he had an excellent foreign minister in *Bernstorff*, who managed to steer Denmark and Norway clear of the Seven Years' War and kept the two kingdoms out of all European complications. Most threatening were relations with Russia. The Emperor at this time, Peter III, was a descendant of the Gottorpian Dukes and the family grudge against Denmark was so thoroughly ingrained in him that he swore he would conquer the country and send the Danish Royal Family to Tranquebar. A Russian army was actually on its way towards Denmark, the Danish fleet had put to sea, and Danish troops were in readiness at the border, when suddenly word came that the Czar had been overthrown and his wife, Catherine the Great, had seized the power from him. With this lady Bernstorff succeeded in coming to terms. She relinquished all Russo-Gottorpian claims to Slesvig and the whole of Holstein, and thus both duchies finally reverted to Denmark – even though the Danish King still had Holstein as a German fief. The Danish border was now at the Elbe.

Frederick's first marriage was to Princess Louise of England, the daughter of George II. She died comparatively young, though not until she had given birth to Frederick's successor, Christian. No English princess had been Queen of Denmark since Eric of Pomerania's Philippa, in fact relations generally between England and Scandinavia had dwindled astonishingly. English interests all lay in other directions, out towards the wide oceans and further to the south of Europe. Only Norway was obliged to carry on a lively trade with English ports. Frederick's second wife was German.

When Frederick died he was lauded by Denmark's budding romanticist poets, and though his achievements were modest compared with those of other Danish Kings, he was nonetheless given the most splendid monument: the French sculptor *Saly's* equestrian statue in Amalienborg Square – an absolute monarch in Roman dress.

Absolute monarchy was put to its most rigorous test immediately afterwards. Frederick V's son, Christian VII, was physically small and slight of build. He had shown peculiar symptoms as a child and it soon became obvious that he was mad. He was not devoid of talent and indeed showed ability in various directions. But at times he became overwrought and his education was completely neglected. He had had a painstaking Swiss tutor named *Reverdil*, but his everyday companions were the flunkeys in the big palace, and his father took very little notice of him. He became King before he was seventeen and everybody expected a great deal from him, for the talents he had shown in various fields, together with the fact that at times he revealed a very winning personality, created the illusion that the two kingdoms were about to have a splendid young king. His chamberlain, *Reventlow*, was no doubt largely to blame for the tragedy that now commenced to unfold itself. Reventlow was stern of temperament and not particularly far-sighted. He believed in using a firm hand and succeeded in cowing the young prince by beating him. Reverdil's considerably more intelligent system of upbringing was not sufficient to counterbalance the ill-effects of the thrashings.

In 1766 Christian married Caroline Matilda, the 15-year old daughter of the English Prince of Wales, Prince Frederick Ludvig, whose sister was Christian VII's mother, Louise of England.

The marriage was ill-fated from the start. At the same time Danish politics were hazarded by Court intrigues, and the wise Bernstorff was almost in despair. All those in positions of any responsibility were appalled when the young King decided to undertake a "European tour" two years after coming to the throne. He went to France and England and to everybody's surprise acquitted himself remarkably well.

The middle of the 18th century saw the awakening both of Denmark's industry and her intellectual life. It saw the founding of the Royal Copenhagen Porcelain Factory, which soon made a name for itself. Early in its existence it executed very demanding commissions, for example an enormous dinner-service, "Flora Danica", which was designed as a gift to Catherine II of Russia, but she died before it was finished, so today it is in Rosenborg Palace, and parts of it are still used at royal banquets. Later on the factory passed through difficult times, but flourished anew and today is known far beyond the borders of Denmark. *Carsten Niebuhr* went east and brought home the first reliable copies of Syrian cuneiform writing. *Captain Norden* went to Egypt and published his drawings of the ancient wonderland in a magnificent book of engravings. Shipping was still flourishing, but the factories were not so fortunate. Nevertheless, the Scandinavian kingdoms were still only on the outskirts of Europe, despite the fact that the art of poetry was beginning to dawn.

Johannes Ewald became Denmark's greatest literary figure of these years, but drama was flourishing too, even though people still swore by the old French tragedies. In Norway a national spirit began to manifest itself (though nobody had thoughts of abolishing the Union) and in the German-speaking province of Holstein the people felt they had natural bonds with Denmark and so there was no opposition there either, in spite of the language. A Holstein bard felt inspired to write a song with the words: "Ich freue mich, dass Dänenblut in meinen Adern fliesst" ("Let me rejoice that Danish blood within my veins doth flow") and a Swede named *Pilo*, who became President of the Academy, headed Danish painting and caused it to be influenced by flourishing artistic circles in Stockholm.

The King, the Queen, and the Doctor

But things went wrong at the top; or rather, there was no knowing what might happen next. Niebuhr, the man who went travelling in Syria, said that Christian VII had the makings of a Caligula in him, but the sick King had not the stature of a Caligula in so far as diabolical deeds were concerned. His illness became worse and he neglected his unhappy young English Queen in a disgraceful manner. The King's Court physician, a German named *Friedrich Struensee*, began to make his presence felt at Court. He was young, interested in politics, beyond any doubt an idealist, but at the same time a soldier of fortune. He took advantage of his position as the King's physician, the man who held the King in the hollow of his hand. He got himself appointed to the post of cabinet secretary to the King and in this capacity all documents pertaining to the government of the two kingdoms passed through his hands. Thus he gradually gained power. In playing this game he made cynical use of the young Queen, who fell hopelessly in love with this gay and gallant young Court physician. To start with, Struensee had without doubt merely regarded the Queen as a means of acquiring greater power over the King, but before long he fell in love himself and thus a full-blown love affair developed between them. It was discovered, and gave rise to a great scandal – one that in no way diminished when the Queen gave birth to her second child, a daughter bearing an unmistakable likeness to Struensee.

From his post as cabinet secretary Struensee moved up to that of *Geheimekabinetsminister*, or Minister of the Privy Council, by the simple expedient of placing the necessary documents before the King and getting him to sign them. After this he secured absolute power for himself by forcing the King (who by this time was getting a bit apathetic) to sign an order to the effect that all laws and decrees were to become valid provided they bore Struensee's signature.

Struensee then set to work to govern Denmark, Norway and Holstein – a fantastic affair even for the Europe of the times. He had himself made a Count, not from vanity, but merely because practical considerations required his holding a social rank commensurate with his office. At the same time he had his friend Enevold Brandt raised to the nobility and given a Court appointment so that he might take care of the sick King every day while Struensee was looking after the two kingdoms – and the Queen.

His rule was not bad. He cleared away a lot of old governmental cobwebs, enacted a whole deluge of new laws and decrees (about 600 in 16 months, according to reports) and dismissed a whole lot of superfluous civil servants – about the most dangerous thing a politician can start doing even in our times. His mind was filled with the ideas of the day concerning the duties and possibilities of enlightened despotism, but his knowledge was superficial and hastily acquired, and his methods jerky. He had a good, clear, swift-thinking brain, but he lacked the ability to evaluate the consequences of his actions. Everything had to be done there and then, and whenever his tempo was slowed down by opposition he regarded it as stupidity. He caused people offence by being a "deist", in other words although admitting to the existence of God he was otherwise irreligious. He met opposition on a point he was unable to judge no matter how great his willingness. He had come to a country where the former leading politician, Bernstorff, had been a German, where the language of the Court was German, and where some of the administration (in Holstein and the southern part of Slesvig) was carried out in German – and he decided the two languages were impractical. He decreed that henceforth the language of the government should be German and thereafter issued all his laws in German. He was unable to appreciate the subtle interplay that went on between Danish and German in the bi-lingual state, and for that matter he was disinterested anyway. On several occasions he was unfortunate, and he revealed more than once that he did not possess any great personal courage. He was not actually dishonest. He lived very modestly in a couple of wretchedly furnished rooms in a side wing of the palace. He did not quietly pile up a fortune for himself (as well he might have done), he secured no land for himself, nor did he build himself any fine manor-houses. He really lived for the government of the country, and in Norway particularly his legislation represented in many respects a great step forward – though here as well he pushed things through too rapidly and with too much confusion. His love affair with the young English Queen was to prove the principal cause of the catastrophe that followed.

She was very young, incredibly naive, and very lonely. She was English and had not been made welcome at the German-speaking Court presided over by the queen dowager. The queen dowager herself was an authoritative and stern woman, and the young Queen found that on several occasions, as soon as she started to strike up some degree of familiarity with her ladies-in-waiting, they were transferred to "other duties". She was let down on all sides and it must be borne in mind that the English Court was really just as much to blame for her unhappy situation as was the Danish. The English Court was perfectly aware that a completely inexperienced young girl was being married off to a madman, so the very marriage in itself constituted a crime on the part of those responsible. She was completely incapable of managing the difficult situation into which her relations with Struensee had brought her, and she behaved with incredible foolishness. It would be reasonable to suppose that by exercising a little discretion she might have been able to carry on a love affair with some measure of success. After all, the practice was not uncommon in European courts at the time. But discretion was not her strong point. She was warm-blooded, hopelessly in love after several years of unhappy marriage, and she felt that she had to demonstrate her youthful happiness to the whole world. She boasted openly of her affair to her chambermaids, demonstrated time and again her deranged clothing (to express things mildly) after each visit the *Geheimekabinetsminister* paid to her rooms, and went riding with him clad in man's attire and tight breeches – a costume which, in view of the fact that she was particularly buxom, suited her abominably. She lived openly and gaily with her beloved Struensee at her various summer residences, behaved foolishly at Court balls, and finally the two of them each fixed themselves up a luxuriously appointed little apartment in one wing of the palace, one floor above the other, but connected by a "secret staircase" about which the whole of Copenhagen knew.

The situation had become untenable, and everybody realized it. Struensee

Den Stormægtigste Dronning **Caroline Mathilde** til Hest.

Derisive picture of Queen Caroline Mathilde on horseback in man's apparel. Behind the prison bars can be seen Struensee; a wet-nurse is carrying the daughter, Louise Augusta.

became more and more unpopular, not least on account of the fact that he took no notice of his opponents at Court and had no notion of how to handle matters diplomatically. The Court spent a last happy summer at Hirschholm in North Zealand, a luxurious palace built in the most elegant rococo style, and the young couple, perhaps sensing that their sands had very nearly run out, stayed on at this summer residence until well into November.

At New Year 1772 a conspiracy was formed and action taken. After a masked ball at the palace the conspirators broke into the sick King's bedchamber, scared him practically out of his wits and got him to sign the necessary arrest orders. Thereafter they marched with soldiers to the apartments of the two lovers. Struensee was seized and imprisoned in

183

Copenhagen's military stronghold, the Citadel, and Caroline Matilda was taken to Kronborg Castle. A court of law started an inquiry. The Queen denied having had anything whatsoever to do with Struensee, but Struensee realized the foolishness of trying to deny and therefore confessed all. The marriage between the sick King and Caroline Matilda was declared null and void.

And then the English Court finally decided to intervene in the matter, concerning which it had naturally been well-informed for some time. George III expressed (somewhat belatedly) his concern for his sister's unhappy plight. A request was sent that she be repatriated, and an English ship came to fetch her. However, the English Court had no desire to have such a "fallen woman" in London, so George III arranged for her to go and live at Celle, in Hannover, which at the time was English. There she stayed, quietly and much beloved by all, for three years, at the end of which time she died, apparently of smallpox. She had to leave her two children behind her in Denmark: her son *Frederick*, who was the King's son, and heir to the Danish throne, and *Louise Augusta*, the daughter she had with her adored Struensee and who later married the *Duke of Augustenborg*.

Struensee and his friend Enevold Brandt were brought before a tribunal. Their guilt was plain, so the sentence passed was not in itself unjust. Struensee had assumed power in the two kingdoms by gross abuse of the King's illness, and he had furthermore transgressed His Majesty's conjugal privacy. Had he been banished from the country, or sentenced to prison, nobody would have raised any objections. But he was condemned to death together with his friend, and so savage was the hate people bore him that the sentence was carried out with mediaeval cruelty. First his right hand was lopped off, and thereafter his head. His body was quartered and broken on the wheel, an act of incredible stupidity. Through this demonstration of crude barbarity, unique in Danish history of later times, much damage was done to the country's prestige throughout Europe. The young Queen's tragic fate aroused great displeasure at the English Court towards Denmark, a feeling of deep resentment which doubtless should be borne in mind when attempting to understand the situation which arose between England and Denmark some few decades later.

After Struensee's fall a Dane named *Guldberg* headed Danish politics.

En nöÿagtig Forestilling af Executionen som skeede uden for Kiøbenhavn paa Stadens Ostre-Fælled paa Grævene, Struensee og Brandt, Den 28 April. A.º 1772

Accurate vorstellung von der hinrichtung der beiden Grafen, Struensee und Brandt, welche den 28 April 1772 vor dem Oster Thor auf dem Felde vor Coppenhagen vollzogen wurde

Execution of Counts Struensee and Brandt at Nørre Fælled. Contemporary print.

He was a man of absolute integrity, but a reactionary. Practically all Struensee's laws and decrees were abolished and things generally restored to their former state.

But he was also ahead of his times. Guldberg enacted one or two laws revealing real perspective, among them a *naturalization law* that is still in force and which decrees that nobody may assume public office in Denmark without having been born in the country or having acquired Danish citizenship. At the time the law naturally applied equally to Danes, Norwegians and Holsteiners.

At this time Bernstorff the Younger (a nephew of the elder Bernstorff) was foreign minister, and he had a difficult problem to deal with. America was engaged in her War of Independence with England, and England demanded that all foreign powers should forbid their ships to call at ports in the United States. Russia was furious and Catherine II proposed an alliance in order to enforce complete navigational freedom, but Bernstorff decided that a conflict with England would be worse than the interruption of trade with America. Guldberg therefore had him dismissed from his post.

Coup d'Etat

But a group of leading men in Denmark soon found Guldberg's honest but short-sighted rule just as unfortunate as Struensee's. The Crown Prince, Frederick, celebrated his sixteenth birthday, thereby coming of age with a right to a seat in the Council of State. This lad, slight of build, was not lacking in courage. During the first meeting of the Council in which he was allowed to participate he personally managed to bring off a *coup d'état*. He used Struensee's effective method, that of placing a document before the mad King and getting him to sign it. His half-brother, the heir-presumptive, jumped up and tried to grab the document, but the Crown Prince managed to get it out of the room and away to his friends. Thus Bernstorff once more became foreign minister and Guldberg was dismissed. The Crown Prince took over the government in 1784 and ruled the country – first as Crown Prince and subsequently as King – for 55 years.

The two kingdoms were making good progress. Shipping was expanding steadily, trade was flourishing, and the Crown Prince and his friends set to work energetically on the most important issues, namely the improvement of peasant conditions and the modernization of agricultural methods. Ever since the time of Christian VI the peasants had been 'adscript' or 'bound to the soil' which meant that, partly in order to assure the existence of a permanent, stable labour force, and partly to facilitate military conscription, all men living in rural areas were 'bound' to remain living on the same estate or within the same district for the entire period of time during which they were liable for military service. Admittedly this was not quite so oppressive as it may sound today, for peasants moved very seldom then anyway. Even so, their freedom of movement had been impeded. Now however, they were allowed to live wherever they liked and at the same time their relationship to landowners and to the state was normalized. Most farmers were *copyholders*, in other words, a farmer often held a copyhold on the farm he rented so that his son could take it over from him at his death. In certain circumstances a landowner might transfer a farmer from a good farm to one that had been neglected in order that he might re-develop it. Part of the rent, known as "manorial dues" was worked off by the farmer on the land belonging to the manor or the state.

Danish peasants during the first half of the 19th century.
Drawing by the Danish painter Marstrand.

This might often mean neglecting his own harvest, although the lord of the manor naturally was not interested in the farmer's being obliged to neglect his own land to such an extent that he ended up being unable to meet his rent. It was now decreed by law that farmers could *buy* their own farms and land, and at the same time agricultural methods generally were revolutionized. The way rural settlements were organized had not really altered since the Middle Ages. Peasants lived closely side by side in small villages and had "co-operated" ever since ancient times. All land belonging to the village was cultivated by the community as a whole and in accordance with decisions made by the peasants themselves at their village *thing* meetings. But now, each peasant was given the opportunity of consolidating his various fields into one whole. Many farms thus moved from the village out to the land, whereby the entire Danish landscape began to alter appearance. With their own land and the right to decide for themselves how hard they toiled, the peasants immediately became more interested in their work, and at much the same time new methods of cultivation, new farm implements, and better ploughs came into being, and improved methods of working the land enabled old, unused soil to be used anew. Fresh soil came under the plough and generally speaking the Danish peasantry was given a new lease of life. Everything promised well. In order to commemorate the introduction of these peasant reforms an obelisk was erected in gratitude to the Crown Prince. This monument, the "Liberty Memorial", is now in the centre of Copenhagen. Originally it was placed outside the city where the countryside began, but Copenhagen has since expanded around and beyond it.

"Liberty Obelisk", a monument to
the liberation of the peasants.

VIII. THE WARS AGAINST ENGLAND

Bernstorff was still foreign minister, and he had plenty of difficulties. After the American War of Independence came the French Revolution. It was in this same year, curiously enough, that absolute monarchy was introduced in Sweden. A few years later the Swedish King was murdered at a fancy-dress ball in Stockholm – the year before Louis XVI was executed in Paris. These were troubled times. Europe's kings had every reason to be nervous, and from several quarters the twin kingdoms of Denmark and Norway were urged to join in the general confusion of war. While Bernstorff adroitly managed to keep his kingdoms out of all entanglements, the Danish shipping industry earned enormous profits, Danish and Norwegian provincial towns passed through a period of tremendous prosperity, the trading companies made money, and on all the seven seas the most commonly seen flag after the British was that of Denmark-and-Norway.

But then England demanded that Dano-Norwegian ships cease calling at ports in France or French possessions, and in order to enforce her will started seizing Dano-Norwegian merchant vessels. Bernstorff did his best to keep matters continually in the process of negotiation. But in 1797 the wise old statesman died and was deeply mourned. Henceforward Dano-Norwegian reaction to English seizures became sharper. Denmark decided to have her merchant shipping convoyed, for the state of affairs at sea was becoming rather similar to the German concept of "unrestricted submarine warfare". In other words, all mercantile navigation undertaken was at the risk of ship, cargo, and crew. This time Denmark entered into an alliance with Russia as an active member of the Armed Neutrality Pact whose motto became 'free ship, free cargo'. That the situation was rapidly becoming critical was clearly realized by everybody.

The Battle of Copenhagen

Early in 1801, England sent a fleet into Danish territorial waters under *Admiral Parker* and *Admiral Nelson*. It cast anchor off Elsinore and demanded permission to pass Kronborg Castle. The commandant replied that he could not permit a battle fleet bound for an unknown destination to pass his guns. Parker waited until a favourable wind enabled him to sail close in alongside the Swedish coast, and as he passed through the straits he bombarded Elsinore. He only scored one hit on the town and that was on the house of the British Consul.

The arrival of the British fleet in Danish waters had been strategically timed. The Russian fleet was still ice-bound at St. Petersburg and could not come to the assistance of Russia's ally. The Danish fleet was still in winter quarters at the naval harbour in Copenhagen. Crews had for the most part been demobilized and ships dismantled. In great haste, volunteers were recruited and guns were mounted in the ships, which were duly warped out of harbour and anchored in line to form a blockade of floating batteries capable of firing broadsides from one side only, their movements restricted to hauling and drawing on the anchor lines. *Admiral Olfert Fischer* was in command of the Danish fleet.

Parker headed the English fleet south towards Copenhagen and sent Nelson into action with 35 ships, 1,192 guns, 14 mortars and 8,885 experienced men, most of them with several years of naval service to their credit, hardened to the rigours of both war and sea. The Danish force comprised 630 guns and 5,234 men, the majority of whom were newly enlisted volunteers.

Nelson had sounded the depth of the water at the southern end of the line the night before. The way in which he exploited the situation was masterly. He lined his ships up opposite the anchored Danish vessels, whereupon the bombardment soon became intense. The people of Copenhagen crowded along the harbour moles and up on the ramparts of the Citadel, craning their necks to catch a glimpse of what was happening, but all they saw was a tremendous cloud of gunpowder smoke that hid both the fleets:

only the mast-tops and their pennants still remained visible. It took Nelson about 1½ hours to manoeuvre into position, but by 11 o'clock the battle was in full swing. It lasted some 5 hours and fighting was violent on both sides. Despite the Danes' inferior strength and their inability to manoeuvre, Nelson on several occasions found himself in difficulties. Parker signalled

Forestilling af Slaget d. 2^den April 1801 om Eftermiddagen Klokken 3. da Admiral Lord Nelson fendte Parlementer Baaden i Lund.
1. Krigskibet Kroner. 2. Krigskibet Dannemark. 3. Fregatten Iris. 4. Blokskibet Dannebrog. fejler fra Battalien da Ilden var udbrudt og kort efter sprang i Luften 5 Lord Nelsons Skib. 6. Admiral Parker's Skib. 7. det store Batterie. 8. det lidet Batterie. 9. Parlementer Baaden med trende Engelske Officerer

Contemporary naive print of the Battle of Copenhagen. Nelson's parleyers are rowing ashore with a white flag.

to him to break off the fight, but it was on this occasion that Nelson put his telescope to his blind eye and said: "I see no signal." Finally he terminated the action himself by sending a message ashore to say that if the fight were continued he would set fire to the Danish floating batteries that had been captured, together with their crews. The Crown Prince gave instructions to Olfert Fischer to sound the cease fire, whereupon Nelson declared himself the victor. Even though some Danish historians have contended that the outcome of the battle might otherwise have been different, it must be remembered that the whole of the rest of the English fleet under Admiral Parker was still intact out in the Sound, and had the fight been continued or resumed with such Danish naval reserves as were ready to put to sea, it would still probably have resulted in an unequal contest for the Danish forces. Losses on both sides were considerable. Out of 5,324

Danes, only 2,215 returned ashore unscathed; 370 died in action and a further 106 died of wounds shortly afterwards. The English losses, though believed to have been greater, are not known with exactitude. A total of 1,200 dead and wounded was reported, although Parker later, in the course of his controversy with Nelson, claimed the figure to have been

"Defenders of the Fatherland, 2nd April 1801". By the Danish painter Eckersberg.

2,237. H.M.S. "Ardent" and H.M.S. "Monarch" alone lost 94 and 220 men respectively. Nelson himself reported his own officer and "civilian functionary" losses as being 51 dead and wounded and the Danish losses as 32.

The outcome of the battle was a Danish defeat, but the moral effect in Denmark and Norway of "The Battle of Copenhagen" on Maundy Thursday, April 2, 1801, was tremendous. Negotiations were partly conducted ashore. Nelson met the Crown Prince and accepted gifts. While negotiations were still in progress a message was received to the effect that Czar Paul had been assassinated. His successor, *Alexander I*, was pro-English – so Denmark stood alone. Even if she had won the battle she would still have had to give in. The Danes suffered one bitter disappointment, long remembered: a Swedish fleet was supposed to come from Karlskrona and relieve the Danish fleet, but although thousands of pairs of eyes peered hopefully across the Sound, it never arrived.

Peace between the Wars

The French Revolution had ended with Napoleon's assumption of power, the foundation of his Empire, and his starting to do just as he pleased with the whole of Europe. There were wars going on everywhere, and it was impossible in the long run to steer the two Scandinavian kingdoms clear of all the flames. Dano-Norwegian trade continued to prosper. Like all the members of Europe's ancient royal houses, Denmark's Crown Prince at first looked with contempt upon the corporal upstart on the imperial throne of France. He made up his mind that if the situation should become untenable he would, despite the 1801 affair and all English pressure on our mercantile trading, side up with England – partly out of liking, and partly because a war against the world's greatest maritime power would be catastrophic for Denmark and Norway, whose greatest asset was their merchant navy, the second largest in the world. But at the *Treaty of Tilsit* in 1807, France and Russia secretly decided that Denmark and Norway were to close all their ports to English ships. Napoleon knew that the Scandinavian kingdoms would refuse and therefore gave orders to Marshal Bernadotte, who was in northern Germany at the time, to the effect that, if it should prove necessary, he was to march north into Jutland and force the Crown Prince to obey.

The Bombardment of Copenhagen – Loss of the Fleet

Nothing was known about the Franco-Russian agreements in London, but the English perhaps wished to keep one jump ahead of anything in that line – even though Denmark was entirely blameless. England therefore sent a fleet – consisting of 25 ships of the line, 40 frigates, several smaller vessels and 377 transports – to Denmark. It passed Kronborg, where fleet and fortress exchanged courtesy salutes – after all, we were on friendly terms with England. At the same time an English envoy arrived in Kiel to speak to the Crown Prince who was there with the Danish army. The envoy demanded that *Denmark enter into an alliance with England*, thereby merely anticipating somewhat brusquely what the Crown Prince already had in mind. At the same time however, the English envoy demanded on behalf of his government that Denmark and Norway *hand over the entire Dano-Norwegian navy in pawn* for the duration of "the present situation". This last demand was a bit too much for the Crown Prince. He said that he was not in a position to commit himself to an immediate answer and referred the envoy to the Council of State and the King in Copenhagen. Thereupon he himself departed with all speed for the capital.

He arrived just as the huge English fleet was casting anchor in the Sound. Copenhagen was not prepared for an attack. The situation was precisely the same as on the occasions when Charles X and Charles XII of Sweden had threatened the city. Once again the army was down by the southern border, this time in readiness to meet Marshal Bernadotte's troops. Copenhagen's defence ramparts, though admittedly intact, were overgrown with beautiful green trees. There were very few guns ready for action. Above all, there were no troops worth mentioning stationed in Zealand, where no danger was anticipated. After all, the big threat had seemed to be the war in Europe, which was constantly getting closer to Holstein. Bombarded in turns by representatives of both the English and French governments, the Crown Prince made the necessary arrangements, placed the defence of the city in the hands of *General Peymann* with orders not to shoot first (for he still could not bring himself to believe that England really meant her threats in earnest) and then went back to the army in Holstein, this time taking his mad father and the members of the Council of State with him.

In the Danish capital, paralysis changed to indignation. Everybody became seized with violent feelings of patriotism. But the paralysis was still there. 150 years previously, when Charles X had drawn up his troops outside the city and prepared to lay siege, Frederick III had remained with his subjects. This time everybody had left. A volunteer corps was nevertheless formed, and block-ships positioned to the north and south of the city actually succeeded in keeping the English fleet at a distance. Thus the city could not be bombarded from the sea, and the English did not wish to risk another naval battle in the harbour like the one fought in 1801. Instead, English forces consisting of a Hannoverian corps sent up from northern Germany landed at *Vedbaek*, a few miles up the coast, and at *Koege*, to the south of the capital. In the course of a not particularly bloody skirmish known in Danish history as "the wooden-shoe battle of Koege", a regiment of Zealandic "militia", armed but otherwise untrained peasant lads, was put to flight by the English troops. The English invasion force

Contemporary print of the bombardment of Copenhagen entitled: "The Friendly Bombardment of Copenhagen by the English on the 2nd, 3rd and 4th September, 1807".

amounted to 30,000 men under the command of General Wellesley, later the *Duke of Wellington*. Against them Zealand was able to muster some 12,000 men, of which only 5,000 were professional soldiers, the rest being civic guards, gamekeepers, and members of the Danish Voluntary Corps. The English artillery had taken up positions by September 1, and the English battery commander sent the commandant of Copenhagen a final note demanding the surrender of the Danish fleet. He received an evasive answer, whereupon he gave orders to commence the bombardment of the city, behind whose old ramparts the dwellings of some 100,000 inhabitants were densely crowded. For three days bombs rained down upon the city. The fire brigade was unable to cope with all the fires, the streets were blocked by people attempting to flee, and still the bombs continued to fall. With the exception of a few short intervals, the bombardment was kept up from half-past seven on Wednesday evening until five o'clock on Saturday afternoon. The Church of Our Lady*), the University, and considerable areas in the Noerreport quarter were all reduced to rubble, 300 buildings were totally destroyed, and 1,600 badly damaged. Of the city's active defendants, 188 were killed and 346 wounded, and of the civilian population, 1,600 men women and children lost their lives and a further thousand were badly wounded. General Peymann gave up and sent negotiators over to the English camp. The terms were still the same, i.e. the fleet was to be handed over, but this time unconditionally. No longer was it to be accepted in pawn. It was to be war booty.

Danes will be Danes. They were seething with indignation and bitter with sorrow, but on Monday, two days after the last bombs had fallen on the city, while flames were still crackling in the houses and smoke was still pouring through the streets, while approximately 2,000 corpses still lay unburied and more than a thousand people lay wounded wherever space could be found for them, and despite the fact that not a single family in the city had failed to suffer from the catastrophe, hundreds of Copenhageners wearing their Sunday best nonetheless strolled out in the September sunshine through the west gate of the city in order to visit the lovely royal park of "Soendermark" near Frederiksberg Castle and have a look at all the kilted Scots in their picturesque camp.

The English seized the Royal Dockyard and all the naval storehouses and magazines, and likewise occupied the naval harbour. All ships were made ready for sea. The entire contents of the naval storehouses – sails, ropes, mast-timber, guns, cannon-balls, powder, provisions, every single thing, even down to charts, telescopes and octants – was stuffed on board, and what they were unable to take with them they destroyed on the spot. Five ships still on their stocks were overturned and their costly timbers hacked into and rendered unserviceable, whereafter the entire Dano-Norwegian fleet then stationed in Copenhagen was hauled out of the harbour for the last time. There went the pride and joy of the twin kingdoms, gliding out to sea. The people of Copenhagen looked on in silence and Danish naval officers wept. The fleet sailed northwards up through the Sound, and by the time it passed Kronborg on this final

*) rebuilt after the fire of 1728.

196

voyage, the beaches were black with people watching in deathly silence as their beloved vessels slid slowly past. It was still hard to realize what had actually taken place. The whole affair seemed so absurd. After all, Danish and Norwegian sympathies were more or less *with* England.

The English booty, strictly speaking, did not include the entire Dano-Norwegian fleet. Although the majority of its vessels were in port at the

"The last deed of the English in Copenhagen, 1807" – ships on stocks in the Naval Harbour being destroyed. Eckersberg.

time, not all were. In total, 15 good ships of the line, 10 frigates, 5 corvettes and 14 smaller ships were taken to England. One vessel the English gallantly left behind: this was a pleasure frigate that had been presented as a gift by the English King to his nephew the Crown Prince. That same year, Denmark sent it to England manned by a crew of repatriate English prisoners-of-war, together with a note to the effect that "this vessel would appear to have been inadvertently forgotten".

The equipment removed from the naval harbour in Copenhagen filled, *over and above* what was stuffed aboard the warships, 92 transports and weighed 20,000 tons.

However, the English did not manage to take everything. This was partly because their ships could not hold any more, partly because some of the equipment was out-dated, and partly because they did not know their way round the Danish naval depot. The Danes actually succeeded in hiding quite a lot. After the English had pulled out there still remained some 1,000 guns complete with mountings, 26,000 cannon balls and bombs, 6,000 pounds of gunpowder, a large supply of saltpetre and sulphur, likewise quite a lot of serviceable timber. And so the Danes immediately started building new ships, not ships of the line, but gunboats. Voluntary gifts and donations came streaming in to support the enterprise.

A final point: even though the plundering of the naval base by the English far surpassed anything the Danes would ever have dreamed possible, the English did not, beyond the fact that they seized booty and carried out military operations, behave in a hostile manner. In fact one record says that "... on the whole the English army observed good discipline and paid for everything which was supplied for the support of the troops; moreover upon its departure commissaries were left behind to settle all legal claims." In England the course of events was regarded on the whole as satisfactory, but protests were heard in several quarters. Seven members of the House of Lords refused to sign the address of thanks submitted to the country's military leaders, pointing out that no proof had existed either of Denmark's hostile intentions or of the necessity of attacking Copenhagen.

The Seven Years' War of the North

After this there could be no doubts as to where Denmark stood. The Crown Prince joined up with Napoleon. This was doubtless stupid of him, but nevertheless understandable, for Danish grief and indignation got the upper hand of plain political sense. From 1807 to 1814 Denmark and England were engaged in open war, but as the Danish navy had been reduced to nil, the English navy was able to control Danish territorial waters. From 1807 onwards, Denmark waged *a gunboat war*. A number of small gunboats and other smaller craft were quickly built (there was neither time, timber or money to build larger ships) and hundreds of Danish merchantman captains were granted letters of 'marque and reprisal' and had their ships fitted out with guns. This 'private' fleet alone amounted to 600 vessels of varying sizes carrying a total of some 1,000 guns, though of course they were by no means as effective as 1,000 guns mounted aboard proper naval ships. By means of this gunboat warfare the Danes managed to inflict quite a lot of damage on English shipping. Denmark was able to console herself with a number of successful skirmishes at sea and the conquest of a few small naval craft (nine brigs and several smaller vessels and boats) but it was not of much help as regards turning the tide of the war. Norway had been hardest hit, for her ports and coastlines were blockaded by the English navy. All imports had to be smuggled into the country. Norway had insufficient breadstuffs herself and so a shortage arose – in fact in many districts there was famine.

Denmark was sucked into the European whirlpool, but Norway remained passive and closed off. There were several battles in northern Germany, but no matter how many the reports of victories won, the situation remained unsolved and the losses unrepaired. Denmark's days of prosperity were over. The war had completely destroyed her maritime trade, her tiny, distant tropical colonies were practically cut off from the mother country, and the national economy was in danger.

At the same time, Denmark and Norway once more found themselves at war with Sweden, and were thus in a predicament. Napoleon therefore sent an auxiliary force up into Jutland under the same Marshal Bernadotte who not so long previously had been on his way, not to lend assistance, but to occupy Jutland. The plan this time was that he should attack Scania, but his auxiliary army, consisting of 23,000 Spanish and French troops, got no further than the island of Funen. It was supposed to cross over to Zealand, but the English were blocking the Great Belt. In the meantime the Spanish troops heard news (tactically passed on by the English) of the rebellion in Spain and gratefully accepted offers of passages home aboard English ships. Apart from burning down Jutland's last Renaissance castle, the big fortress of Koldinghus, the auxiliary force achieved nothing.

Denmark still had one ship of the line left. The "Prince Christian Frederick" had not been in Denmark in 1807. She was now given orders to decoy the English ships away from Great Belt so that Bernadotte could get across. Late one evening, the "Prince Christian Frederick" found herself surrounded by five English men-o'-war off a spit of land known as *Sjaelland's Odde*. There were 200 green, untrained recruits on board which merely served to increase the enemy's superiority. The commander of the "Prince Christian Frederick", Captain Jessen, had decoyed the English away from Great Belt as instructed, but now he was obliged to stand and fight. That evening, March 22, darkness had already fallen by 7 p.m. Firing commenced half an hour later. At 10.30 p.m., after three hours' fighting, Jessen ran his ship aground and surrendered. More than a third of his crew were dead or wounded. The English tried to get the vessel afloat again, but she caught fire and exploded. Those who died were buried in a churchyard on *Sjaelland's Odde*, just opposite where the battle took place. *Lieutenant Willemoes*, the young Danish naval hero of the Battle of Copenhagen, died in this fight.

The Separation of the Twin Kingdoms

Sweden's anti-French King had been deposed. Sweden had to surrender Finland to Russia, and the King's uncle was elected to the throne as *Charles XIII*. But he had no children. For a time there was a vague plan afoot to establish Scandinavian unity by electing a Dane as heir to the throne, but a new candidate was then unexpectedly manoeuvred into the picture. Sweden wanted to remain on good terms with Europe's lord and master, Napoleon, and therefore chose one of his marshals, *Bernadotte* (already known to the Danes) as successor to the Swedish throne – a selection which caused some surprise. Marshal Bernadotte accepted, arrived in Sweden, and almost immediately broke with Napoleon. This altered the position in Scandinavia. Bernadotte was French, completely unfamiliar with Scandinavian history and traditions, and, being a pupil of Napoleon, did not take such matters too seriously anyway. As Sweden's new leader he felt he ought to make some sort of gesture to his new people, whose language was practically unintelligible to him. Sweden had lost Finland to Russia, and that was of course a matter with which it would be inadvisable to meddle. But, with a map spread out in front of him, Bernadotte realized that he would be able to appease some of the Swedes' bitterness at their loss of Finland by the simple expedient of making them a present of Norway. Denmark had been greatly weakened by the war. In Norway, which had suffered badly, there was a certain amount of unrest, and in many Norwegian circles it was realized that

BRIGGEN LOUGEN
COMMAND... CAPT:LIEUT: IESSEN ANGREBET UNDER ST THOMAS af 2DE ENGELSKE FREGATTER SOM EFTER EEN SKAR
CANONADE NODES ILDE TILREDTE AT FORLADE SAMME.
DETE FOREFALDEN DEN 3DE MARTY 1801.

*The Danish brig Lougen (The Law)
putting two English ships to flight
after a violent exchange of gunfire off
St. Thomas, the Virgin Islands. 1801.*

*Silver cup donated to the University of
Copenhagen by King James of Scotland
in 1590, melted when the University
burned down in 1807 during the English
bombardment. National Museum.*

Scottish camp in Soendermarken, 1807. They brought their wives and children with them.

Danish gunboats attacking an English convoy during the war years, 1807 to 1814.

Denmark and Norway could not maintain the same interests for ever. The war with England had been catastrophic for Norway on account of the disruption caused in trade relations between the two countries. Denmark's former attacker and helper, Bernadotte, wanted Norway, and the European powers saw no reason why hindrances should be placed in his way. Bernadotte had turned his back on his old Emperor and drawn himself up into line with the victorious nations. Denmark was the loser.

Eidsvoll Manor in Norway, where the Norwegian Eidsvoll Constitution was signed in the spring of 1814.

Frederick VI's young cousin, *Prince Christian Frederick*, was viceroy in Norway, ruling the country with the assistance of a group of Norwegians. The situation was critical. Although it had been agreed in the councils of Europe that Bernadotte was to have Norway, things were now blowing up into a regular war between her and Sweden. To Bernadotte's military mind there was nothing strange in the thought of *conquering* Norway. There were a number of border incidents in which the Norwegians, despite their inferiority and poor equipment, acquitted themselves remarkably well. Christian Frederick then took over control of Norway as an independent King. This naturally pained his cousin Frederick in Denmark, but everything ended less violently than anticipated. The Norwegian Estates of the Realm met at *Eidsvoll* and agreed upon a free constitution under Christian Frederick's leadership, "the freest in the world", a *Basic Law* for the Kingdom of Norway. Christian Frederick received a letter from Frederick VI dated March 21, 1814, which constitutes one of the most human and nobly inspired documents in the hard-boiled history of these years. In it, King Frederick advises his cousin to yield. The whole situation was in Norway's disfavour, the outcome was inevitable, and Norwegian independence in the face of Europe's promise to Bernadotte was quite simply beyond the bounds of possibility. Frederick advised him merely to negotiate wisely, to procure for Norway as much independence and freedom within the limits of a real *union* with Sweden as he possibly could, and to "... seize every opportunity, endeavour to uphold Norway's independence, see to it that Norway obtain from the King of Sweden such terms as will allow of Norway's becoming a federative state under the Swedish King, seek to obtain for Norway all possible advantages in respect of trade and shipping, see to it that the country's taxes be not raised, that the army remain as it stands, that it be not used for purposes other than the defence of the country, that public servants be chosen from amongst the nation's own native subjects, that the university retain its right of existence, see to it that thou securest everything thou possibly canst for thy people and for the land of Norway ... then shall I see in thee a great man, one that hath spared Norway from anarchy and done everything within his power to save the fates of 900,000 people. God, Who knoweth my heart, will not, when we come before His Judgment Seat, fail to appreciate this my conduct."

This is Frederick's farewell to Norway and the Norwegian people. Bernadotte yielded and did not succeed in incorporating Norway within the Kingdom of Sweden as a conquered country. He was obliged to endorse the Eidsvoll Constitution and acknowledge a Norwegian self-governing parliament – in other words, accept an equally balanced union. Just how glaringly Frederick VI's attitude contrasted with that of his contempories, at a time when the borders, nations, and human fates of Europe were handled like chessmen, can be judged from the remarkable fact (seen from a present-day viewpoint) that England, in order to console Frederick VI and get him to relinquish Norway and thus satisfy Bernadotte, proposed that Denmark, in compensation for her loss, could be given: *Holland*. Frederick said he did not feel he could really accept this gesture.

For Denmark, the seven years of war and the way they terminated proved an almost unbearable defeat: Norway gone, the fleet destroyed, maritime trade crushed. For England, the advantages to be obtained in meeting Bernadotte's wishes and thus, by effecting the separation of Denmark and Norway, splitting the world's second largest merchant navy, could not be ignored. The opportunity which the twin kingdoms had had of dominating world maritime trade was thus shattered.

That England, in the final phase of the war, should become Denmark's ally and render Denmark considerable support during her conflict with Sweden, was too abrupt and paradoxical a switch for the Danes to accept unhesitatingly. The British Embassy in Copenhagen had its windows smashed. Nevertheless, England's support, in view of the fact that Dano–Norwegian maritime trade had now been crushed, was a great help in Denmark's predicament.

The decisive fact remained that the Crown Prince had allied himself with the losing side, i.e. Napoleon. Denmark nevertheless managed to take part in the Congress of Vienna, but the damage was already done.

The war was over. The 439-year union between Denmark and Norway was dissolved. The dissolution would have come about in due course anyway, for Norway was already beginning to liberate herself nationally from Denmark. But if things had been allowed to develop more harmoniously, Norway would probably have obtained her complete independence straight away. As things turned out, she was now to find herself involved in another union for a further 91 years.

The Danish position at the outbreak of nearly every war may puzzle some people: did the Danes then never learn? Time and again the same strategic situation, time and again apparently the same mistakes, e.g. the army inconveniently in Holstein just when the attack was being launched in Zealand. The difficulty is the geography of the country, unique in Europe: the Scanian provinces, Jutland and the five hundred islands. Until 1658 Denmark's borders to the south and east were threatened, and since then the kingdom's weak point has been the southern border at the root of Jutland. It is here that the army should be stationed in readiness. If the enemy should launch his attack elsewhere, against Copenhagen, for instance, the army cannot just march to the scene of action for it has to be *shipped*. The moving of troops from one end of Denmark to the next has always been complicated for it involves maritime transportation and it is impossible to have a fleet of transports lying eternally in readiness. Time and again this fact has decided Denmark's destiny.

The situations are often similar, yet each time they develop in a fairly logical and explainable way. Too much confidence was probably placed – just as the English in England as an entity – in Zealand's being an island and therefore naturally protected. And then there was no interest in military matters, for an earthbound, sober outlook makes for little interest in war. The Danes are not militarists and in reality never were. When in olden days the King sent out a call to arms the peasants responded and fought, feuds might brew and provoke people into taking sides, and in times of stress the odd thing might happen. But it always took time to get started. Later on, during the 17th and 18th centuries, the fleet was generally in good shape, in fact during the wars against Sweden it was definitely the superior force. But when England attacked Denmark the country had been enjoying a period of peace for almost a hundred years. Her ships were good enough, and so were her crews, but they lacked battle experience and nobody wanted war, for it was regarded as destructive and pointless. Even as far back as the Viking Age, under Sweyn Forkbeard, the "peace party" formed by the Danish peasants was seemingly a very big one. In 1814, when Denmark was separated from Norway, it was felt to be pointless to join in the major European strife. But the most contributory factor has probably been the ingrained peasant-thrift mentality that regards money spent on arms as money spent unwisely. One sometimes has the feeling that the Danish outlook has never developed beyond the idea that, in time of war, you take your rusty battle-axe down from the wall – or go and try to find it in the woodshed where it has been serving a useful purpose – and sharpen it on a grindstone. It is difficult to make people realize – in peacetime – that newer forms of war require materials and preparations which cannot be produced at short notice – as in ancient times when the enemy suddenly appeared in your paddock. Preparedness has seldom been a strong point in Danish history. The Danes are too tied up with everyday life, are blessed with too great a sense of humour to be eternally *en garde*. Their mentality dictates their fate.

Something was still left to Denmark of the old Scandinavian kingdom, for when Bernadotte was presented with Norway, he was not given the old Norwegian dependencies as well. Denmark retained *Greenland*, *Iceland*, and the *Faroe Islands*, and still owned small colonies in the tropics: the *Virgin Islands* in the West Indies, some trading stations on the coast of *Guinea*, the Indian trading stations of *Tranquebar* and *Fredericknagore*, and the *Nicobars*. But the Danish colonies were not worth very much, the prime reason for their lack of success being that they were much too small. Denmark had put a stop to the import of negro slaves on its West Indian islands in 1792 – the first country in the world to forbid slave-trading – and together with the falling off of the slave trade, one of the Guinea coast's most lucrative sources of income disappeared.

Medallion commemorating abolition of slave-trade in 1792.

IX. THE FINAL YEARS
OF THE ABSOLUTE MONARCHY

Denmark was alone. The country was regarded as being impoverished and on the verge of disintegration. In 1813, while the war was still on, the Danish state had gone bankrupt. Her finances simply collapsed. Reconstruction after the war proceeded but slowly at first. General conditions were extremely poor, and throughout the land things seemed to be at a standstill. Not quite everything: shipping began to pick up slowly again, and during the war Danish literature and art had unfolded, developing richly romantic schools. Patriotic feelings were aroused, poets wrote laudatory verses, literary salons sprang up in idyllic rural surroundings, and culture radiated from literary manor houses and vicarages.

At the same time, a contrasting nationalism began to arise. The loss of Norway resulted in a threat to upset Denmark's internal balance. The old monarchy had consisted of Denmark, Norway, and Holstein. Now that Norway had gone, the German Holstein element began to make itself felt in the life of the country to a far greater extent than hitherto. During the past generation, the Norwegian element had been very pronounced, both in intellectual life and amongst the country's civil servants. Numerous Danes had been civil servants in Norway, but just as many Norwegians had been civil servants (priests, in particular) in Denmark. This Scandinavian interchange was now over. Instead, many Holstein civil servants and business people started making their appearance in Danish towns. On the one hand, the Danes now began to be aware of this danger of a pure Germanization; on the other, a national spirit began to grow up amongst Holsteiners in the province of Holstein, inspired naturally enough by the German national rising in conjunction with the romanticist movement and the Napoleonic Wars. Holsteiners saw greater visions towards the south. In increasing numbers, they began to regard any form of contact with tottering Denmark as unfortunate.

Frederick VI sat on his throne, the absolute monarch of his people. Despite the fact that he was no genius and no doubt often made wrong decisions, his integrity was beyond question. He symbolized the fact that the country still existed; he was a contact with the past, and this at a time when the country could see the past collapsing unmercifully. The mighty rococo palace of Christiansborg had been gutted by fire, the Church of Our Lady lay in ruins, Hirschholm Castle had been built on too soft soil and began to show cracks, the fleet had gone, and so had Norway. But Danish poets discovered that the ancient Nordic past could be a substitute for classical Greece. Tragedies were written about Nordic gods and goddesses, and writers "... became conscious of the spirit and conscience of Scandinavia". And there on his old throne sat King Frederick, with his "dearly beloved family" about him. He was a father to his two peoples, the Danes and the Holsteiners. He was their commander-in-chief, departmental manager and administrator, was aware of *everything* that went on, and did *everything* himself, even the most trivial of tasks. Just like old Christian IV, he issued an endless stream of ordinances and orders concerning matters both large and small, right down to petty details which one would think could have been attended to by persons on the spot, such as: "... the linen articles belonging to the field hospital which are stored in Glückstadt (in Holstein) shall be aired once or twice during fine weather in order that no harm be occasioned them by damp." And every night, on the simple, white-painted, deal writing-desk in his bedchamber, were placed the keys to the four gates of the city of Copenhagen.

But it was here, over the course of the next 50 years or so, in this atmosphere of modest demands and thriftiness, that *Hans Andersen* wandered round the streets and talked to the inventor of electro-magnetism, *H. C. Oersted*, here that *Soeren Kierkegaard*, the theological philosopher, and *Grundtvig*, the spiritual revivalist of the Danish people, both strolled, here that *Oehlenschläger*, Denmark's national poet, lived and wrote, here that the news was received with a mixture of pride and joy that *Thorvaldsen*, in his studio in Rome (after an Englishman with the promising name of *Sir Thomas Hope* had provided him with working capital by commissioning his first major work, "Jason", in carrara marble) had started to revive classical Greek sculpture. It was at this time that *Eckersberg*, the father of modern Danish painting, was living in Copenhagen and painting pictures for Denmark's bourgeois homes, picture after picture, always of sailing ships (what else did the Danes want him to paint?) ship after ship, endless

Caricature of the theological philosopher and author, Søren Kierkegaard, drawn by Marstrand.

flotillas of white-sailed men-o'-war ploughing through the water, in and out amongst the bright green islands, always in beautiful sailing weather, peacefully, Eckersberg's great idyll of the Danish Armada, balsam on the deep Danish wounds, sailing ships painted with the precision and detail of rigging diagrams – they had to be, for those who commissioned them knew every plank.

When old Frederick VI died, he was genuinely mourned throughout the country. With him, a whole era passed to the grave, a Denmark that was never to return, an era of reverses and deep disappointments, one during which many errors were committed. But then people realized too, that it was asking a lot to try and steer a ship of state unscathed through the typhoon that Napoleon chose to let loose over Europe. Danish peasants carried their King's coffin along the last part of the road from Copenhagen to the Cathedral in Roskilde, the burial place of Denmark's royal heads.

Frederick VI's cousin Christian, the Eidsvoll prince who gave Norway her free constitution, became *Christian VIII*, whereupon everybody hoped he would give Denmark a constitution too. Nobody had felt they could be so brutal as to ask old Frederick about it and moreover he had made known his own views on the matter by his precise, self-confident declaration: "We alone know what is for the good of the people."

The cartoonist Fritz Jürgensen captured the bourgeoisie of Copenhagen in a series of drawings during the first half of the 19th century. Here "A Game of Chess".

But Christian VIII was by now a middle-aged man, disappointed, subject to spells of melancholic bitterness. He was concerned about the growing German nationalism in Holstein and the southern part of Slesvig; he observed with some displeasure the youth of the capital demonstrating enthusiastically its approval of 'liberty'; he provided bursaries out of the money-box in his own writing-desk for artists and writers so that they could spend a number of years abroad and thereby improve their talents. In order to pave the way for complete liberty, assemblies of the Estates of the Realm had been introduced during the reign of Frederik VI. Christian himself did not feel that he was empowered to go any further. His "language decrees" were an attempt to pacify the unrest prevailing in Slesvig, but, not having been formulated with much foresight, the effect they produced was contrary to his intentions.

The situation was obviously once more very critical. Admittedly Denmark had once more succeeded in recovering from her troubles with astonishing rapidity, shipping was prospering once again, merchants and shipowners in the provincial towns were making good money, the citizens of Copenhagen were doing very nicely, the peasants were continuing their efforts to make agricultural progress, and intellectual movements were dawning. But even so, there was a paralysing bitterness behind it all. Writers wrote and people read, but no matter how idyllic everything appeared, the people could not get over the grave shocks and losses the country had suffered, despite the white sails that once more could be seen tacking in and out between the five hundred islands. It was much too obvious that Denmark's position amongst European nations had sunk so low that she hardly counted as a country any more. Foreigners came visiting and described what they found in disdainful tones. In people's hearts was still the memory of how things had been before the catastrophe, but it was seldom they allowed their feelings to manifest themselves.

Sarcastic criticism of the old autocratic system had already commenced to break out in many circles during the reign of Frederick VI, and during Christian VIII's reign such criticism increased – not only in Denmark, but also in Holstein. And when Christian VIII died, the crisis came to a head.

X. THE CONSTITUTION
THE SLESVIG WARS

Christian VIII's son, *Frederick VII*, was neither loved nor admired. He had wrecked two marriages, was known to be somewhat vague and moody, and was not considered reliable. In fact nobody knew quite how to handle him. Revolutions in Denmark have a habit of taking place in their own special way. In 1660, when absolute monarchy was introduced, the King merely had a talk with some of the leading men in the country and then announced that from then on there would be absolute monarchy - and that was all. In 1848 there was unrest all over Europe. Shots were ringing out in the streets of Berlin and Paris. In Denmark, feelings mounted to such extraordinary heights that a number of honest citizens donned their top hats and frock coats, went to see the King, and told him that from now on they wanted a free constitution. They got it.

A number of meetings were held in the capital and a "constituent assembly" gathered in order to draw up the new constitution. Almost at the same time however, an uprising broke out in Holstein. The *Prince of Noer* assumed power by informing the garrison in Rendsborg that the citizens of Copenhagen had risen in rebellion and were threatening the King.

A curious state of affairs arose: just as Denmark was winning her political liberty, she went to war against the Holstein rebels, who were not interested in Danish liberty, merely in their own. From a Danish standpoint the situation was logical enough, though seen through foreign eyes it must have seemed a little peculiar. A Schleswig-Holstein revolutionary government was set up, whereupon the political situation became very complicated for one very definite reason: Denmark virtually had nothing against the German province of Holstein's wishing to pursue its German sympathies, but a document signed in 1481 now took on the character of a time-bomb. When Christian I first tried to settle the eternally muddled Slesvig question, he had decreed that the two duchies should remain forever undivided. His idea naturally was that Slesvig was ancient Danish territory, and that by binding the two provinces together, Hol-

Fallen Danish soldier. Sketch by the Danish painter Simonsen, who accompanied the troops in the field.
Opposite: Danish riflemen in an open wood.

stein would thus become permanently bound to Denmark. But he did not say so in so many words, and so now the Holsteiners pointed at the old document and said: "Now we're leaving you and going over to Germany, and we're going to take the whole of Slesvig with us – because the two provinces are to remain forever undivided, *up ewig ungedeelt.*" Despite the fact that Denmark fully respected Holstein's German character and German sympathies, it was nevertheless felt that the old state of affairs, i.e. both duchies being joined to Denmark, should be sacrosanct.

During the foregoing years the southern part of Slesvig had gradually become Germanized. The province was generally administered by German-speaking civil servants, and Christian VIII's misunderstood "language decrees" had irritated the population to such an extent that in Angel for instance, everybody had deliberately gone over to speaking German – for in the border country everybody was (and is) able to speak both languages. It was in order to retain Slesvig that Denmark went to war against the revolutionary army that had been mobilized. Volunteers streamed in from the German states to help the Holsteiners and the Germans in South Slesvig, and the "Schleswig-Holstein question" became a matter dear to the heart of every German.

The first battles were won by the Danish army, but when Prussia declared war on Denmark and marched up through Slesvig, the position became untenable. The war lasted three years, but there was only fighting

during the summer months. The rebel army surrounded the old fortress town of Fredericia, but the Danish army managed to launch a sortie resulting in an important victory which had great moral effect. Prussia withdrew from the war and left matters in the hands of the revolutionary army. On July 25, 1850, the two armies met at *Isted Heath* for the decisive battle. The Danish army numbered slightly more than 40,000 and the Schleswig-Holstein forces approximately 27,000. The front was three miles long and the battle lasted all day, starting at 3.30 a.m. It ended in a victory for the Danes and the retreat of the Schleswig-Holstein forces. The war was thus over, even though there were a few more minor skirmishes. By the terms of the peace treaty, Slesvig and Holstein became Danish once more, and in Denmark the victory was regarded as complete.

During the course of the war the "constituent assembly" completed its work, and on June 5, 1849, the new constitution was agreed upon and signed. From now on, Denmark was to be ruled by a governmental assembly consisting of two chambers to be known as the *Folketing*, or Lower

House, and the *Landsting*, or Upper House. The King's position was laid down "constitutionally", and all Danish *men* aged 30 and above were granted the right to vote on the basis of 'one man, one vote'.

Thus Denmark's absolute monarchy, having been in force for 190 years, was finally overthrown. It was already out-dated at the time of its fall, but the reason why it fell as late as it did and why it was retained for so long, was that it was never abused to the point of being intolerable. During the 190-year period, none of Denmark's Kings had been tyrants, and the administration of justice had never become arbitrary. In fact Molesworth, the scorner of Denmark's system of absolute monarchy, admitted, as mentioned, that her state of legislation was better and more reliable, and her courts of law more approachable and cheaper, than in England, despite England's political freedom. Nothing could take place without passing through the law courts; nobody could be imprisoned or executed without due legal procedure being taken and judgment being passed. All the absolute monarchs had been upright men within the limits of their abilities. Most of them managed to procure themselves the services of good, at times excellent, ministers. Even under the mad King, Christian VII, the government of the country did not collapse, and the period during which it was abused, i. e. the Struensee episode, was only a short interlude. Most of the autocratic monarchs worked energetically and conscientiously in the interests of their twin kingdoms, and it had thus been difficult to work up a sufficiently powerful opposition when everything appeared to be proceeding peacefully and reasonably well. Moreover, although it is correct, from a political standpoint, that democracy was introduced in Denmark in 1849 with the signing of the new constitution, it was in reality based upon very ancient traditions that provided a foundation upon which Denmark's new political democracy could rest: for hundreds of years (or thousands, more likely) the ancient Danish rural settlements had been independent. After the Viking Age and the establishment of a united Danish Kingdom, centuries were to pass before monarchy and newer forms of administration took a firm hold on the country's self-governing settlements, a self-government which continued through village *thing* meetings and through town councils. Throughout the land, people were accustomed to discussing matters at meetings and making decisions. One valuable tradition in particular had been maintained, a tradition that happens to be one of the most difficult to introduce in newly established democracies, in fact almost impossible: there had always existed an ancient, unfailing ability to choose more or less the right leaders. Election propaganda was of very little importance, for

A series of drawings told the home front about the war going on "over there". The pictures were always unwarlike and rather jolly. Here, a platoon advancing through the country as if on a carefree outing.

people had a knack of picking sober-minded, sensible men, and no time for fly-by-nights. A political system and political practice may be disinterested in, even irritated by, this ancient, genial tradition, may even to a certain extent try to counteract it in order to push forward a party candidate, but the old tradition is always there in the background. Without it, Danish democracy would have been helpless.

Even so, the men who were entrusted with the government of the country after the three years of war were politically untried. They were not given a chance to practise quietly on peaceable, everyday problems. Naturally there had been political parties and group-dictated viewpoints even before the signing of the constitution – after all, the constitution had been the result of awakening political thought. The difficulty was still the Slesvig question, for although the majority of Danish citizens assumed that Denmark had won the war, the peace treaty stated the plain facts. It said, amongst other things, that *Denmark was not to bind Slesvig any more closely to herself than she bound Holstein*. And as Holstein was German territory with the Danish King as its Duke, there were very clear limits as to how intimately the two provinces could be incorporated within the realm. In other words, Denmark had not succeeded in re-covering Slesvig for herself unconditionally – a task which the Kings of Denmarks had been attempting for almost 700 years. When the rebellion and the war were over, Slesvig's administration had to be re-established. Royalistic, Danish-minded civil servants were therefore appointed to various posts. The ducal family of Augustenborg and some 30 revolutionary leaders were exiled from the country, but otherwise no form of judicial settlement was attempted and nobody was accused or sentenced for actions carried out during the rebellion and war years. The language problem was more difficult to solve, and the new government did what it could to get the matter under control. It was decreed that in the northern part of Slesvig the official language was to be Danish, and in the southern part, German. In the narrow strip across the province where the two languages mingled, it was decreed that the language in schools should be Danish. This was promptly contested in German propaganda attacks. An unforeseen difficulty cropped up in the actual system of government: it had been assumed that the new democratic constitution would apply to the whole of Denmark *including* Slesvig, but to this Prussia and Austria protested, declaring that it would serve to bind Slesvig closer to Denmark than Holstein. So in Slesvig the King was obliged to continue ruling autocratically in collaboration with the Estates of the Realm. This meant that Slesvig was attached to Denmark through the person of the King – and Frederick VII had no sons. Therefore Denmark decided that the question of the succession to the Danish throne must be approved and guaranteed internationally.

Between the Wars

The London protocol dated August 2, 1850 and signed by Denmark, the Swedo-Norwegian Union, England, France and Russia, confirms the

Battle of Isted, 1850.

*Money chest from the
Sound Customs
House at Elsinore.
Now at the museum
at Gothenburg.*

Danish soldiers man-handling a gun during the retreat from Danevirke in 1863.
Painted by Simonsen. Frederiksborg.

Entrenchment at Dybboel after the storming of April 18, 1864. German photograph.

desire of the signatory parties to "uphold the integrity of the Danish monarchy", and by the Treaty of London dated May 8, 1852 (also signed by Austria and Prussia) the signatory parties acknowledged *Prince Christian of Glücksburg* as heir to the Danish throne. Both he and his wife belonged to the old Royal Danish House. The Danish parliament voted its approval of the London Treaty, and the Duke of Augustenborg promised that he would refrain from making any further claims to the throne on behalf of his family provided he received, in return, compensation for his estates on the island of Als.

In this way it was presumed that the unity of the realm had been assured. A few defections however, had already taken place. During the 17th century, Denmark, as mentioned, had tried to take part in the race for colonies in the newly discovered lands overseas, and had actually managed to secure a foothold – but no more – in several places. It was the countries bordering on the Atlantic (for whom navigational conditions were much more favourable) that were able to help themselves to the rich, fabulous, strange worlds overseas. The Danish colonies and trading posts managed to exist and trade, but they never became very big. Sweden had tried too, but had been obliged to give up.

From 1845 to 1847, a Danish corvette, the "Galathea", commanded by Steen Bille, sailed round the world on a scientific expedition similar to the voyages of the "Beagle" and the "Challenger". Although this was a fine chance of displaying the Danish flag all round the globe, the captain nevertheless had the painful duty, in India, of striking the Danish flag at the fort in *Tranquebar*, which had been sold to the English East Asiatic Company for 2 million Danish *kroner*. It had proved impossible to develop the colony successfully as it was too small and prices were often forced down by the English trading company, which naturally enough was only interested in its own prosperity. The old Danish fort at Tranquebar still stands to this day and there are Danish tombstones crumbling away in the old churchyard. In 1850 Denmark sold her three colonial outposts on the coast of Guinea, *Christiansborg, Augustenborg*, and *Fredensborg*, to England. Here too, the old white fortresses are still standing, and old Danish guns, covered with verdigris and bearing the initials of Danish kings, still crown the walls.

As mentioned before, Denmark had tried several times to build a colony out of the island group south of India known as the *Nicobars*. A final serious effort was made from 1846 to 1856, but upon the expiration of this 10-year period the project was given up and the islands abandoned. In 1869 they were occupied by England. All Denmark had left were the *Virgin Islands* in the West Indies, and *Greenland*, "the world's largest island", which was not worth much, mainly a tremendous cake of ice, but at least there was considerable fishing and whaling. *Iceland* and the

Grindwhale catch at Vestmannahavn in the Faroe Isles.

Faroe Islands were Danish possessions out in the northern Atlantic. One by one the country lost her outposts, and when the old castle of *Frederiksborg* burned down in 1859, the English seafarer Captain Marryat, who happened to be an eye-witness, told how the Danes stood petrified as they watched their past perish in a sea of flames.

Yet another bit of past history was written off with admirable Danish diplomatic astuteness. Ever since 1429, when *Eric of Pomerania* introduced the Sound Dues, all foreign ships had had to pay toll when passing through the Sound and the Danish Belts. In other words, toll was exacted on all shipping passing in and out of the Baltic. It was a state of affairs that had caused Denmark endless political difficulties, had cost the country all the Scanian provinces (surrendered to Sweden in 1658) and although the dues had constituted an easy source of income, it is an open question

Ships in harbour at Julianehaab in Greenland.

whether an easy source of income is always a good thing for a state administration.

But now the maritime nations of the world had had enough. Sound Dues had been paid for no less than 428 years, in fact their payment was even continued 200 years after Denmark lost control of the Sound (one coast after all was now Swedish) and it is actually incredible that Denmark was able to perform the feat of exacting these irritating dues long after the justification for their introduction had ceased to exist. It is equally incredible that Denmark managed to settle matters with such skill as to render the final result little short of astonishing. All the maritime nations of the world could quite simply have terminated the agreements by declaring that they no longer wished to pay the dues – and just what would Denmark have been able to do?

The result of the negotiations was a treaty dated March 14, 1857, by the terms of which Denmark gave up her Sound and Belt Dues for ever and promised in future "never under any pretext whatsoever" to hinder the passage of a foreign vessel on its way through the Sound or the Belts – with the exception, naturally, of legally justified civilian detentions, or detentions performed for the purpose of avoiding maritime disasters, collisions, wrecks, etc.

In return, the twin kingdoms of Sweden and Norway, Belgium, France, the Netherlands, Prussia and 6 other German states, Russia, Great Britain and Austria undertook to pay Denmark a once-for-all indemnification of 30,476,000 rix-dollars. Converted at the present rate of exchange today this would amount to about £20,000,000. Similar agreements were drawn up with a number of other maritime nations as well (U.S.A., Portugal, Venuzuela, etc.) who likewise undertook to pay an indemnity. But today, a hundred years after the event, a couple of the high contracting signatory countries have still not paid up in full.

The discontinuation of the Sound Dues had one local effect: in Elsinore, the old toll port-town where nearly all the toll was collected, the abolition of the dues was catastrophic. Elsinore had been the most international town in Denmark. All ships had been obliged to cast anchor in its roadstead, which in turn had made for bustle and life in its streets, profits for its tradespeople, and a general stir of activity in the town and its taverns that was practically unique.

The Sound Dues had been introduced in their time by way of compensation for Denmark's obligation to provide lighthouses. The motivation for the large sum paid in commutation was that Denmark, with her 500 sea-washed islands and many shallow channels, was still obliged to maintain a very complicated lighthouse service for the benefit of international traffic. The Danish lighthouse service was already in the process of being expanded, charts were being improved, currents and shoals marked in. (The first Danish lightship had been placed in position off the island of Laesoe in 1829 after insistent demands from abroad, particularly from England). The Danish life-saving service, founded in 1852, was modelled on the English salvage company in Shields that had been established in 1789. Danish waters were feared by seafaring folk, particularly the waters round Bornholm and off the west coast of Jutland. Year after year, sailing ships went aground on the long, harbourless coastline and were reduced to matchwood, their crews usually being drowned in the heavy surf. The biggest wreck in the history of the west coast of Jutland was during the war against England, on Christmas night, 1811, when H. M. S. "St. George" and H M. S. "Defence" were cast up upon the sandbars. Of the combined crews of the two ships, only 11 men were rescued – 1,600 were drowned. But the wrecks did not cease. During a storm on October 4, 1860, 14 ships ran aground all within a comparatively short stretch of coastline – a disaster that exceeded the capacity of the newly started life-saving organization. But the service was gradually expanded, with the result that today there are 55 rescue stations spread round the coasts of Denmark. From its start in 1852 and up until the first world war in 1914 – the last glorious years of the great sailing ships the Danish life-saving service brought almost ten thousand people safely ashore. (To this day the service has still not outlived its purpose: as recently as 1956 the boats had to go out no fewer than 31 times.)

The Danish merchant fleet had recovered. Many merchantmen were sailing round the world and many of them came from the smaller provincial Danish ports. At the same time agriculture was developing steadily and industry was likewise gradually picking up. In 1802 the world's first serviceable steamship, a tug named the "Charlotte Dundas", was chugging on the Clyde. In 1807 Robert Fulton sent the era of the steamship sailing into the mouth of the Hudson River, and Denmark's first steamship, the "Caledonia", was acquired in 1819. Stephenson had completed his first locomotive in 1814, and the Manchester-Liverpool railway was opened in 1830. Denmark's first railways opened in the Slesvig-Holstein provinces: the Kiel-Altona line in 1844. The Copenhagen-Roskilde line was started in 1847. Norway's first railway line was opened in 1854 and Sweden's in 1856. In all spheres of activity, despite all disappointments, despite all territorial depreciations, Denmark was beginning to find her way.

XI. DEFEAT AND REVIVAL

The constant headache was the Slesvig question. The German Confederation (of which Holstein was a member) was constantly interfering with Denmark's relationship with her two southern provinces. This interference did not confine itself to the member state of Holstein, but was also extended to the affairs of Slesvig, which was *not* a member and therefore, so to speak, no business of the German Confederation. It was obvious to everybody that the aim was to drag Slesvig into the Confederation. Finally the Danish government's patience was exhausted. It was decided to settle the question once and for all, radically, by incorporating Slesvig definitively in Denmark, allowing it to share equally in the country's political democracy, and thereby put an end to all the eternal trouble. This step, though perhaps understandable, was nonetheless dangerous. It meant that Denmark would be breaking the peace treaty, extending the authority of the Danish government down to the River Eider, and separating Slesvig from Holstein.

Naturally the Danish government realized that the decision was a serious one and might have serious consequences. The act was passed in the Danish parliament on a Friday evening, November 13, 1863. On Sunday the 15th, two days later, at Glücksburg Castle, before having had time to sign the act, King Frederick VII died.

Everybody realized that the situation was extremely grave. When the news reached Copenhagen by telegraph on the Sunday evening, all theatres stopped their performances, guns on the coastal fortresses thundered out a mourning salute for the last King of the old Royal House, and tens of thousands of people filled the streets leading in towards Christiansborg Palace, where the prime minister, *Hall*, with the traditional cry of "The

King is dead, long live the King!" proclaimed Prince Christian of Glücksburg King of Denmark, *Christian IX*, according to the provisions for the succession agreed upon in London.

The situation was acute, opinions were sharply divided, and furthermore some resentment was caused by the fact that the young King hesitated for three whole days before making up his mind to endorse the new act involving Slesvig's incorporation, known as the "November Constitution".

The effects were immediate – not in Slesvig, but down in Germany. The new act was a violation of the treaty, and the *Duke of Augustenborg*, whose father had renounced all his rights, had himself proclaimed Duke, not only of Slesvig, but of a united *Schleswig-Holstein*. There was one person with whom the Danish government had not reckoned, nor could hardly have been expected to reckon, for the simple reason that he was as yet an unknown factor in European politics: that person was *Otto von Bismarck*. Bismarck had just become Prussia's minister of state, and he saw his chance in what had taken place. For a start, he lent his support to the Duke of Augustenborg and furthermore persuaded Austria to join in the affair, as Austria too had been a party to the agreements after the first Slesvig War. Denmark was presented with a carefully calculated ultimatum, a demand that the new act be repealed. But the respite given was so short that a withdrawal, even from an administrative point of view, would have been quite impossible. But Bismarck did not want the Danes to retreat. He wanted war, for he needed to win prestige. He had built up a new Prussian army without having previously obtained completely clear grounds for the concessions granted, and he wanted to prove, both to the Prussian King and to the Prussians themselves, just what the new army was worth. And he also wanted a chance of trying out his new army.

In Denmark, the government resigned and a new one was formed. The Danish army immediately withdrew from Holstein (in order to demonstrate clearly that we had no desire to hold on to this member state of the German Confederation) and took up a position along the southern border of Slesvig, along *Danevirke*, the more than 1,000-year old border defence embankment. The army numbered some 40,000 men and was supposed to hold a front about 60 miles long. On February 1,

1864, the combined Austro-Prussian army crossed the border at the River Eider and marched northwards under *General Wrangel*.

Danevirke, the ancient Danish defence line, did not extend along the entire length of the border, only along the eastern part. To Danish minds, *Danevirke* was a myth surrounded by historical romanticism. In itself the embankment was useless. In most places it had long since collapsed or been washed away by rain so that it merely formed a faint wavy line across the fields. Originally, only the eastern boundary had required defending, for the country to the west was all bog and marshland. But now it had dried up considerably, and furthermore the meadows and marshes froze over and thereby became as firm as the rest of the land. The border was too long, and impossible to hold against the enemy's force of 60,000 men.

The Danish army managed to ward off a couple of minor attacks and skirmishes, but the situation was untenable. The commander of the Danish forces was *General de Meza*, who, as a young artillery cadet, had stood upon the battlements of Kronborg Castle and cheerfully fired away at the English fleet, thereby earning himself a stiff reprimand for wasting gunpowder. Later, during the 3-year Slesvig War, he acquired a reputation for being an efficient, fearless, but at the same time a calm commander. He would spend his time at his headquarters setting French sonnets to music or designing ivory handles for his broom. He was meticulously careful about his health, fussed endlessly over his uniform and his white gloves, yet every morning rode fearlessly through the defence lines so utterly unaffected by the fact that a war, after all, was supposed to be on, that after one such morning ride, somewhat closer than usual to the enemy positions, he wrote in his diary, slightly nettled: "I was shot at. I do not understand what they think they are doing."

But despite his strange ways he was an excellent general, a courageous, conscientious, serious man, and an officer who enjoyed everybody's full confidence.

The government had given him orders to hold his position – with the proviso however, that he was to keep the army intact and ready to fight in the spring. This in itself was an impossible order. The prime minister came to inspect the defence positions – and then the situation took a strange turn. A council of war was held, and it was decided to evacuate

Danevirke and retire to a more easily defended position at *Dybboel*. The only one to vote against the resolution was the artillery general, because it meant leaving a considerable amount of his artillery behind.

The retreat was carried out in good order during the night of February 5, along roads that were completely iced up, and with a snowstorm

*In an entrenchment at Dybboel. Contemporary woodcut in
"Illustreret Tidende".*

blowing from the northeast – in other words straight in the faces of the endless, trudging columns of soldiers. For some strange reason they did not use the railway. It was there, all ready, and orders had even been given that the train was to comply with any military instructions that might be given. But presumably the officers had never thought of using a railway in a war – after all, it was very new. The march through the winter night thus acquired a tragic touch of absurdity by reason of the fact that there they were, marching through the snow and ice, while the railway line, along which a train could have easily covered the whole distance ten times over in the course of the night carrying everything – artillery, equipment, and wounded – simply remained unused.

The withdrawal was effected so stealthily that the enemy noticed nothing until the following morning. Austrian cavalry was sent in pursuit of the retreating army, but at *Sankelmark*, a cavalry attack was fought off by the rearguard in the course of a hard and somewhat bloody skirmish. The army took 18 hours to march to Flensborg, and after a rest in the town continued out to Dybboel Hill. Here there was a chain of ten rather small earthworks.

Rearguard action at Sankelmark during the retreat from Danevirke. Contemporary woodcut.

In Copenhagen, and throughout Denmark, the news of the withdrawal from *Danevirke* had a completely paralysing effect. It gave the old myth surrounding the defence line a bad jolt, and that was more than people could bear. The government hurriedly made a scapegoat of the deeply conscientious General de Meza and had him dismissed. This in itself constituted an unpleasant political step and a grievous injustice. Furthermore, the wisdom of changing the command of the army at a moment of such gravity as this was very questionable indeed.

As already indicated, the Danish army was considerably smaller than the Prussian army. The Prussian troops were moreover equipped with infinitely superior arms. The Danish army was still using muzzle-loaders, whilst the Prussians had breech-loading rifles that not only were capable of firing off a dozen or more rounds for every one fired by the Danes, but in addition were far more accurate and could shoot much further. Worst of all however, was the fact that the German artillery was modern and vastly superior. Almost all the Danish guns were muzzle-loaders of a type similar to those which most European nations had at their disposal. Many af the German guns were breech-loaders and therefore able to shoot much further than had been thought possible up to then, a fact which was to prove catastrophic for the Danish defence positions at Dybboel, for the enemy was able to fire across a wide fjord and score hits *in behind* the earthworks without the Danish guns being able to make any sort of retaliation.

There was, naturally enough, some lively diplomatic activity going on behind the war. Russia was not interested in seeing Germany force her way up into Jutland, and the Danes kept hoping that England would either send help or offer to arbitrate. But Queen Victoria's Coburg husband naturally regarded "the Schleswig-Holstein question" from a German standpoint, with the result that even after his death the Queen's views continued to coincide with his. Incidentally her great-aunt Caroline Matilda's tragic fate as Queen of Denmark is said to have given Queen Victoria a marked distaste for the country. During the 19th century, after Denmark had completed her last war with Sweden (1813-1814), the twelfth war between the sister nations within historic memory, a romantically influenced Nordic movement grew up, "Scandinavianism", whose aim was to work towards peace and a more intensive unity between the three Scandinavian countries. Many people became seized by this "Scandinavianism", but it was principally a literary, academic movement that had no roots in *real-politik*. Many Norwegian and Swedish volunteers took part in the first Slesvig War on the side of the Danes. Many volunteers from both countries fought and fell for "Scandinavia's ancient boundary" on Dybboel Hill, but the twin kingdoms of Norway and Sweden did not actually take any active part in the war. After the many fine speeches that had been delivered at Scandinavian banquets and after all the auspicious verses that had been composed by the poets, Denmark naturally rather hoped that they might do so, but she ended up standing alone. For eight weeks the Danish army defended the small earthworks, which within a short space of time were completely destroyed by the German artillery. Day after day soldiers marched up the highway and relieved each other in the shattered redoubts, lay encamped on the bare, muddy, winter fields, and let themselves be shot at. A couple of trial attacks were beaten off, and the German army dug itself into proper zig-zag trenches no more than a few hundred yards from the Danish positions.

At sea, the Danish fleet remained superior, blockading the German coastline and thereby seriously inconveniencing German trade and imports. But it was at Dybboel that the war had to be decided. A Danish army

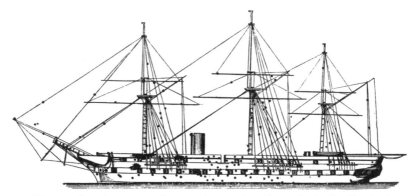

Hits scored on the Austrian frigate Schwarzenberg during the battle off Jutland.

corps succeeded in drawing a considerable part of the Austrian forces up into Jutland, away from the Dybboel front, but on April 18, after eight weeks of siege and shelling, a main attack was finally launched. The Danish army's new commander, *General Gerlach*, was suffering so badly from rheumatism at the time the attack came that he was literally *hors de combat*, so his second-in-command, *General du Plat*, suggested that he temporarily hand over the command, whereupon he, du Plat, would then, alone and on his own responsibility, withdraw from the position and spare Danish soldiers from a meaningless blood bath. But Gerlach refused. De Meza's fate seemed to him too bitter. The attack turned into a race between the Danish and the German soldiers to reach the entrenchments, for, as a result of the bombardment, many of the Danish troops had retired behind the shattered earthworks. The Danish army was forced back, but when one wing was in danger of being completely cut off from the road leading down to the bridge over to the island of Als, Danish troops made a counterattack which, though forcing the German army far enough back to enable a considerable number of those who had become trapped to get down to the bridge, nevertheless resulted in the attacking force's being thoroughly disintegrated and suffering considerable losses. However, the operation really did succeed in enabling a consider-

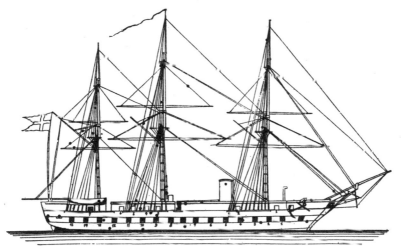

Hits scored on the Danish frigate Jylland during the battle off Helgoland.

able part of the Danish defence force to withdraw in safety over the bridge. The Danish navy prevented German ships from interfering. But Dybboel was lost. General du Plat remained standing by the roadside watching the retreating army until he himself was shot. The fight for the earthworks and the positions behind them lasted four hours, during which time the Danish forces suffered a total of 4,486 casualties, including missing and wounded, and of these, some 1,700 died. About 1,200 enemy soldiers lost their lives.

The war was not over. The Germans were in control of Jutland, but did not cross over to the islands. The German army prepared to cross Als Sound and conquer the last bit of Slesvig. Meanwhile a Danish squadron became engaged in a skirmish with an Austrian naval detachment off the island of Helgoland. Helgoland had orginally belonged to the Dukes of Slesvig, but had been conquered by the Danes in 1714. In 1807 the island was occupied by the English, and in 1814 handed over to

England by the Danes. (In 1890 the English gave the island to Prussia in exchange for large German territorial concessions in Africa. England did not realize at the time, nor could hardly have been expected to do so, the enormous strategic importance the island would have had in English hands during the two world wars against Germany). Thus on May 9, 1864, the island was English, and as the Austrian flagship had been set on fire, the Austrian squadron retreated in towards the safety of English territorial waters. A number of English men-o'-war, which had been observing the fight from a distance, manoeuvred in between the combatants and thereby put an end to the battle. The Austrian fleet took no further part in the action. The Battle of Helgoland served to strengthen Danish morale slightly, but its military importance was not great. That same day a truce was signed, and England summoned a conference in London in order to bring the war between Denmark and Prussia/Austria to a close. A compromise was suggested. Prussia and Austria declared themselves willing to a division of Slesvig, but only one that would allow Denmark to retain negligible territories up in the north of the province. Denmark, for her part, demanded Slesvig down as far as Danevirke. France and England proposed a somewhat similar division, but the Danish prime minister, *Monrad*, was obsessed by the thought of Slesvig's ancient Danish nationality, and in a fit of understandable (though politically unwise) bitterness, refused to accept a dividing line further north than that which he had agreed on with the Danish King. The arbitrators gave up, whereupon the war recommenced afresh. But this time it was completely pointless. The enemy crossed Als Sound in June, and during the fight for the island Denmark lost an additional 800 men. The German losses amounted to 400. Denmark was thereafter forced to accept a peace treaty in Vienna at which she surrendered all three duchies – Slesvig, Holstein and Lauenborg – to Austria and Prussia.

The duchies were lost to Denmark, whereupon the Duke of Augustenborg once more came forward. But Bismarck, with brilliant impudence, had his "legal advisers" prove that the Augustenborg family had long since relinquished all its claims. The lawful lord and master of the duchies was Christian IX of Denmark, who had, after all, surrendered his rights to Prussia and Austria at the Peace of Vienna, whereby Bismarck's grounds for going to war against Denmark were undeniably removed. But the provinces now belonged to Prussia and Austria, and two years later Prussia went to war against Austria, whereby she obtained the duchies for herself.

But *Napoleon III* had a clause inserted in the Austro–Prussian peace treaty, a paragraph 5, to the effect that the northern part of Slesvig was to be returned to Denmark "later", after a plebiscite. However, the Prussian army defeated the French in 1871, and eight years later, with Austria's agreement, Bismarck deleted this paragraph 5; Slesvig was German.

Political fights

In Denmark, the immediate effect of the war was paralysis. Nobody could see any way of starting afresh. The country had been reduced to one of Europe's smallest nations, and the general expectation was that she would subside completely and become obliterated, perhaps divided up between Germany and Sweden.

A natural outcome of the defeat in Denmark was a feeling of deep bitterness. But this, from a superficial viewpoint at any rate, did not last long. The political outcome was that the party which had been in power up to now, the National Liberals, was obliged to accept responsibility both for the policy pursued and the resultant defeat. The party was more or less dissolved, and a more conservative policy followed. The big land-owners acquired a considerable amount of political power and in opposition the "Venstre" (or "Left") party was formed. The Danes became involved in a political struggle that was to be kept up vigorously for decades. It was centred upon an ambiguously formulated phrase in the Constitution that read: "The King shall choose his ministers freely." Taken literally, it could mean that the King was allowed to choose his ministers regardless of the outcome of the elections and regardless of the relative strengths of the parties in parliament. But the "Venstre" party claimed that the phrase could only be construed to mean that "normal parliamentary practice" was to be followed on this point, i.e. that the King could choose his ministers freely from amongst the members of the party holding a majority in parliament. But the Conservative party stuck to the literal wording of the constitution, and so for many years a peculiar situation prevailed whereby the country's ministers had most of the members of parliament against them. Thus it was not even possible to put through the annually proposed budget. In other words, strictly speaking, the government was unable to govern. It managed as well as it could by making use of an emergency paragraph permitting the passing, in emergency situations, of "provisional", or temporary laws which only required the signatures of the ministers responsible and the King. They were supposed to be approved by parliament at a later date "when the occasion to do so shall arise", and for a number of years Denmark was thus governed by means of "provisional laws". The situation was naturally an impossible one in the long run, and political feelings ran higher and higher. But the government took advantage of these years to put through various projects, amongst them the *fortification of Copenhagen*, which consisted of the building of fortresses on the coast and a military defence line on land surrounding the entire capital, so that at any rate a situation similar to that in which Copenhagen had found itself in 1658 and in 1701, when the Swedes suddenly landed in Zealand, or in 1801 and 1807, when the English attacked Copenhagen, should not be able to recur and find Copenhagen completely defenceless. On the other hand no new defence system was built down on the German border. The very thought of a new war with Germany seemed so hopeless that it was considered at all events unwise to start provoking, by the erection of heavy fortifications, the new German Empire which, within but a few decades, had risen to be the victorious, warlike, and ambitious Great Power of the European mainland.

Revival

But behind all the political activity the defeat had another effect. Once again, Denmark's strange ability to recover quickly from disasters and catastrophes revealed itself. Under the motto "what is outwardly lost is inwardly won", work was commenced on the consolidation of the country within the extremely limited framework available. A start was made on the wide, barren moors of Jutland, and within a few decades large sandy stretches of heathland had been broken up. Forests were planted, the soil cleared, and crops sown, with the result that the moors rapidly began to shrink in size. Work was started all over the country drying out the bogs

Two Greenlanders, painted in Copenhagen, 1724. National Museum.

The Russian naval fregate Alexander Newsky aground on the west coast of Jutland, 1868. 722 were saved. Contemporary woodcut.

The Royal Family at Fredensborg. Amongst those in the front row are King Edward VII, Czar Alexander III and King Christian IX.

A meeting at the Folk High School at Askov.

and marshlands and damming up shallow bays and inlets so that large areas of what previously had been marshland or shallow sea now became arable land. Behind this agricultural uprising stood the Danish Folk High Schools. During the course of several decades this educational movement had developed into a strong, nation-wide organization. Practically all young people in rural districts now enrolled in the Folk High Schools for additional, post-school education. Not only did they learn practical farming, but history and literature too, in fact what spread through the land and turned the "regeneration" process into a task everybody came to regard as a duty, was a tremendous, deeply enthusiastic elevation of intellectual standards. The shipping industry was modernized, the merchant navy expanded, industry began to get seriously under way, towns began to expand explosively, commercial methods and trade organizations were modernized, factory-workers began to form a new social class – here as everywhere in Europe – and the country's agricultural adaptability was exploited to good advantage.

Until now Denmark had mainly produced cattle and corn, but from the new countries, particularly from the vast American prairies, enormous quantities of cheap corn now began to flood the markets of the world, and against this competition Denmark was helpless. So, within a short space of time, the country's agricultural effort was diverted into other channels. With determination and efficiency, Denmark now began to specialize in "quality farm produce", in other words butter, eggs and bacon. In fact production was organized so successfully that soon Denmark was able to offer products that were first-class and at the same time uniform in quality.

Behind this abrupt switch and production drive stood not only the Folk High Schools, but also the "co-operative movement". The Danish "village community" system had been abolished towards the close of the 18th century, but so ingrained in people's minds was the ancient Danish tradition of communal endeavour, that when the "co-operative idea" was first put forward, it was regarded neither as unfamiliar nor unacceptable, and therefore spread rapidly. "Co-operative dairies" were built all over the country, in other words every district had its own big dairy where all the local farmers delivered their milk. They moreover owned the dairy between them, and thus were their own wholesalers, had all the profits for themselves, were able to control marketing and sales, and each had a personal interest. At the same time the country acquired "co-operative bacon factories", and the co-operative movement was extended to include poultry and eggs, and even the farmer's own domestic purchases at "co-operative stores". By means of all this, Denmark climbed into position around the turn of the century as one of the leading agricultural nations of the world. During this period the fishing industry was modernized too. Motorized fishing-cutters took the place of the old open boats, and throughout the country, in all spheres of activity, the work of renovation and modernization proceeded apace. The many small shipping companies in the provincial port towns naturally lagged behind somewhat in their efforts to compete on the oceans of the world, and whereas in former times Danish merchants in Copenhagen and the provincial towns had personally owned one or more ships, from now on, here as in other countries, the big, financially powerful shipping companies began to assume control. The Danish ship-building industry began to assert itself. In 1911 Holland and England succeeded in launching a couple of small ships fitted with Diesel engines, and the following year a big Danish shipping firm, the East Asiatic Company, sent the world's first large ocean-going motor-ship, the "Selandia", out on a voyage to the Far East.

It was at the close of the 19th century that Danish literature reached one of its peaks. At the same time Danish contributions to the sciences were considerable. Thus progress was being made throughout this small, well-organized country, and the defeat that had been suffered was no longer outwardly noticeable, although it still remained a factor lodged in the minds of the people.

The Danish Royal Family led a remarkable career during these years. Old King Christian IX's elder daughter, *Alexandra*, became *Queen of England* by marrying *Edward VII;* his second daughter, *Dagmar*, became *Empress of Russia* by marrying *Alexander III;* and one of his sons became *King George of Greece*, later assassinated at Salonica (in 1913). During the first years of the 20th century the union between Norway and Sweden was dissolved. The rupture caused considerable tension between the two countries, and in some circles in Sweden there was even a mood for war brewing, but finally the dissolution was effected peaceably. As their new

King, the Norwegians elected Christian IX's grandson, duly crowned in 1906 as *Haakon VII*.

Thus for a number of years, Fredensborg Palace, the Danish Royal Family's idyllic country seat in North Zealand, became the centre of European court life. The King of England, the Czar of Russia, and the various children and connections of the Danish Royal Family were all guests at the palace at one time or another.

XII. THE WORLD WARS &
DENMARK TODAY

.

Denmark carried on peacefully and in a state of relative prosperity, in the face of which the belligerent mood of 1914 seemed absurd. When war broke out, Denmark realized once more, just as she had done for the past 1,000 years, the vulnerability of her position at the entrance to the Baltic. Germany threatened to lay mines in Danish waters unless Denmark undertook to close them off herself. After discussions in England, Denmark decided to adopt the latter course.

During the war years, as the front became solidly established in France, it became clear that the danger of war in Scandinavia was not imminent. Like other neutral countries, Denmark earned enormous sums of money by trading with the belligerent nations, and succeeded in keeping her balance. But the war years left their mark on life in Denmark, who had really tried to ensconce herself behind her wall of peaceful obscurity; they had been hectic from an economic point of view, but were not without their hardships. Even though the country's losses could not be compared with those of the belligerent nations, Danish shipping was nonetheless hard hit as a result of German submarine warfare. Approximately 100 Danish ships were torpedoed, as a rule without any consideration being shown for their crews.

Two things happened during the war: in 1915, Danish women were granted the right to vote on an equal footing with men, and in 1916, the West Indian islands were sold to America. This step caused some resentment. It was considered bitter that the Danish flag should have to be struck on Denmark's last tiny, tropical, colonial outpost. However, the matter was finally decided by popular vote and the sale was carried through.

236

The Return of North Slesvig to Denmark

When the war was over, everybody realized that it produced a problem. Germany had been defeated: what was to be done about Slesvig now?

The population of Slesvig had gone through 56 strange years. It had been incorporated within the German Empire and naturally had been governed as a German province. That more than half of the population happened to be Danish-speaking and Danish-minded was a fact that lay beyond the extent of German administrational interest – or, as a German prince expressed it in a speech at Soenderborg: "What the German eagle gets its claws into, it never releases."

The province was relatively poor. It was in an out-of-the-way corner of Germany, possessed no assets of any value, and therefore Germany took no great interest in it. The administrative authorities worked methodically on the task of Germanization, but failed to understand that force was not the most appropriate way. All sorts of obstacles were placed before the Danish population: Danish meetings and gatherings were, as far as possible, prevented or forbidden, in fact the authorities went to the extent of imposing fines if people painted their houses in such a way as would result in the colours red and white coming too close to one another. This kind of petty maliciousness actually had the effect of keeping Danish nationalism alive. Large hordes of Slesvigians went up to attend Folk High Schools in Denmark and came back with an insight into Danish culture and mentality. At one time a burning question arose, that concerning conscription: were Danes in Slesvig to allow themselves to be conscripted as German soldiers, or should they emigrate? A wave of emigration commenced, but was checked by Danish leaders in the province, who pointed out that if Danish youth emigrated, the Danish element in the population would have lost the fight, because the German population would merely fill up the gaps in the ranks. Young Slesvigians therefore did their German military service in order to retain their position and civil rights in the province. During the world war they were sent to the front on which they least wished to fight, but when it was over, Slesvigian leaders went to Copenhagen. The Danish government approached the nations assembled at Versailles and requested that the right of selfdetermination be applied to Slesvig, in other words that a settlement of Slesvig's national affiliation be decided by means of a plebiscite. After a year of international administration a popular vote was taken and more than half of Slesvig (North Slesvig) voted for a return to Denmark. The border was found to coincide almost precisely with the language border, approximately where it would have been drawn had a division been made according to popular opinion in 1864. Only the big town of Flensborg, as a result of an influx of Germans, had expanded and become Germanized to such an extent that it came to lie south of the border.

Naturally the border could not hope to be a pure dividing line. There were those with Danish sympathies to the south, and those with German sympathies to the north, but from the voting there appeared to be very few: the border was surprisingly clearly demarcated. In 1920, the Danish King, Christian X, rode across the frontier on horseback, and North Slesvig was reunited with Denmark – this time not as a separate duchy, but incorporated properly within the realm.

North Slesvig had been ravaged by war and badly neglected. For five years all its menfolk had been at war; there had been nobody to take care of its farms, and the province as such was very backward compared with Denmark anyway. New farms and new roads were badly needed everywhere. Five thousand North Slesvigians had lost their lives in the war.

National Crisis and the Interwar Period

When the war was over, the Danish national economy once more found itself going through a crisis. All Danish industrial production and commercial activity had been adapted to the abnormal conditions that had prevailed during the war and the unstable, easy opportunities of profit that had accompanied them. Large sums of money had been earned unsoundly, had often ended up in the wrong hands – not always particularly efficient hands – and a number of crashes had to be survived before the country's finances became more or less re-organized. Denmark's producers had to a certain extent abused the simplicity of the situation, and it had become necessary to re-establish respect for Danish wares.

This too was accomplished, although Denmark, together with the rest of the world, was obliged to go through a number of currency crises which constituted particularly hard blows to Danish agriculture.

The interwar period was, despite all the crises, one of reckless optimism. During the era of the League of Nations, Denmark, like other countries, embarked upon the task of renovation: new architecture, new literature, new painting, functionalistic furniture. Everything had to be new and serve a definite purpose. The past was renounced, for it had led to a world war. In the modern, ideal world, sober-mindedness and foresight were called for. The arch-enemy, Germany, had been beaten, and a certain easy optimism began to spread – despite agricultural crises. The old political parties lost ground, workers' organizations developed as industry expanded, and in 1924 the Danish Social Democratic Party managed to obtain the government. So far so good. Danish ships were once more sailing round the world, a fact that aroused remarkably little interest on the part of the Danish population, but the general public outlook, due to the many defeats, had narrowed. The Danes realized that Denmark was a small country, but smiled indulgently at the thought and continued to dream of taking their place in a great, united Europe.

Danish agriculture had long since discovered its best customer to the west of the North Sea: England. Danish butter and Danish bacon had become established facts in the Danish business world; the Danes began cultivating an interest in England. The wars with England at the beginning of the 19th century were something belonging to the distant past. Perhaps they had not been exactly forgotten; but they were regarded more as having been an unfortunate error of judgment on England's part. After all, England had had so many matters to think about during those years – what with the Napoleonic Wars and all the rest of it. At the beginning of the 19th century, Danish intellectual life evinced a deep interest in German romanticism. This came naturally, for after all, German Holstein formed part of the Danish monarchy. After the fighting for Slesvig during the middle of the century and the subsequent tension between Denmark and Holstein, interest in German affairs and culture waned, and was replaced by a corresponding interest in French culture and literature. But after the collapse of France, and after commercial relationships with England increased, English – and in due course, American – literature took the lead. A great deal of English was read, for after all, the language was taught in Danish schools, and much English literature was translated into Danish. Shakespeare featured permanently in the repertoire of Denmark's Royal Theatre; in fact the Danes became generally familiar with English intellectual life and thought.

That a corresponding English interest in Denmark was not observed (to put the position mildly) did not affect Danish interest in the literature of England and America, be it classical or modern. England was regarded as a sort of sister nation. After all, everybody knew that there was quite a large drop of Danish blood flowing in the veins of every Englishman. At the same time it was borne in mind that Angles from South Slesvig, and later other Danes, had emigrated in thousands to England 1,500 and 1,000 years ago respectively, so they could hardly be blamed for having forgotten "the old country" after such an elapse of time. After all, England had had to go through one thing and another since then, and the two countries had gone their own ways, not only in regard to their histories, but also from a prestige viewpoint. It was discovered (with some surprise) that the English really displayed very little interest in their ancient kinsmen and closest neighbours to the northeast, i.e. the Scandinavian peoples, and in fact knew extraordinarily little about them. There was nothing to be done about it. The Danish language now began to absorb several English words, of which a number, curiously enough, turned out to be old Danish words that had been exported westwards a thousand years previously. They now came back, their pronounciation having in the meantime acquired a distinctly English ring.

But in 1933, an Austrian political dreamer began Germany's regeneration under the motto of "Der Tanz ins Glück". It would be unfair to reproach Danish politicians for not having appreciated the perspectives straight away in view of the fact that no leading statesmen in any of the larger European countries had managed to do so. The first repercussions were felt in North Slesvig. The German minority north of the border had been accorded all reasonable privileges: it had its own church services, its own German-speaking schools that received financial support from the Danish state in just the same way as ordinary Danish private schools, and no Dane would have dreamed of doing anything so foolish as to prevent the German minority's freedom of speech or freedom of assembly. The

German minority, despite the fact that numerically it hardly qualified for a mandate, was represented in the Danish parliament. The latest, blaring, brassy tones from the south caused the German minority, naturally (and very understandably) to listen with interest and to start dreaming that their turn for reunification with Germany would soon be coming too. There was no shortage of German orators who more than intimated that the days of Danish triumph would soon be over.

World War II and the Occupation

During the last years before the war, every ordinary citizen realized clearly what apparently no politician could get into his head: that war was imminent.

It came in 1939. Just before it burst, Hitler had made Denmark a present of a "non-agression pact" which Denmark accepted without displaying much enchantment and perhaps should have turned down – the way several other countries did. But by now, any treaty bearing Hitler's name had come to be regarded as worthless anyway. So it seemed to make little difference whether one said yes or no, and why merely make a madman even madder?

On April 9, 1940, Hitler marched north. His objective was Norway, and his path lay through Denmark. Early one morning, German troops streamed in over the Danish border, German ships entered the harbour at Copenhagen, and while German bombers circled low over the capital, Danish politicians were forced to sit down and negotiate. There was some skirmishing in North Slesvig, a few airfields were bombed, and the Germans exchanged some rifle-fire with soldiers of the Royal Life Guards below the King's windows in Amalienborg Square. During the course of the morning the government gave in and the business of occupying Denmark was over.

This reaction was not fully understood abroad. The Danes hardly understood it themselves that sunny spring morning, when their peaceful, well-organized little country suddenly discovered that she had suffered the same fate as Czechoslovakia – something to which every Dane had given careful thought during the years prior to the war, but never seriously believed possible. The reaction that morning was really very Danish.

Just as Christianity was introduced in Denmark by means of a decision at a *thing*-meeting, just as the Reformation was brought about more peacefully than anywhere else in Europe, just as absolute monarchy was introduced by an announcement in 1660 and discarded again in 1848 at the request of a delegation of honest citizens clad in top hats and frock coats, thus, in a similar fashion, did Denmark react on April 9, 1940.

OPROP!

Til Danmarks Soldater og Danmarks Folk!

Uten Grund og imot den tyske Regjerings og det tyske Folks oprigtige Ønske, om at leve i Fred og Venskab med det engelske og det franske Folk, har Englands og Frankrigets Magthavere ifjor i September erklæret Tyskland Krigen.

Deres Hensigt var og blir, efter Mulighet, at treffe Afgjørelser paa Krigsskuepladser som ligger mere afsides og derfor er mindre farlige for Frankriget og England, i det Haab, at det ikke vilde være mulig for Tyskland, at kunde optræde stærkt nok imot dem.

Af denne Grund har England blandt andet stadig krænket Danmarks og Norges Nøitralitæt og deres territoriale Farvand.

Det forsøkte stadig at gjøre Skandinavien til Krigsskueplads. Da en yderlig Anledning ikke synes at være givet efter den russisk-finnske Fredsslutning, har man nu officielt erklæret og truet, ikke mere at taale den tyske Handelsflnates Seilads indenfor danske Territorialfarvand ved Nordsjøen og i de norske Farvand. Man erklærte selv at vilde overta Politiopsigten der. Man har tilslut truffet alle Forberedelser for overraskende at ta Besiddelse af alle nødvendige Støtepunkter ved Norges Kyst. Aarhundredes største Krigsdriver, den allerede i den første Verdenskrig til Ulykke for hele Menneskeheden arbeidende Churchill, uttalte det aapent, at han ikke var villig til at la sig holde tilbake af «legale Afgjørelser eller nøitrale Rettigheder som staar paa Papirlapper».

Han har forberedt Slaget mot den danske og den norske Kyst. For nogen Dager siden er han blit utnævnt til forausvarlig Chef for hele den britiske Krigsføring.

On April 9, 1940, the Germans dropped "Opraab!" pamphlets over Denmark and Nor-way, a kind of explanation of German motives and intentions. The text of the message was incredibly naive and the language used was a hopeless mixture of Danish, Norwegian and German – so the effect it had was the precise opposite of that intended.

It was an extremely sober reaction, and a sober estimation of the immediate situation: there was no hope of defeating Hitler's Germany, and help from abroad was something Denmark had on previous occasions waited for in vain. No nation helps another unless such help happens to suit its own book. April 9, 1940 may have cost human life, but the country had not been annihilated. The King and the Government remained untouched, the country remained intact, merely with foreign guests in its midst, guests who promised solemnly that they would only behave as guests and not interfere with either the independence or the government of the country. It remained to be seen how things would develop in the future.

This unheroic, common-sense reaction could not help causing some embarrassment when the news was received that the Norwegians had decided to fight, and that they were continuing to fight. But there is a difference between the terrain in Norway and the terrain in Denmark. You can blow up a Danish road, but guns and tanks only have to drive into the fields and go round the crater. Planes can fly over Denmark from German bases within an hour or two. Norway is further to the north, and her terrain is just as difficult as Switzerland's. Mountain roads can be dynamited so that there is just no way round at all, and a couple of gun batteries and machine-guns can hold a mountain pass almost indefinitely. Even so, despite everything that could be *explained*, the difference in the reaction of the two countries on April 9 gave rise to bitterness.

But then came the collapse of France and England's fantastic withdrawal across the Channel. The Danes realized that, on April 9, Denmark had really had no other alternative except to commit a heroic suicide which would have done nobody any good whatsoever. Never before had the situation in Europe been so murky. England and France, upon whom all eyes were turned, had their backs to the wall; and in Denmark the situation became more and more serious. It soon became evident that the Germans did not intend to respect the terms of the occupation agreement as far as non-interference was concerned. A Danish Nazi Party had already been formed before the war, and it now tried to exercise its influence, but its leaders were men of such meagre calibre that not even the Germans had any use for them. In Norway the situation after the collapse became even more serious than in Denmark. The leader of the Norwegian Nazi Party, *Vidkun Quisling*, was officially instated as chief of the Norwegian government, and the country found itself engaged in a struggle for life and death, man against man. In Denmark, German demands became more and more impertinent, and the German petty-mindedness which had made itself so well-known to the people of North Slesvig during their struggle and 56 years of exile, did not fail to reassert itself. The Allied colours, red, white and blue, were forbidden, and children were arrested for wearing hats in these colours. Had the Germans been large-minded enough to refrain from these and a thousand other similar acts of petty foolishness, they might have found things much easier. As it was, their actions were not only irritating, but also very revealing: they

243

served to give the Danes a feeling of mental superiority which, justified or not, nevertheless spread and had a great effect.

In all critical situations people try to find acceptable explanations. Denmark's position was embarrassing, and the explanation found in this instance was simply that the wrong policy had been pursued. As is usually the case when explanations have to be sought, this one may have been right and may have been wrong – probably both. That is why the Danes, instead of rallying round their elected leaders in parliament, fell back on tradition and rallied round the person of the King. Christian X was no longer a young man. He had lived quietly through the waves of cultural renovation that had characterized the 1920's and 1930's – waves which had not been so very royalistic. While his brother, King Haakon, had had no alternative when Norway collapsed other than to abandon his country and go to England, Christian X remained in Denmark. Every day he rode on horseback through the streets of the German-occupied capital – not that this was anything new. He had done so every morning of his life whenever he happened to be in Copenhagen. But he continued to do so, despite occasional outbursts of firing in the streets. Danes stopped on the pavements and lifted their hats to their old King as he rode calmly past them, alone and unattended, without any guard or any form of escort. A small thing in the tremendous drama that was being enacted in Europe, but to the people of German-occupied Denmark it meant a great deal.

This was not the time for discussions. The Danish dream of occupying a place in a united Europe, now that people saw it beginning to take on the form of a nightmare, was dead. It was appreciated that Denmark was possibly going through the final, irrevocable chapter of her long and eventful history.

Denmark and Norway were involved in this second world war, but Sweden was not. From Copenhagen, blacked-out and bearing the marks of German occupation, the Danes were able to look out every evening across the waters of the Sound and see lights twinkling in the old Danish towns of Malmö and Hälsingborg. Every night an illegal traffic of small boats took refugees over to Sweden and maintained contact with the free world via Sweden. The Swedes, who were neutral, took care of all Danish and Norwegian refugees with a display of hospitality that knew no bounds. The refugee stream was soon brought under control. Only those who had serious reasons for escaping were allowed to cross the Sound, though of course a number did so on their own initiative.

Germany naturally turned her attention towards the big Danish colony of Greenland in view of its proximity to America. But Greenland's status was decided before Germany could take any action. When Denmark was occupied, Denmark's ambassador to the United States declared that as his government was not in a position to act freely, he would take upon himself the responsibility of acting on Denmark's behalf and placing Greenland under U.S. protection. The Faroe Islands and Iceland were occupied by the Western Powers in the same way, thus preventing Germany from obtaining bases in the North Atlantic.

The Germans began plundering Denmark systematically. Denmark's agriculture and industry had lost their principal outlet, i.e. Western Europe, and a trading arrangement was therefore entered into with Germany, who offered high prices to be paid through Denmark's National Bank. In practice this meant that the Danish state paid Danish suppliers for goods they delivered to Germany. Naturally the official agreement was that Germany would refund the Danish state in due course, but nobody was in any doubt as to the real truth of the matter.

A Clearer Policy

In the beginning, the government hoped that it would really prove possible to steer the country through its difficult predicament on the basis of the German assurances – more or less, at all events. But as time went on it became more and more obvious that the agreement was worthless. A game of double-dealing was initiated, but it was difficult for many Danes, naturally enough, firstly to understand, and secondly to follow, the treacherous course of a policy of this nature.

The population gradually became impatient. Denmark's fleet and army were both intact, but remained passive. The position became increasingly absurd. A resistance movement began in the form of small, privately organized, independent groups, which though not capable of much to start with, soon developed into useful sabotage units. This initial active resistance was, strictly speaking, against the agreement entered into on

245

April 9. But the position had altered since then. When the government started condemning acts of sabotage and all forms of resistance, and ordered the police and the law-courts to intervene actively, both the government and its official organs began to lose their authority over the population.

It became steadily more evident that a diplomatic course involving continual pointing at the agreement of April 9, was no longer practicable. Even the government gradually began to realize that any attempt to pursue an astute, diplomatic policy was a waste of time. In August 1943, there were "disturbances" and "popular strikes" in several Danish towns, including the capital, whereupon the German occupation force lost its head. Many civilians were killed as a result of shooting in the streets, and some 500 persons were seized as hostages. The Germans took over official control of the country after the Danish government had resigned. Army barracks and naval depôts were suddenly attacked by German troops, during which action 23 Danes lost their lives. The fleet scuttled itself in the harbour on August 29.

Denmark was now being governed by the German occupation force. To begin with, the Germans were at a complete loss as to how to tackle the problem. For the Danes themselves however, the whole state of affairs had now suddenly become infinitely clearer, and the break was felt as a tremendous relief. September 18 saw the formation of Denmark's *Freedom Council*, a self-organized body whose purpose was to direct the countless sabotage and resistance groups which in the meantime had sprung up all over the country. Acts of sabotage were naturally intended to impede German plans in Denmark and delay German exploitation of Danish industry and agriculture; but the "Fight for Freedom" was also intended to demonstrate clearly to the rest of the world on which side of the fence Denmark wished to be.

Even though conditions in Denmark never acquired that deeply shocking stamp of cruelty which characterized the German occupation of other countries, matters nevertheless became serious enough. On October 1, the Germans committed one of their most serious stupidities by taking action against Denmark's Jews in accordance with the dictates of the Nazi programme. Prior to the German occupation Denmark had no "Jewish problem", and when the action was launched, most Danish Jews, thanks to assistance from all sides, were enabled to escape over to Sweden.

At this time the "export" of Danish prisoners to German concentration camps was increasing, and together with them were despatched the relatively few Jews on whom the Germans managed to lay their hands.

The position now became tense. Reports were received of deaths resulting from torture in German-occupied Danish prisons, and the first

During the occupation the official Danish press was under German censorship, but a swarm of illegal newssheets spread all over the country. The paper and printing were not always of the best, but the text as a rule was well-written, concise, and as reliable as possible. These illegal newssheets rendered the German censorship completely worthless.

death sentences to be passed on Danish saboteurs were carried out by shooting. Masses of small illegal news-sheets were distributed to all Danes and supplied information concerning everything the official newspapers were not allowed to print, likewise corrected versions of articles inserted in the daily press under German pressure.

On January 4, 1944, the Germans committed another of their completely incomprehensible acts of stupidity by dragging the Danish poet, playwright and clergyman, *Kai Munk*, out of his home on the west coast of Jutland and "liquidating" him with a bullet through the back of the neck. His body was found in a ditch at the side of a country lane. Even the most cautious and hesitant of Danes could now no longer harbour any doubts as to the path that lay ahead.

Sabotage activity increased, whereupon the Germans started carrying out "counter-sabotage", i.e. wanton destruction of Danish property in order to revenge acts of sabotage to factories and railways. The towns of Denmark changed character. Even though the extent of the destruction naturally cannot be compared with the catastrophic bombing of Europe's cities, damage was nonetheless considerable and the loss of human life increased steadily. Wanton acts of vengeance became more and more common, but by sheer virtue of the methods used the effect was invariably the direct opposite of that intended. German troops would appear in a Copenhagen street, close it off, drag out a number of persons at random, and shoot them. Or German "counter-saboteurs" would buy a railway ticket and board some train. As services had been greatly reduced on account of the war, all trains were badly over-crowded. The "counter-saboteur" would have a time-bomb in a suitcase and then get off at some station and leave the suitcase behind in the train, with the result that one or several coachfuls of men, women and children would be blown sky-high. Nocturnal arrests were common. Every single morning the newspapers would print short announcements to the effect that the following persons, at times a dozen or more, had been shot in their homes during the night. On the other hand, saboteurs' bombs exploded every single night in factories that were working for the Germans. The Germans had broken up the Danish police force and sent a large number of its personnel to concentration camps in Germany. Those on whom the Germans did not manage to lay their hands went underground and many became active saboteurs and members of the Danish resistance movement.

General Strike

Towards the end of June 1944, a serious crisis developed. The formation of a voluntary corps of Danish Nazis had aroused a great deal of indignation, and there had been demonstrations. The Germans countered by imposing a curfew on the capital. German patrols started firing in the streets and succeeded in wounding about a thousand people. Danish workers retaliated against the imposition of the curfew (by which people were forbidden to leave their homes in the evening or at night) by downing tools at their place of work earlier than normal every day "because

Dannebrog being struck at St. Thomas, March 31, 1917, Danish marines on the left.
The somewhat lop-sided company on the right are Americans

King Christian meeting stout North Slesvig veterans at the reunion of 1920.

Despite the occupation Christian X rode alone through the streets of Copenhagen every morning. In the air: a German aircraft.

they had to tend to their gardens and allotments". The Germans tried to offset the resultant decrease in production by extending the curfew until 11 p.m. But just then the news was received in Copenhagen that eight Danish saboteurs had been executed. All work stopped. The Germans replied by surrounding the capital, preventing all supplies from entering and all persons from leaving, whether by bus, car or rail. Copenhagen was in a state of siege. The most extraordinary atmosphere of mutual co-operation to be manifested during the whole war spread through the isolated city. People went and fetched water in the lakes and ponds, milkmen started their own system of rationing the meagre supplies available so that mothers could fetch milk for their children round by the back door, and everybody helped everybody else. At this time the trade unions attempted to make the workers go back to work. In reply, Denmark's *Freedom Council* drew up a clear list of the demands made by the "strikers", in other words, the Danish population. These demands were to be satisfied before work would be resumed. Everything was at a standstill. Leading politicians broadcast appeals to the workers, begging them to go back to work and pointing out the terrifying consequences a continuation of the strike would entail. But the strike went on. Finally the Germans gave in. A proclamation was issued by the Freedom Council and the workers went back to work. Once more the situation had been shown up in stark relief: the Freedom Council, and not Denmark's politicians, constituted the one authority that carried any weight with the population.

The Germans continued their murders and executions. A police force was formed known as the *Hipo* (*Hilfspolizei*), recruited from unpleasant elements amongst the Danish population, mainly ex-convicts. This corps of toughs was used by the Germans against the civilian population.

To begin with, Danish sabotage work had naturally been amateurish. Its objectives were selected at random, haphazardly. But soon a system of collaboration with England was organized, and thenceforward all sabotage was directed by radio from England. Danes went over to England, were trained, and then returned to Denmark by parachute. The dropping of arms became common, resistance groups contacted one another, and a definite system was developed, particularly in regard to the sabotaging of important railway junctions, so that Danish saboteurs succeeded to a great extent in keeping the Jutland railway network out of function – a factor of considerable importance to the maintenance of German communications with occupied Norway.

As the German fronts gradually collapsed in one part of the world after another, hopes in occupied Denmark naturally rose. But at the same time the fact was clearly faced that Denmark might very well be selected as a battlefield for the last desperate fight in Europe. The situation improved, and in Sweden, Danish refugees were organized into a proper, thoroughly trained regiment armed with the finest modern Swedish military equipment. A number of shortages were beginning to make themselves felt in Denmark by now, especially in respect of coal and coke. There was also a shortage of clothes and a number of other items, though once again it must be emphasized that these shortages bore no comparison with the needs that were felt in other countries. In April 1945, the Swedish Red Cross, under the leadership of Folke Bernadotte, succeeded in obtaining permission to go and fetch Norwegian and Danish prisoners from German concentration camps, including Danish Jews. People in Denmark realized that the German Empire was in the process of disintegration. Just at this time, German refugees began streaming northwards into Denmark. They arrived by train and by ship, thousands upon thousands of them. The Germans requisitioned schools and other buildings and converted them into barracks. These refugees brought disease with them, but despite their strange behaviour, their macabre wretchedness could arouse nothing but pity. Many of them were suffering from bombing wounds; they were starving, incredibly filthy, full of lice, in rags, and miserable. Their children died off like flies. They were human beings in such pitiable condition that it was difficult to regard them as enemies, but more like extras in an appallingly realistic filmic reconstruction of Eastern Europe in 1812. The whole thing was too unreal. This refugee stream probably opened the eyes of many Danes to the fact that the inhuman ruthlessness of this war had inflicted much more suffering in other parts of the world, horrors which, despite all that Denmark had been through, the Danes quite simply had not had an opportunity of picturing for themselves. At the same time it was clearly realized that Germany had been struck a mortal blow, and that these were the inhabitants of a country in the process of dissolution. But – with all due human compassion – these ragged hordes continued to pour into Denmark, thousands upon thousands of them. For the most part they were Eastern Germans, very strange both in outward appearance and mentality. If these human masses were to remain in Denmark, the population of the country would become altered beyond recognition for all time.

The German Collapse

By German orders, the news of the deaths of Hitler and Mussolini was announced simultaneously in Denmark. Of course the Danes had already heard it on the wireless broadcasts from London. While everybody realized that the war was now practically over, it was still not known for certain where the final act would take place. It was not impossible that Germany's leading Nazis and military officers might decide to fight to the bitter end in Denmark and Norway, for they had some serious accounts awaiting settlement. In Denmark, these were naturally exciting days during which everybody followed the progress of the front from hour to hour as it gradually came closer and closer to the Danish border. And the final phase was enacted, quite literally, on the border. British planes were already in the process of bombing German motorized and armoured columns heading northwards up through the Danish province of North Slesvig when the news was broadcast from London on the evening of May 4, 1945, clean through the German jamming stations, to the effect that the German forces in *Northern Germany, Holland*, and *Denmark*, had capitulated on *Lüneburg Heath* to *Fieldmarshal Montgomery*. Admittedly the capitulation was only supposed to take effect as from 8 o'clock the next morning, but nobody cared. That evening and the following day were incredible. Denmark was still blacked out. Copenhagen and the other big towns were merely murky blotches on the landscape that warm May evening as dusk began to fall. In those days everybody had a supply of candles, for one never knew when the Germans might cut off all power supplies again. Spontaneously, nobody knows quite how, people started putting all their candles on their windowsills, whereby the towns and cities of Denmark suddenly became illuminated by a soft golden glow coming forth from the windows of houses throughout the land. Nobody stayed at home, everybody went running through the streets, cheering and laughing – though some more quietly, for there was still some lively shooting going on in the streets. Resistance groups settled accounts with Danish Nazis and *Hipo* members. German officers and Danish Nazis roared through the streets in their motor-cars in order to try and reach the German border before 8 a.m. the next day. The following morning the whole country was in a state of wild jubilation. Shooting continued. Cars tore round arresting informers and others with whom it was desired, for excellent reasons, to exchange a word or two. These incredible days cost several hundred human lives. But Denmark was free.

There was one dampener on the general rejoicing: the capitulation did not include Norway. That came a few days later. The Danish refugee regiment returned from Sweden, armed to the teeth, but its services were no longer necessary. Flags were flapping all over Denmark.

With the exception of one place: just as Denmark was being liberated, Russian women pilots swept in over the island of Bornholm and ordered the German commandant to capitulate to the Russians. He refused, where-upon the Russians bombed the two towns of Roenne and Nexoe to bits. Bornholm was occupied by Russian troops.

In the midst of all the rejoicing it seemed meaningless. It made people realize that Denmark was still not yet completely out of her difficulties. But it must be said that after a couple of hectic days the first Russian invasion troops were replaced by more peaceful Russian forces. Of course there was no knowing whether the Russians intended to occupy Bornholm for an indefinite period. However, they withdrew from the island after a year or so. Incidentally, the occupation of the island was carried through without any difficulties, in a correct and disciplined manner. At any rate one of the first things the Russians did was to evacuate every single German refugee. They stuffed them into Russian ships and everything they could find in the way of a boat on Bornholm and sent them over to the German coast.

On the other hand the 200,000 German refugees in the rest of Denmark, where the liberation had been effected by British troops, were interned in big camps, where they remained for more than a year before the English and American occupation forces were able to take charge of them.

Still remaining was the settling up of accounts with pro-German elements in the Danish population, such as informers and German stooges.

When the liberation came, Denmark had no official government, although unofficially the government and local administrational bodies had continued to function, for the simple reason that the Germans had not been able to cope and had therefore put up tacitly with the continued functioning of the Danish authorities – with the exception, of course, of the police force, which the Germans had disbanded of their own accord, thereby causing themselves more inconvenience than anybody else.

The Danes looked to their Freedom Council as the principal authority in the land. In fact the first government to be formed after the liberation took over members of the Freedom Council as ministers in order to avoid any unpleasant political tension.

A judicial settlement was difficult, because the situation in Denmark during most of the occupation had been "officially obscure". The severe attitude adopted to begin with therefore quickly became milder, and the whole affair finally proved unsatisfactory both for those who had insisted on a harsh policy and for those who had held more lenient views.

Denmark became a member of the United Nations, and yet another problem concerning foreign policy came into the foreground as a result of the German collapse: the rest of Slesvig, or "South Slesvig", i.e. the part which did not become Danish in 1920.

The Allies are said to have offered Denmark the whole stretch of territory on condition that she would agree to accept all the German refugees that had arrived from all corners of their war-torn country and were then jammed together in South Slesvig. The reason why South Slesvig, which had voted clearly at the reunion of 1920 to remain German, could once again constitute a problem for Denmark was that public opinion within the province itself had changed since then. After seeing something of the endless columns of refugees from Eastern Germany, many South Slesvigians felt that after all they perhaps had closer ties with Denmark and the other Scandinavian countries. Danish majorities appeared in both town and parish councils south of the border. A cry was heard from the province itself that now it would like to come north again, and in Denmark this could not avoid irritating an old, practically healed wound. South Slesvig was discussed violently, both politically and privately, and opinions were sharply divided. But the government did not wish to become involved in untenable border changes based on temporary swings in public opinion. It was felt that the abnormal situation existing at the time could not be accepted as sufficient grounds for any action. But the Danish minority south of the border had grown considerably; a cultural programme was therefore drawn up providing for subsidies for Danish schools, Danish church services, and so forth.

For the German minority north of the border, in the Danish part of North Slesvig, Germany's collapse and the subsequent arrival of peace on May 5, 1945 was a serious matter. This German minority had very understandably declared its friendship with the occupying power, and this, equally understandably, could not be construed otherwise than as an act of disloyalty towards Denmark. But the minority had also supported the occupational forces actively. Its position after the cessation of hostilities was therefore difficult, and for a number of years a deep bitterness existed on both sides. However, it was eventually smoothed out. Germans north of the border were given back their old privileges in respect of education, religious worship, and politics. They then made a declaration of loyalty towards Denmark, and even though a few individuals have since expressed the opinion that the declaration was "forced out of them", the matter has gradually been allowed to rest.

The Aftermath of War

During the war Denmark had the painful experience of seeing Iceland terminate the union between the two countries unilaterally. Iceland and Denmark had been united ever since 1380, and during the course of the previous 50 years or so, the relationship existing between them had been legally revised in order to enable Iceland to become an independent, self-governing country whose union with Denmark amounted to no more than a "personal union". In other words, the connecting link was merely that they had the same King. In the treaty signed by the two countries and known as the "Union Act", it was clearly stated that the Union could be dissolved by mutual negotiation. It was realized in Denmark that in due course Iceland would wish to free herself completely from her connection with Denmark, and this desire was considered only natural. It was therefore felt to have been all the more unkind on Iceland's part to consider it necessary to dissolve the 564-year old connection unilaterally, especially at a time when Denmark was engaged in a hard struggle for her own existence. For the announcement of the dissolution was not made at the commencement of the German occupation, when both Denmark's attitude and the outcome of the war were still open to doubt, but on February 26, 1944, at a time when the situation in Denmark was the gravest imaginable, when Germany's defeat was more than probable, when Denmark's own efforts to liberate herself were clearly visible and the day when Iceland would be able to negotiate with a free union partner and have her wishes fulfilled could obviously not be very far off. In Denmark, the termination of the union was felt to have been rather like kicking a man when he is down. However, King Christian merely sent off a hearty congratulatory telegram and the matter was therewith regarded as closed.

After the war, Greenland developed into a serious problem for Denmark. The agreement into which Denmark's ambassador to the U.S. had entered was that America should take Greenland under her protection and in return be permitted to establish her military bases there "for the duration of the present situation". But "present situations" have a habit of lasting more or less indefinitely. Voices were heard in the American Senate advocating the occupation of Greenland on military grounds. This was not felt by Denmark to be a direct threat and is hardly likely to have been one. But by means of an amendment to the constitution, Greenland's status was altered too. The country is thus no longer a Danish colony, but quite simply a Danish county, a part of Denmark just like Zealand or Jutland. At the same time a programme was initiated for the modernization of Greenland in order to bring education, hospitals, trades and local administration on to a level with conditions in the rest of Denmark. Greenland now has representatives in the Danish parliament just like the other Danish provinces. On the other hand the Faroes are a self-governing entity within the Danish body politic.

Simultaneously with the amendment of the constitution to incorporate Greenland within the Danish realm, an alteration in Denmark's own system of government was introduced. Of the two former parliamentary houses, one was abolished, leaving only the *Folketing*, previously the Lower House. The constitutional powers of the King and his ministers were left as they were, but the law governing the royal succession was

255

altered to give women equal rights with men, just as in England. King Christian X died in 1947 and was succeeded by his son, Frederick IX, who has no sons. In 1953 the Law of Succession was changed, so that his daughter Margrethe is now heir apparent.

After the war, with the abrupt change in the international situation and the division of the world into two somewhat rigidly opposed spheres of interest, one in the east and one in the west, it was obvious that Denmark would have to take her place, and equally obvious, without any discussion whatsoever being required, to which camp she belonged. But Denmark's position remains the same old, dangerous position that has governed the course of her history for the past thousand years: that of keeper of the gates of the Baltic. Russia is no doubt extremely interested in seeing just how these gates are kept open – or closed.

By way of an attempt to stay outside the two big world coalitions and keep Scandinavia clear of all political groups, a Scandinavian, or Nordic Defence Union was considered. The idea was an obvious one, but Norway was not keen and was more interested in pursuing a policy clearly aligned to that of the Western Powers. It was a great disappointment to Denmark and Sweden that the plan could not be realized, despite the fact that from an economic standpoint it would almost certainly have meant a greater burden. While Sweden maintained her unconditional neutrality outside all groups, Denmark and Norway became members of NATO. Denmark and Norway, having endured the same trials during the war, had developed a firm friendship. Thus it was felt natural, not only for this, but also for political reasons, that the two countries should pursue the same policy.

From the point of view of trade, Europe has been unsettled since the war. Perspectives have been constantly changing, and the old feeling of security which Denmark once enjoyed, the feeling that the majority of her agricultural products could always be sold to England, no longer exists. Denmark has been exporting considerable amounts to the allied occupation forces in Germany since the war, but this is not a state of affairs which can last for ever. A small country must face facts and realize that its products run the risk of becoming superfluous on a world market, and that they must therefore be made indispensable with the help of intelligent marketing and by sheer virtue of their qualities. Danish agriculture, which by the turn of the century had established such a reputation for itself, must once again make an abrupt change of course and it will succeed, once again, in bringing about such a change. Industry is on the watch-out for new markets, and Danish shipping, though naturally subject to the same conditions as those affecting the rest of world shipping, is in full swing. The country has undergone a process of reconstruction since the war: social welfare legislation has been extended considerably; popular enlightenment and education are making steady progress, and the old Folk High Schools are enjoying a revival of their popularity all over the country; there are public lending libraries everywhere, and experimentation is being conducted in the field of primary school education with a view to blazing new trails; at the same time, higher education is seeking to make new thrusts via the natural sciences, as the liberal subjects have not undergone the same rejuvenation.

During and after the war, Danish literature, just like the literature of other countries, was of the enquiring type. The very world situation offered writers difficult working conditions; intellectual theories collapsed, and others were found to lead nowhere. But book production, which rose sharply during the war, has remained at the same level during the post-war years. Danes read a lot.

With the country's relatively sound potentialities, steady production, comparatively high standard of living and generally stable conditions, no political questions manage to achieve particular urgency; and thus, together with the gradual elimination of the insecurity and tension of the war years, interest in politics has dwindled correspondingly. The serious housing shortage, one of the most immediate of post-war problems, is gradually being met. Denmark's obligations in respect of her membership of NATO, her greatly expanded social welfare programme, and the steadily increasing number of persons drawing fixed salaries for their services in state and borough administration, all place very great demands, just as in other countries, on the taxpayers of the nation. Even so, there is reason to believe that Denmark's future, providing the international situation permits, should not be too gloomy.

Present Status

To resume briefly: Denmark has maintained her position throughout her 1,000-year long history. Her inhabitants represent one of the few peoples in Europe that have never suffered from large-scale invasions or population transfers and so today can really claim for the most part to be the descendants of the "Danes" of the Stone Age. This is one of the explanations of their calm, congenital confidence (at times bordering on the reckless), the belief that, in Denmark, things can never go really wrong. Somehow she has always managed to pull through in the past, even when things were looking their blackest. Thanks to her position at the entrance to the Baltic, Denmark has found herself, time and again, involved in the political strife of Europe. Nevertheless, just like the other Scandinavian countries, Denmark lies so far to the north of the main European arena that most of the big European catastrophes and revolutions manage to do no more than send waves of repercussion up over the border. For centuries, Denmark had to maintain a two-front position involving constant threats both from the northeast and from the south. It was as though a pair of gaping pincers had been suspended over the country. Time and again, Denmark and Sweden have fought for the supremacy of Scandinavia and the Baltic, until finally, when the importance of the Baltic to the maritime trade of the world began to dwindle, the struggle ceased to have any meaning. Denmark was in due course obliged to surrender the Scanian provinces to Sweden, the most serious territorial loss she ever sustained. On the southern border the position is that, despite having Europe's big, dynamic, central power, in other words Germany, as her neighbour for nearly a thousand years, Denmark has only had to retreat from *Danevirke* to the present border, a distance of some 28 miles. Taking the comparative strengths of the two countries into consideration, and regarding the matter in a sober light, this is perhaps quite an honourable result. In the course of her history Denmark succeeded, for relatively lengthy periods, in establishing a position of power for herself in Scandinavia. That position has been lost. But even though the central, basic land of Denmark has been obliged to cede various territories, the nation is nevertheless still there. She has often been ravaged by foreign troops, often written off as an independent state by her neighbours, but she has never been completely wiped out, never completely conquered and subjected to foreign dominion. After each catastrophe – including the last – she has always managed to recover. With every inch of her soil marked indelibly by the lives, conditions and history of her inhabitants throughout the course of 15,000 years, she has always managed to pull through – Jutland and the five hundred green islands, Denmark, the Land of the Danes.

THE KINGS AND QUEENS OF ENGLAND AND DENMARK

The sovereigns of England can be traced back considerably further than those of Denmark, but then during the early centuries England was divided into several kingdoms of varying sizes. Alfred the Great was the first to stem the Danish onslaught, and after him followed a number of Saxon kings. In 975 came Edward the Martyr (slain by Danish Vikings).

Listed below, from this Edward onwards, are the kings and queens of England side by side with those of Denmark. This may help English readers to get their bearings in Danish history.

ENGLAND		DENMARK	
SAXON KINGS		Gudfred.. died approx.	810
Alfred the Great	871– 901	Gorm the Old died app.	940
Edward the Martyr ..	975 – 978	Harald Bluetooth app.	935– 985
Ethelred the Unready	978–1013 (1016)	Sweyn Forkbeard app.	985–1014
DANISH KINGS			
Sweyn Forkbeard ..	1013–1014	Harald	1014–1018
Canute the Great (1014)	1017–1035	Canute the Great	1018–1035
Harold Harefoot	1035–1040		
Hardicanute	1040–1042	Hardicanute	1035–1042
		Magnus the Good ..	1042–1047
SAXON KINGS		Sweyn Estridson	1047–1074
Edward the Confessor..	1042–1066	Harald Hén	1074–1080
Harold Godwinson ..	1066	Canute the Holy	1080–1086
		Oluf Hunger	1086–1095
NORMAN KINGS		Eric Egode	1095–1103
William I	1066–1087	Niels	1104–1134
William II	1087–1100	Eric Emune	1134–1137
Henry I	1100–1135	Eric Lamb	1137–1146
		Sweyn Grathe,	
Stephen	1135–1154	Canute, Valdemar I ..	1146–1157
HOUSE OF PLANTAGENET		Valdemar I (the Great)..	1157–1182
Henry II	1154–1189	Canute VI	1182–1202

ENGLAND		DENMARK	
Richard I	1189–1199	Valdemar the Victorious	1202–1241
John	1199–1216	Erik Ploughpenny ..	1241–1250
Henry III	1216–1272	Abel	1250–1252
Edward I	1272–1307	Christopher I	1252–2159
Edward II	1307–1327	Eric Clipping	1259–1286
Edward III	1327–1377	Eric Menved	1286–1319
Richard II	1377–1399	Christopher II 1320–1326, 1330–1332	
		Valdemar Atterdag ..	1340–1375
HOUSE OF LANCASTER		Oluf	1375–1387
Henry IV	1399–1413	Margaret 1387–1397 (1375–1412)	
Henry V	1413–1422	Eric of Pomerania ..	1397–1438
Henry VI	1422–1461	Christopher of Bavaria	1439–1448
HOUSE OF YORK		HOUSE OF OLDENBURG	
Edward IV	1461–1483	Christian I	1448–1481
Edward V	1483	Hans	1481–1513
Richard III	1483–1485	Christian II	1513–1523
		Frederick I	1523–1533
HOUSE OF TUDOR		Christian III	1535–1559
Henry VII	1485–1509	Frederick II	1559–1588
Henry VIII	1509–1547		
Edward VI	1547–1553		
Mary	1553–1558		
Elisabeth	1558–1603		
HOUSE OF STUART			
James I	1603–1625	Christian IV	1588–1648
Charles I	1625–1649		
THE COMMONWEALTH			
(Oliver Cromwell,			
Lord Protector ..	1653–1658	Frederick III	1648–1670
Richard Cromwell ..	1658–1659)	Christian V	1670–1699
		Frederick IV	1699–1730
Charles II	1660–1685		
James II	1685–1688		
William III (and Mary II			
until 1694)	1689–1702		
Anne	1702–1714		

ENGLAND

HOUSE OF HANNOVER
(House of Windsor from 1917)

George I	.. .. ..	1714–1727
George II	.. .. ..	1727–1760
George III	.. .. ..	1760–1820
George IV	.. .. ..	1820–1830
William IV	.. .. ..	1830–1837
Victoria	.. .. ..	1837–1901
Edward VII (Coburg)	..	1901–1910
George V	.. .. ..	1910–1936
Edward VIII	.. ..	1936 (abd.)
George VI	.. .. ..	1936–1952
Elisabeth II	.. .. ..	1952–

DENMARK

Christian VI	.. .. ..	1730–1746
Frederick V	.. .. ..	1746–1766
Christian VII	.. ..	1766–1808
Frederick VI	.. ..	1808–1839
Christian VIII	.. ..	1839–1848
Frederick VII	.. ..	1848–1863

HOUSE OF GLÜCKSBURG

Christian IX	.. .. ..	1863–1906
Frederick VIII	.. ..	1906–1912
Christian X	.. .. ..	1912–1947
Frederick IX	.. ..	1947–

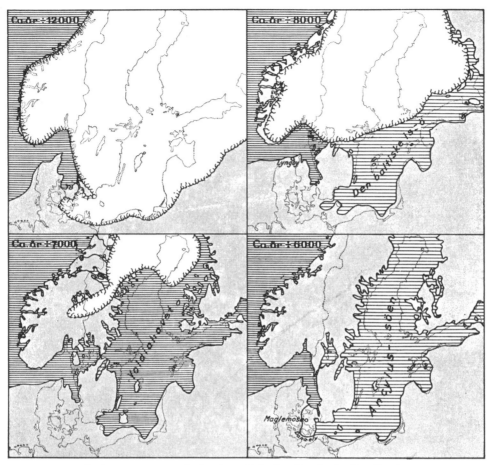

Various stages towards the close of the last Ice Age in Scandinavia.
1: About 12,000 B. C.   2: About 8,000 B. C.
3: About   7,000 B. C.   4: About 6,000 B. C.

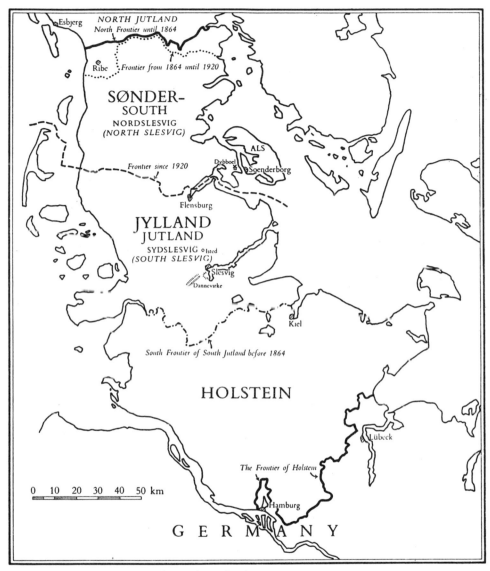

Map of South Jutland (100 km = 62.14 miles)

Holstein more or less united to Denmark since the Middle Ages, as a rule with the Danish King as Duke. Wrenched from Denmark 1864 and incorporated into Germany. Slesvig originally Danish soil, administered since the early Middle Ages as an independent duchy, during recent centuries with the Danish King as both King and Duke, but closely bound up with Holstein. Conquered by Germany i 1864. In 1920, after a plebiscite, divided into North and South Slesvig; the former reincorporated in Denmark, the latter in Germany.

265

INDEX

Abel 92, 93, 104
Absalon 71, 72, 73, 74, 75, 76, 79, 92, 96
Absolute Monarchy 166, 189, 206, 211, 214, 242
Adam of Bremen 63
Adolf of Holstein, Count 115
Adolph, Duke 144
Age of Chivalry 67, 96
Aggersborg 52, 53, 64, 65
Agriculture 18, 19, 20, 21, 24, 26, 77, 80, 148,
    151, 187, 221, 233, 234, 239, 245, 256
Akershus Castle 135
Albrecht, King of Sweden 101, 103, 106, 107
Alexander I, Czar 192
Alexander III, Czar 233 a, 234
Alexandra, Queen 234
Alfred the Great 46, 47, 53
Als 217, 228
Als Sound 229, 230
Amager 126, 177
Amalienborg Square 178, 241
Amber 24, 34, 37, 39
Ambrosius Bookbinder 137, 141
American War of Independance 189
Andalusia 38
Andersen, Hans 207
Angles 8, 41, 42, 56, 60, 157
Anna Cathrina, Queen 154
Arkona 72
Arnfast, Abbot 94
Assandun 55
Asser Rig 71
Atterdag, Valdemar, see Valdemar Atterdag
Augustenborg, Dukes of 184, 216, 217, 223, 230
Augustenborg, colonial outpost 217
Augustus the Strong 169 a, 171

Baffin Bay 156
Baltic, The 12, 13, 16, 24, 28, 42, 43, 58, 64, 68,
    70, 83, 100, 101, 106, 130, 172, 219, 236, 258
Basileia 24

Battle-Axes 25, 26
Belts, The 110
Beowulf, Song of 41
Berengaria, see Berngerd
Berg, Claus 121 a, 123, 130
Bergen 102, 125
Bergenhus 125
Bernadotte, Folke 250
Bernadotte, Marshal (later Karl 14 Johan) 193–
    194, 199, 201–202, 204
Berngerd, Queen 83, 92
Bernstorff, J. H. E. 177, 179, 181
Bernstorff, Lady 178
Bernstorff (the Younger), Andreas Peter 185,
    186, 189
Bille, Steen 217
Bishop of Bremen 161
Bishop of Roskilde 92
Bishop of Slesvig 79
Bismarck, Otto von 223, 230
Black Count, The 88
Black Death 99
Black Plough 69, 70
Black Sea 48
Blekinge 10, 146, 163
Bluetooth, Harald, see Harald Bluetooth
Bodil, Queen of Denmark 66
Bogs 35, 40, 41, 61
Bohemia, King of 81
Bohuslen 10, 32
Bombardment of Copenhagen 193, 194, 195
Bonifacius, Pope 96
Bookbinder, Ambrosius 137
Bordesholm Altar 123
Bornhoeved, Battle of 89
Bornholm 11, 42, 66, 96, 163, 164, 221, 252
Bothnia, Gulf of 15
Brahe, Tycho 149, 154
Brandt, Enevold 181, 184, 185
Bremen, Archbishop of 63, 66

Britons, ancient 8
Brochdorff, Ditlev 136
Broemsebro, Treaty of 159
Bronze Age 26–37, 41
Brunke Hill, Battle of 115
Brüggemann, Hans 123, 130
Bugislaw, Duke 73, 74
Bugislaw of Pomerania 112
Burial customs 22, 23, 24, 26, 29, 32, 48 a, 49 a

Calvin 142
Canterbury 54, 63
Canute, son of King Niels' son Magnus 70–71
Canute Lavard 68, 69, 70, 71, 79
Canute VI 73, 74, 76, 77, 78, 79, 85, 86
Canute the Great 52, 54–59, 62–64, 76–78, 87, 90
Canute the Holy 63, 64–65, 78
Caroline Matilda, Queen 179, 182, 183, 184, 227
Catherine II of Russia 178, 179, 186
Catholic Church, Fall of 141, 142
Celle 184
Celtic Iron Age 35–37
Celts, The 8, 34–39, 41, 60
Charles of France 48
Charles II of England 167
Charles V, Emperor 126, 132, 135
Charles X of Sweden 161, 163, 194
Charles XII of Sweden 169 a, 171, 172, 194
Charles XIII of Sweden 200
Charlottenborg Palace 169
Christian I 115, 116, 212
Christian II 125, 126, 128, 129, 130, 131, 132,
    134, 135, 138, 139, 140, 141, 145, 146
Christian III 140, 141, 142, 143, 144, 145
Christian IV 134, 151, 152, 152 a, 153 a, 154,
    156, 157, 158, 159, 160, 161, 174, 207
Christian V 167, 168, 169, 170
Christian V's Danish Law 167
Christian VI 176, 177, 186
Christian VII 178, 179, 180, 182, 186, 188, 214
Christian VIII 209, 210, 211, 212
Christian IX 223, 230, 233 a, 234, 235
Christian X 238, 244, 248 a, 249 a, 256
Christian Frederick, Prince 201
Christian of Glücksburg, Prince 217, 223
Christian of Oldenburg, Count 114
Christianity 51, 56, 60, 62, 63, 77, 92, 104, 124,
    175
Christiansborg Castle 176, 207, 222
Christiansborg, colonial outpost 217
Christina, Queen of Sweden 120, 121

Christina, Leonora 167
Christopher I 92, 93, 94, 96
Christopher II 97
Christopher of Bavaria 112, 113, 114
Christopher of Oldenburg, Count 139, 141
Church, The 62, 64, 66, 67, 69, 74–75, 77–78,
    80–81, 90, 91, 92, 93–94, 96, 104, 108, 121–
    124, 137–138, 143
Church-building 66–67, 74–75, 77–78, 81, 90–91
Church of Our Lady 207
Cimbrians, The 37, 38, 43
Clement, Captain 139, 141
Coat-of-arms, Danish 85, 146
Coat-of-arms, Norman 85
Colleoni 116, 120 a
Colonial policy 218
Conrad, Emperor 56
Constantine, Emperor 42
Constantinople 66
Constitution of 1849 215
Co-Operative Movement 234
Copenhagen 75, 93, 163, 176, 177
Copenhagen, Battle of 191–193, 200
Copenhagen, Fortification of 232
Copenhagen, Siege of 141
Copenhagen, Storming of 163–166
Counts' War, The 139, 140, 141, 142, 148
Cranach, Lucas 127
Cretaceous Period 11
Crusades 66
Czechoslovakia 241

"Dagger Age" 27
Dagmar, Queen 81, 89
Dagmar, Empress of Russia 234
Danevirke 72, 89, 217 a, 223, 224, 225, 226,
    230, 258
Danish Law, Christian V's 167
"Danegeld" 52, 53, 54, 55, 56, 60
Danelagh 44, 46, 47, 48, 52, 55
"Dannebrog" 84, 119
Danzig 102
Death cult 22, 23
Diet of Worms 138
Ditmarshes 117, 118, 119, 120, 146
Dolmen 22, 23
Dragomir, see Dagmar
Dybbøel 217 a, 225, 226, 227, 228, 229
Dürer, Albrecht 130, 131
Dyveke 125, 126, 127
Daa, Claus 159

Ebbesen, Niels 98
Ecclesiastical Art 123
Eckersberg, C. W. 192, 197, 208
Edward VII, King 233 a, 234
Egede, Hans 175
Egode, Eric 63, 65, 68, 71
Egypt 179
Eider, River 222, 224
"Eider Stone" 59
Eidsvoll Constitution 202
Elbe 178
Elisabeth, Queen of Christian II 126, 131, 132, 133, 145
Elisabeth, Queen of England 137 a, 150
Elsinore 110, 111, 135, 147, 190, 216 a, 220
Elsinore Castle, see Kronborg
Emune, Eric 69
Engelbrechtson, Engelbrecht 111
England, Viking conquest of 51–56
English East Asiatic Company 217
Erasmus of Rotterdam 131
Eric XIV, King of Sweden 145, 146, 152
Eric Clipping 95
Eric Egode 63, 66, 68, 71
Eric Emune 69
Erik Jarl 54
Eric Lamb 69, 70
Eric Menved 96
Eric Ploughpenny 92, 93
Eric of Pomerania 107, 109, 110, 111, 114, 120, 147, 178, 218
Erlandsen, Jacob 94
Esbern Snare 71, 75, 81
Eskild, archbishop of Denmark 71, 72, 73, 74, 80
Eskimoes 175
Estonia 83, 84, 92, 99, 101, 119
Estrid, Sister to Canute the Great 57
Estridson, Sweyn, see Sweyn Estridson
Ethelred the Unready 52, 53, 54
Ewald, Johannes 179

Falkoebing, Battle of 107
Falsterbo 102
Faroe Islands 204, 218, 245, 255
Finderup barn 95
Finland 200
Fisher, Olfert, Admiral 190, 191
Fishing 102, 103, 135
Flanders 46
Flanders, Count of 64
Flensborg 136, 226, 238

Flint 17, 19, 20, 21, 24, 25, 27, 34
Fodevig, Battle of 69
Folk Ballads 91
Folketing 213, 255
Folk High Schools 233, 237, 257
Fonts 64 a, 67, 74
Forest Hunters 13
Forkbeard, Sweyn, see Sweyn Forkbeard
Fredensborg, colonial outpost 217
Fredensborg Palace 233 a, 235
Fredericia 162, 213
Fredericknagore 204
Frederick, Duke (later Frederick I) 117, 118, 132, 133, 134
Frederick I 133, 134, 135, 136, 137, 138, 144
Frederick II 137 a, 145, 146, 148, 150, 151
Frederick III 161, 162, 164, 166, 194
Frederick IV 169 a, 171, 172, 173, 174, 175, 176
Frederick V 177, 178
Frederick VI 184, 186, 193, 194, 196, 198, 200, 201, 202, 203, 204, 207, 208, 209, 210
Frederick VII 83, 211, 216, 222
Frederick IX 256
Frederick Ludvig, Prince of Wales 179
Frederiksberg Castle 177, 196
Frederiksborg Castle 154, 164, 218
Frederikshald 173
Freedom Council 246, 249, 253
French Revolution 189, 193
Friis, Johan 148
Frisians 93, 117
Frøj 50
Fulton, Robert 221
Funen 67, 89, 90, 92, 94, 158, 162, 168 a, 199

"Galathea" 217
Gallehus 35 a, 42
George II 178
George III 184
George of Greece, King 234
Gerlach, General 228
German Emperor Otto 49
German Emperor 72, 73, 74, 79, 81, 88
Gert, Count 97, 98, 99
Gjedde, Admiral 156
Glimminge Castle 131
Glücksburg Castle 222
Glückstadt 207
Gorm the Old 46 a, 49, 50
Gothic Period 121, 122
Gotland 10, 42, 100, 101, 112, 154, 159

Gottorp Castle 132, 134, 144
Grade Heath 71
Grand, Jens, Archbishop 96, 97
Grathe, Sweyn, see Sweyn Grathe
Great Belt 12, 16, 162, 163, 199
Great Nordic War 170, 171, 172, 173
Greenland 47, 48, 150, 156, 175, 204, 218, 219, 245, 255
Gregory of Tours 42
Griffenfeld, Peder 167, 168, 169
Grundtvig, N. F. S. 207
Gudbrandsdalen 153
Gudmonsson, Lave 93
Guinea 204, 205, 217
Guldberg, Hoegh 184–186
Gundestrup 37, 42
Gurre Castle 104
Gustav Vasa 129, 131, 132, 145
Gustavus, Adolphus 153, 158, 159
Gyldenstierne, Knud 135
Gøye, Mogens 140

Haakon VII, King of Norway 235, 244
Haderslev 138
Hagenskov Castle 94
Hakon, King of Norway 100, 101, 105, 106, 107
Halland 10, 160, 163
Hall, James 156
Hall, C. C. 222
Hammershus Castle 96
Hans, King 116, 117, 118, 120, 121, 121 a, 122, 123, 124, 125, 134, 136, 144, 146
Hanseatic League 100, 101, 102, 103, 106
Harald Bluetooth 46 a, 49, 50, 51, 54, 58, 62, 65, 76, 93
Harald Hén 63
Haraldsted 68
Hardicanute 57, 58
Hardradi, Harald 58, 59
Haruds 37
Hastings 48
Havn, see Copenhagen
Hedeby 49, 51, 61, 93
"Hel" 58
Helgesen, Poul 138
Helgoland 229
Helgoland, Battle of 230
Helvig, princess of Slesvig 99
Hén, Harald 63
Henrik Loeve 73
Henry IV 111

Henry VIII 135
Hesselager, Castle 148
Hilfspolizei 249
Himmerland 38
Hirschholm Castle 183, 207
Hitler, Adolf 241, 242, 251
Hjelm 95
Hjortspring 41
Hoby 39
Holberg, Ludvig 174, 175
Holgerson Ulfstand, Jens 131
Holland 126, 130, 134, 202
Holmegaard Manor 159
Holy Land 66
Holstein 10, 13, 18, 97, 103, 106, 109, 115, 116, 117, 119, 120, 134, 144, 154, 171, 178, 180, 181, 194, 203, 206, 209, 210, 211, 212, 213, 215, 222, 223, 230, 239, 265
Hope, Sir Thomas 207
Horsens 140
Humlebaek 171
Hunger, Oluf 63, 65, 66
Hven 149, 154, 155
Hvide, Stig Andersson 95
Hoegh-Guldberg, see Guldberg
Hälsingborg 110, 111, 244
Härjedal 160

Ice Age 11, 12, 13, 15, 67, 264
Iceland 48, 135, 204, 218, 245, 254, 255
Illerup 40
Ingeborg of Denmark, married to King Philip August 85–87
Ingeborg, wife of the Duke of Mecklenburg 105
Ingeborg of Sweden, Erik Menved's wife 97
Innocent III 86
Invincible Armada 146
Iron age 35, 36, 43
Ironbeard, Adele 120
Ironside, Edmund 54
Isted Heath, Battle of 213, 216 a

Jacob, Anund, King of Sweden 58
Jacob, Count of Halland 95
James I 156
James III 116
James IV 200
"Jammersminde" 167
Jelling 46 a, 50
Jews, Persecution of Danish 246–247
Jews, Danish 250

John the Mild, Count 97, 99
Jomsborg 44, 51, 53, 54, 58
Jonsson, Rane 95
Julianehaab 219
Jutland 11, 12, 16, 17, 24, 26, 36, 38, 40, 49,
    49 a, 50, 58, 60, 65, 67, 69, 82, 89, 90, 92,
    95, 152, 158, 159, 161, 162, 199, 203, 221,
    228, 229, 232, 249
Jutland, South (see also Slesvig) 93
Jutlandic Law 89, 90
Jürgensen, Fritz 209
Jämtland 160

Kalmar Union 104 a, 107, 108
Kalmar War 153
Kaloe Castle 131
Kalundborg 75, 145
Karl XIV, see Bernadotte, Marshal
Kattegat 12
Keppler, Johan 155
Kernen Castle 110
Kierkegaard, Soeren 207, 208
Kipling, Rudyard 62
Knipperdollinck 142
Knutsson, Karl 115
Koege, Battle of 195
Kolberg Roads, Battle of 159
Koldinghus Castle 150, 199
Kongsberg 160
Kragehul 40
Krechting 142
Kringen 152 a, 153
Krogen Castle 110, 111, 147
Kronborg Castle 110, 137 a, 147, 160, 164, 184,
    190, 193, 196, 224
Kruuse, Vibeke 160
Kyrre, Olav 64

Lackland, John 87
Laesoe 220
Lamb, Eric 69, 70
Landskrona 110
Landsting 214
Lauenborg 230
League of Nations 239
Lena, Battle of 87
Leonora Christina 167
Lier 134
Limfjorden 17, 103
Lindisfarne 45
Little Belt 12, 16, 161

Lochlans 45
Lodbrog, Regnar 48
Loeve, Henrik 73
London, Treaty of 217
Lothar, King 68
Louise of England, Princess 178, 179
Louise Augusta 183, 184
Louis XVI 189
Lund 73, 94
Lund, Battle at 168
Lund Cathedral 111
Lurs 33
Luther, Martin 134, 135, 138
Lutter am Barenberg 158
Lyndanisse, Battle of 84
Lyoe 88
Lyrskov Heath, Battle of 58
Lübeck 85,92,102,105,121,130,131,138,139,141
Lüneburg Heath 251
Lützen, Battle of 159

Magna Charta 95
Magnus 68, 69, 71, 100, 101
Magnus the Good 57, 58, 59
Malmö 110, 164, 244
Malpaga, Palace of 116
Mandern, Karel van 152 a
Margaret, Queen 94, 100, 101, 105, 108, 111,
    112, 115, 116, 129
Maria, Duke Galeazzo 116
Marryat, Captain 218
Marstrand, Wilhelm 187, 208
Mary, Bloody 142
Mecklenburg, Duke of 105
Megalithic tombs 23, 26, 27
Menved, Eric 96
Meza, General de 224, 226, 228
Middelfart 99
Middle Ages, Early 61
Migrations 37, 40, 41, 43
Molesworth, Sir Robert 169, 214
Moliére 174
Monarchy, Absolute 178
Monrad, D. G. 230
Montgomery, Fieldmarshal 251
Mule, Asbjoern 74
Munk, Jens 156
Munk, Kai 247
Munk, Mogens 132
Mussolini, Benito 251
Münster 142

Mythology 41
Møn 11, 77
Mönnichhofen, Colonel 153

Napoleon 198, 200, 203
Napoleonic Wars 207
Napoleon III 231
Narva, Battle of 171
National Museum 28
NATO 256, 257
Nelson, Horatio, Admiral 190, 191, 192
Netherlands 126, 130
Nexoe 252
Nicobars 204, 218
Niebuhr, Carsten 80, 179
Niels, King 63, 66, 67, 68, 69, 81
Noer, Prince of 211
Norden, Frederik Ludvig, Captain 179
Nordic Defence Union 256
Nordland 13, 35
Normandy 11, 47, 48, 54
Normans 8, 45
North Sea 12, 14, 15, 16, 24, 26, 83
North Slesvig 134
Northumbria 54
Norway 144, 160, 201, 202, 203
Norway's Free Constitution 201
Notke, Bernt 115
Novgorod 85
Nyborg, 75, 95
Nyborg, Battle of 168 a
Nydam 40, 41

Obotrites 68
Odense 65, 92
Odense Cathedral 121 a, 123
Odin 50
"Odin's Shrine" 65
Oehlenschläger, Adam 207
Oersted, H. C. 207
Oesel 159
Olav the Fat 53, 54
Ol's Church s. 91
Oluf Hunger 63, 65, 66
Oluf III 105, 106
Opdam, Jacob van, Admiral 164
Orkney 116
Otto, Emperor of Germany 49
Otto, Junker 98
Oxe, Peder 146
Oxe, Torben 127, 128

Parker, Admiral 190, 191, 192
Paul, Czar 192
Peasant Reforms 187, 188
Peat-bogs 20
Peter the Great of Russia 169 a, 171
Peter III of Russia 178
Peymann, General 194, 196
Philip August, King of France 85, 86, 87
Philip the Handsome of France 96
Philip II of Spain 145, 146
Philippa, Queen 111, 112, 120, 178
Pilo, C. G. 180
Plat, General du 228, 229
Podebusk, Henning 103
Poland 161
Poltava, Battle of 171
Porcelain 176
Prince Frederick, Crown, later Fr. VI 190
Pufendof, Samuel 163

Quisling, Vidkun 243

railway, Denmark's first 221
Ramsay, Alexander, Colonel 153
Rantzau, Johan 141
Rask, Gertrude 175
Reformation 74, 134, 136–144
Regnar Lodbrog 48
Reindeer 12, 13
Religion 21–22, 31, 50, 80, 142–143
Renaissance 145, 151
Rendsborg 211
Rescue Service 221
resistance movement 245
Reval 85
Reventlow, Anna Sophie 173
Reventlow, Count Ditlev 179
Reverdil 178, 179
Ribe 68, 82, 92
Ribe Church 94
Rig, Asser 71
Rigsraadet 134, 138, 140, 144, 146, 151, 158
Ringsted 82, 83
Roenne 252
Roeros 160
Rolf 48
Rollo 48
Roman Empire 42
Romanesque Period 122
Roman Iron Age 38, 41
Romans 8, 38, 39, 41, 60
Romsdalen 153

Ronneby 146
Rosenborg Palace 137 a, 153 a, 155, 160
Roskilde 73, 74, 108
Roskilde, Banquet of 71
Roskilde Cathedral 208
Roskilde Fjord 16
Roskilde, Peace treaty of 162, 167
"Round Tower" 154, 155
Royal Charter 95
Royal Copenhagen Porcelain Factory 179
Rufus, William 89
Runes 42, 61, 74
Ry Church 140
Rügen 11, 72

"Sagas" 76
St. Alban 64, 65
St. Bartholomews Eve 142
St. Brice's night 52, 54
St. Edmund 54
St. Mary's Church 85, 137
St. Thomas 200 a, 248 a
Salisbury, Earl of 156
Salonica 234
Sankelmark, Battle of 226
Saxe (Saxo Grammaticus) 75, 119
Saxons 8, 41
Scandinavian Union 107
Scania 10, 50, 94, 102, 163
Scanian Law 90
Scanian War 167, 168
Schlentz, Junker 118, 119, 120
Schumacher, Peder 167
Schwerin, Heinrich von, the Black Count 88
Seven Years' War, The 146, 148, 177, 198
Shakespeare, William 174, 240
Shetland 116
Shipping 31, 32, 46, 66, 67, 70, 77, 79, 80, 148,
    154, 164, 176, 179, 186, 189, 206, 210, 221,
    234, 236, 257
Sigbritt Willumsdatter (Mother Sigbritt) 125,
    126, 131, 132
Simonsen, Soeren 212, 213 a
Sixtus IV, Pope 116
Sjaellands Odde, Battle of 199, 200
Skanderborg 82, 98
Skanoer 102, 106
Skaw 12
Skram, Peter 141, 174
Slagheck, Didrick 129
Slave Trade 205

Slesvig 8, 10, 79, 89, 90, 92, 93, 104, 106, 109,
    110, 111, 114, 115, 116, 123, 134, 144, 157,
    178, 181, 209, 212, 213, 216, 222, 229, 230,
    237, 238, 239, 240, 241, 253, 254, 265
Slesvig Cathedral 119, 123
Slesvig War, The First 211
Slesvig War, The Second 223
Sli 93
Smek, Magnus 98, 99, 106
Snare, Esbern 71, 75, 81
Social Democratic Party 239
Soenderborg 140, 141, 237
Soenderborg Castle 136, 140, 145
Soendermarken 196, 201 a
Sophie of Mecklenburg 150
Soroe Abbey 74
Sound Dues 110, 111, 146, 148, 150, 166, 173,
    219, 220
Sound, The 12, 16, 110, 164, 193, 196, 244
Spain 199
Speed, John 157
Spoettrup Castle 140
Stamford Bridge, Battle of 59
Stenbock, Magnus 172
Stephenson, George 221
Stettin 102
Stjerneborg 149
Stock Exchange 154
Stockholm 102, 115, 117
Stockholm Bloodbath 129
Stone Age 8, 12–26, 27
Stralsund 102
Streon, Eadrich 54
Struensee, Johann Friederich 180, 181, 182,
    183, 184, 185, 186, 214
Sture, the Younger Sten 115, 117, 120, 121, 128
Sturlason, Snorre 76
Suneson, Anders, Archbishop 84
Svantevit 72
Svendborg, Battle of 141
Sweyn Estridson, 57–59, 61–63, 92
Sweyn Forkbeard 51, 52, 53, 54, 78, 204
Sweyn Grathe 70
Sweyn Ulfson, see Sweyn Estridson
Syria 180
Sønderjylland 93

Tallinn 85
Tap Hede, Battle of 98
Tavsen, Hans 136, 137
Taxation 64

Teutons, The 37, 38, 40
Teutonic Iron Age 41, 42
Theatre 174
Thing 113
Thirty Years' War, The 158
Thor 47 a, 50
Thorsbjærg 40
Thorvaldsen, Bertel 207
Thyra 46 a
Tilly, Tserclaes von 158
Tilsit, Treaty of 193
Toejhuset 160
Tollund man, The 34 a, 40
tombs, Megalithic 23
Tombs 26
Tordenskjold 172, 173
Torkil the Tall 53, 54
Torstensson, Lennart 159
"Torstensson's War" 159
Tove Prude 57
Tranquebar 156, 178, 204
Trelleborg 52, 53
Trolle, Gustav, Archbishop 128, 129
Trundholm 32
Tryggvesson, Olav 51
Ty 38, 77

Ulfeld, Corfitz 167
Ulf Jarl 56, 57
Ulfson, Sweyn, see Sweyn Estridson
Ulfstand, Jens Holgersen 131
United Nations 253
Uppsala 62, 116, 128
Uranieborg 149
Urban, Pope 66

Vadstena 112
Valdemar Atterdag 97–105, 109–110, 114, 159
Valdemar I, see Valdemar the Great
Valdemar II, see Valdemar the Victorious
Valdemar the Great 70–73, 75, 76, 77, 93
Valdemar the Victorious 79–83, 87, 104, 119
Valdemar the Younger 83, 89
Valleborg Stone 62
Vandals, The 37, 38
"Vandalusia" 38
Varberg Castle 95
"Varingians" 66
Vasa, Gustav, see Gustav Vasa
Vedbaek 195
Vendland 51

Vendsyssel 37
"Venstre" 231
Versailles 237
Vestervig 78
Vesterås, bishop of 69
Vestmannahavn 218
Viborg 95, 136, 140
Viborg Thing 133
Victoria, Queen 227
Viemose 40
Vienna, Congress of 203
Viking Age 43–61, 80, 175, 204, 214
Viking conquest of England 51–56
Viking expeditions 44
Vikings 42
Vinland 48
Virgin Islands 200 a, 204, 218, 248 a
Visby 100, 101, 103
Vognbjærg 36
Volmer, King, see Valdemar Atterdag
Vordingborg 90
Vordingborg Castle 73

War of Independence (America) 185
Watling Street 52, 55
Wellesley, General (Duke of Wellington) 195
Wellington, Duke of 195
Wendland 101
Wends 58, 70, 72, 80, 84, 101
Wessel, Peter 172, 173
West Indian Islands 236
Willemoes, Peter, Lieutenant 200
William the Conqueror 60, 64, 65, 77
Willumsdatter, Dyveke, see Dyveke
Willumsdatter, Sigbritt, see Sigbritt Willums-
   datter
Witchcraft 90
Wittenberg 136
World War I 236
World War II 241
Worm, Ole 157
Worms, Diet of 138
Wrangel, Friedrich, General 224
Wullenwever, Jürgen 139

York, archbishop of Canterbury 47

Zealand 94, 162, 163
Zealandic Law 90

Aalborg 48 a, 141